A LIBERATING SPIRIT

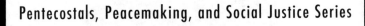

Pentecostals, Peacemaking, and Social Justice Series

PAUL ALEXANDER AND JAY BEAMAN, SERIES EDITORS

Volumes in the Series:

Pentecostal Pacifism: The Origin, Development, and Rejection of Pacific Belief among the Pentecostals

by Jay Beaman

Forgiveness, Reconciliation, and Restoration: Mulitdisciplinary Studies from a Pentacostal Perspective

edited by Martin W. Mittelstadt and Geoffrey W. Sutton

A Liberating Spirit

Pentecostals and Social Action in North America

EDITED BY

MICHAEL WILKINSON

AND

STEVEN M. STUDEBAKER

PICKWICK *Publications* · Eugene, Oregon

A LIBERATING SPIRIT
Pentecostals and Social Action in North America

Pentecostals, Peacemaking, and Social Justice Series 2

Pickwick Publications
An Imprint of Wipf and Stock Publishers
199 W. 8th Ave., Suite 3
Eugene, OR 97401

ISBN 13: 978-1-60899-283-6

Cataloging-in-Publication data:

A liberating Spirit : Pentecostals and social action in North America / edited by Michael Wilkinson and Steven M. Studebaker.

Pentecostals, Peacemaking, and Social Justice Series 2

xiv + 274 p. ; 23 cm. Includes bibliographical references and index(es).

ISBN 13: 978-1-60899-283-6

1. Pentecostal churches—Doctrines. 2. Peace—religious aspects—Pentecostals. I. Wilkinson, Michael, 1965–. II. Studebaker, Steven M., 1968–. III. Title. IV. Series.

BX8765.5.Z5 L53 2010

Manufactured in the U.S.A.

CONTENTS

SERIES PREFACE

Pentecostal and Charismatic Christians comprise approximately 25 percent of global Christianity (around 600 million of 2.4 billion). This remarkable development has occurred within just the last century and has been called the "pentecostalization" of Christianity. Pentecostals and Charismatics experience Christianity and the world in distinctive ways, and this series invites discovery and development of Pentecostal-Charismatic approaches to peacemaking and social justice.

The majority of early twentieth-century Pentecostal denominations were peace churches that encouraged conscientious objection. Denominations such as the Church of God in Christ and the Assemblies of God said "no" to Christian combatant participation in war, and some Pentecostals and Charismatics are exploring this history and working for a recovery and expansion of this witness. The peacemaking aspect of the series focuses on pacifism, war, just war tradition, just peacemaking, peacebuilding, conflict transformation, nonviolence, forgiveness, and other peacemaking-related themes and issues within Pentecostal-Charismatic traditions and from Pentecostal-Charismatic perspectives. We launched the series with a twentieth-anniversary reprint of Jay Beaman's *Pentecostal Pacifism*—an appropriate look back to the generative years of the Pentecostal movement when many denominations believed that nonviolence was a hallmark of the gospel of Jesus Christ.

Some early Pentecostals also confronted the injustices of racism, sexism, and economic disparity. Others perpetuated the problems. Yet the Holy Spirit leads us now, as then, to confront injustice prophetically and work to redeem and restore. Pentecostal-Charismatic Christians around the world are working for justice in a myriad of ways. This aspect of the series focuses on gender, race, ethnicity, sexuality, economics, class, globalization, trade, poverty, health, consumerism, development, and other social justice related themes and issues within the Pentecostal-Charismatic tradition and from Pentecostal-Charismatic perspectives. We understand that peace and justice are not separate concerns but different ways of talking about and seeking *shalom*—God's salvation, justice, and peace.

Forthcoming volumes include both original work and publication of important historical resources, and we welcome contributions from theologians, biblical scholars, philosophers, ethicists, historians, social scientists, pastors, activists, and practitioners of peacemaking and social justice. We especially welcome both scholarly and praxis-oriented contributions from majority world Pentecostals and Charismatics, for this series seeks to explore the ways that Pentecostal-Charismatic Christians can develop, strengthen, and sustain a peace-with-justice witness in the twenty-first century around the world. Royalties from sales of these volumes are often donated to Pentecostals & Charismatics for Peace & Justice (www.pcpj.org), a 501(c)3 network advocating for Jesus-shaped and Spirit-empowered peace with justice.

Paul Alexander

CONTRIBUTORS

ESTRELDA ALEXANDER, PhD (The Catholic University of America), is Professor of Theology at Regent University School of Divinity and Executive Director of the Seymour Pan-African Pentecostal Project. She is author of *The Women of Azusa Street* and *Limited Liberty: The Ministry and Legacy of Four Pentecostal Women Pioneers* and co-editor of *Phillip's Daughters: Women in the Pentecostal Movement*, as well as several articles on race and gender within the Pentecostal tradition. She is a member of the executive committee of the Society for Pentecostal Studies and serves on the editorial board of the *Journal of Pentecostal Theology*. She is an ordained minister in the Church of God (Cleveland, TN).

PETER ALTHOUSE, PhD (University of Toronto), is Associate Professor of Theology at Southeastern University. He is the author of *Spirit of the Last Days: Eschatology in Conversation with Jürgen Moltmann* and numerous articles on Pentecostalism in *Pneuma* and *Journal of Pentecostal Theology*.

MELISSA D. BROWNING is a doctoral candidate in Christian Ethics at Loyola University, Chicago. Her current work focuses on HIV/AIDS, women, and faith-based initiatives in East Africa. As an ethicist and an ordained minister in the Baptist tradition, Melissa focuses on the ways in which religion and faith shape the lives of women around the world.

ANDREA HOLLINGSWORTH is a doctoral candidate and Lecturer in Constructive Theology at Loyola University, Chicago. She is author of

The Holy Spirit (with F. LeRon Shults), the latest book in W. B. Eerdmans' "Guides to Theology" series. Her articles have appeared in such journals as *Pneuma* and *Zygon*.

PAMELA M. S. HOLMES, PhD (University of Toronto) is an instructor in Systematic Theology and Spirituality within the departments of religious studies and theological studies at Queen's Theological College (Queen's School of Religion), Queen's University, Kingston, Ontario where she also directs the Supervised Practice of Ministry Program and coordinates the Flora Jane Baker Minister in Residence Fellowship. She is an ordained minister with the Canadian Fellowship of Christian Assemblies, co-founder and minister-at-large of Quinte Community Christian Church, Belleville, Ontario, an active member in the Society for Pentecostal Studies having recently founded its Women's Caucus and a board member on the Ontario Multi-Faith Council. Pam has published several articles relating to feminist critical theory of religion and Canadian Pentecostalism.

DERRICK R. ROSENIOR, PhD (Howard University) is Assistant Professor of Communication and director of the Lewis Wilson Institute for Pentecostal Studies at Vanguard University of Southern California. He is a member of the Society for Pentecostal Studies.

ADAM STEWART is a doctoral candidate at the University of Waterloo and Adjunct Professor of Religious Studies at Master's College and Seminary, Toronto, Ontario. He is a recipient of the Joseph-Armand Bombardier CGS Doctoral Scholarship, awarded by the Social Sciences and Humanities Research Council of Canada.

STEVEN M. STUDEBAKER, PhD (Marquette University) holds the Howard and Shirley Bentall Chair in Evangelical Thought and is Assistant Professor of Systematic and Historical Theology at McMaster Divinity College, Hamilton, Ontario. He is an active member in the Society for Pentecostal Studies and the editor of *Defining Issues in Pentecostalism: Classical and Emergent*, author of *Jonathan Edward' Social Augustinian Trinitarianism in Historical and Contemporary Perspectives*, and of several articles on Pentecostal theology. He is ordained with the Assemblies of God.

A. J. SWOBODA is a doctoral student at the University of Birmingham, UK and adjunct professor of theology and biblical studies at George Fox Evangelical Seminary, Portland, Ore. As an active contributor in the

Society of Pentecostal Studies, he is currently researching and writing on the issues surrounding a foundational Pentecostal and Charismatic eco-theology. He is a licensed pastor in the Foursquare movement.

CLINTON N. WESTMAN, PhD (University of Alberta) is Assistant Professor in the Department of Archaeology and Anthropology at the University of Saskatchewan. He is the author of several articles on Pentecostalism and other issues within Aboriginal society.

MICHAEL WILKINSON, PhD (University of Ottawa) is Associate Professor of Sociology, director of the Religion in Canada Institute, and coordinator of the Canadian Pentecostal Research Network at Trinity Western University, Langley, British Columbia. He is the author of *The Spirit Said Go: Pentecostal Immigrants in Canada* and editor of *Canadian Pentecostalism: Transition and Transformation* as well as scholarly articles on globalization and Pentecostalism in *Pneuma, Journal of Pentecostal Theology, Transformation,* and *Asian Journal of Pentecostal Studies.*

ACKNOWLEDGMENTS

We would like to thank the contributors for working with us to develop this important volume on social action and Pentecostalism. Everyone has worked diligently to see the project come to completion. We also want to thank the series editors, Paul Alexander and Jay Beaman, for their passion and vision for peacemaking and social justice. We hope this work will make a contribution to our understanding of how Pentecostals in North America can work towards social action that understands the social and cultural context of their theologizing. The introduction appeared in an earlier version and was published in *The Ecumenist: A Journal of Theology, Culture, and Society*. Permission to use that material was graciously granted from the editor and the journal.

Finally, we acknowledge the support of our families in our work.

Michael thanks Valerie for her encouragement and patience.
To Victoria, Ethan, Alex, and Grace—be peacemakers
in a world that needs to know the love of God.

Steve thanks Sheila for support and understanding for the time
taken away from family in the production of this volume.

1

Pentecostal Social Action

An Introduction

Michael Wilkinson and Steven M. Studebaker

INTRODUCTION[1]

Some suggest that North American Pentecostalism represents an anti-culture posture arising from an experience of deprivation or marginalization from mainstream culture.[2] One response to cultural marginalization is the adoption of conservative politics and the materialistic values of consumer culture. A sense of disenfranchisement often leads to withdrawal from society or to a spiritual triumphalism.[3] On the other hand, there are

1. An earlier version of this chapter was published as "A Liberating Spirit" by Wilkinson and Studebaker.

2. See Anderson, *Vision of the Disinherited*. For a recent and thorough overview of religion and class issues, see McCloud, *Divine Hierarchies*.

3. Triumphalism among Pentecostals may be understood spiritually and politically. Early Pentecostals saw themselves as restorationists returning Christianity back to what it was supposed to be. This was often in opposition to the so called spiritually

1

those who argue that Pentecostalism outside North America is developing a "theology of liberation" in response to social issues.[4] These Pentecostals are described as "progressive Pentecostals" who engage issues of poverty, inequality, and ecology.[5] The focus on these Pentecostals, however, is primarily in Africa, Asia, and Latin America with little discussion about North America. Is there a North American equivalent? In what ways are Pentecostals in North America engaging issues of race, class, gender, and ecology? What theologically motivates North American Pentecostals to respond to these issues? What categories best explain Pentecostal responses to these issues in North America? How do they compare to Pentecostal responses elsewhere?

The authors of this book critically evaluate whether there are "progressive Pentecostals" in North America. Is there evidence of a Pentecostal "theology of liberation" that explains Pentecostal engagement in North America? Are Pentecostals in North America as "progressive" as their counterparts elsewhere? Do these categories fit North American Pentecostal responses to social issues or are others more suitable? In what ways are Pentecostal responses to social issues unique to North America or similar to Pentecostals elsewhere in the world?[6] This book, therefore, is an effort to understand and assess theologically and socially the contemporary relationship between North American Pentecostalism and culture with reference to global trends. This introduction provides an overview of some of the literature and issues to be explored as we move toward an assessment of "progressive Pentecostalism" in North America.

LIBERATION THEOLOGY AND PROGRESSIVE PENTECOSTALISM

Liberation theology represents an important shift in Christianity, especially among Roman Catholics but also Protestants, beginning in the middle of the twentieth century.[7] The goal of Liberation theology is most certainly social justice rooted in a preferential option for the poor with the

dead denominations they left. However, it may also be understood politically in North America when there is a close tie between religion and the political realm, especially in the United States.

4. Anderson, *Introduction to Pentecostalism*.

5. Miller and Yamamori, *Global Pentecostalism*.

6. Robertson uses the terms particular and universal to highlight sameness and difference in his analysis of globalization. See *Globalization*.

7. Ferm, *Third World Liberation Theologies* and Berryman, *Liberation Theology*.

base ecclesial communities the primary location for theological application. Liberation refers to the belief that personal salvation is inseparable from the social struggle for justice. Salvation is social and personal and is incorporated into a theology of the Kingdom of God. While Liberation theology is often associated with Latin America it was in fact far more global in nature. Latin American writers included Gustavo Gutiérrez, Juan Luis Segundo, Leonardo Boff, Hugo Assmann, Jon Sobrino, José Miranda, and Rubem Alves.[8] In Africa John Mbiti, Kofi Appaiah-Kubi, and Allan Boesak were important figures.[9] In Asia Kosuke Koyama, C. S. Song, and Kim Yon-Bok wrote on themes of liberation for Asian Christians.[10]

There is some question as to whether or not themes of liberation found a home in North America. How could it be possible for a theology rooted in the colonial experience to be applicable in a "core" region like North America?[11] How could North Americans understand the economic injustice experienced in Latin America? Gregory Baum argued in *Religion and Alienation* that forms of domination and oppression in North America must be understood for their own historical particularities.[12] While Latin American oppression is primarily rooted in the world economic system, Baum says it is not at all clear that a single dominant form is evident in North America. Is there a common variable to explain the experiences of women, African Americans, gays and lesbians, Québécois, and Aboriginal peoples? Baum says "It is unrealistic, in my view to look for a single form of oppression in North America, to which all others

8. For example, see Alves, *Theology of Human Hope*; Gutiérrez, *Theology of Liberation*; Miranda, *Marx and the Bible*; Assmann, *Theology for a Nomad Church*; Segundo, *Liberation of Theology*; Boff, *Jesus Christ, Liberator*; and Sobrino, *Christology at the Crossroads*.

9. Mbiti, *Concepts of God in Africa*; Appiah-Kubi and Torres, *African Theology En Route*; and Boesak, *Black and Reformed*.

10. Koyama, *Waterbuffalo Theology*; Song, *Third-Eye Theology*; and Yong-Bok, *Minjung Theology*.

11. Liberation theologians are influenced by Marxist social interpretations including an analysis of the world economic system. Immanuel Wallerstein is an important social theorist who has written extensively on the world economic system which divides the world into three regions including the peripheral, semi-peripheral, and core. The relationship between these regions is characterized by dependency with the core regions benefiting economically from the other areas. See Wallerstein, *Modern World System*. For a critique of Wallerstein's global perspective, see Robertson, *Globalization*.

12. Baum, *Religion and Alienation*, 216.

are subordinated."[13] Following Max Weber, Baum argues for a particular understanding of oppression and domination in North America which is not simply explained as "liberation" from economic injustice. "What we have is a complex intermeshing of technocratic depersonalization and immobility, economic domination and exploitation, racial exclusion and inferiorization, and other forms including the subjugation of women."[14] It should be clear that while Latin America, Africa, and Asia share some commonalities, all these regions need to be evaluated for their own particularities as well.[15]

While Liberation theology represents one transformation in Christianity, inspiring an important discussion especially among academics, Pentecostalism may turn out to be one of the most important shifts for religion in the twentieth century. Liberation theology opted for the poor, says Donald Miller and Tetsuano Yamamori, but the poor opted for Pentecostalism.[16] As more people in Latin America, Asia, and Africa adopt Pentecostalism as their expression of faith, will Pentecostals be able to deal with the economic and social issues they face? What challenges confront Pentecostals as they grow and expand throughout the world? What is it about Pentecostalism that is attractive to the poor and marginalized?

David Stoll raised our attention to the shift in Latin America when many Catholics were joining the Pentecostals.[17] Stoll argued that a collision between Liberation theology and Evangelicalism was going to occur and needed to be understood as part of a wider religious transformation. He also argued that Latin American politics would change. David Martin likewise examined the explosion of Pentecostalism in Latin America and identified some of the early tensions between the radical elements of Liberation theology and Pentecostalism.[18] One response was to offer a less revolutionary option for the Charismatics in the Catholic Church

---

13. Ibid., 218.

14. Ibid., 218–19.

15. *Third World Liberation Theologies*, 1–2. Also see Beyer, "Defining Religion in Cross-National Perspective," 163–88.

16. Miller and Yamamori, *Global Pentecostalism*, 12. For a similar argument about the relationship between Liberation theology and Pentecostalism, see Shaull and Cesar, *Pentecostalism and the Future of the Christian Churches*.

17. Stoll, *Is Latin America Turning Protestant?*

18. Martin, *Tongues of Fire*.

to pre-empt members from leaving the Church.[19] Both Stoll and Martin illustrate the tensions between Catholics and Pentecostals when Latin Americans were opting for a different kind of Christianity.

While Pentecostalism was often critiqued negatively by Protestants and Catholics, Cheryl Bridges Johns argued that Pentecostals in Latin America actually shared with Liberation theology some important commonalities.[20] Pentecostalism, according to Bridges Johns, is a major force in the conscientization of the oppressed in the context of a Spirit-filled faith community.[21] Adopting the views of Paulo Freire, Bridges Johns argued that Pentecostals need likewise to engage his ideas as they work among the marginalized of the world. Bridges Johns argues that Pentecostalism, beginning with its historical roots among the poor in North America, was always a movement of conscientization.[22]

By the mid-1990s an important transformation occurred and Pentecostalism was now being taken seriously by scholars outside of the movement.[23] The widely read and discussed book *Fire from Heaven* by Harvey Cox illustrated this shift in our understanding of Pentecostalism as a movement of liberation.[24] Cox pointed out that Liberation theology and Pentecostalism share in common the idea that Christians are responsible for continuing the ministry of Jesus, the centrality of the Kingdom of God in their respective theologies, as well as the importance of changing social patterns and not just converting individuals. The difference, according to Cox, is found in the politics of each group with liberation theologians leaning to the left and Pentecostals to the right. Some Pentecostals, however, according to Cox, have mounted a counterattack to the rightwing politics of other Pentecostals by formulating a Pentecostal Liberation Theology. Two important early writers discussed by Cox include Eldin Villafañe and Murray Dempster, who both argue for a social ethic that roots itself in the power of the Spirit and avoids the triumphalism of conservative politics.[25]

19. Ibid., 25–26.

20. Johns, *Pentecostal Formation*.

21. Ibid., 12.

22. Ibid., 65.

23. See Beyer, "Movements, Markets, and Social Contexts."

24. Cox, *Fire From Heaven*.

25. See Dempster, Klaus, and Petersen, *Called and Empowered* and Villafañe, *Liberating Spirit*.

The idea of "progressive Pentecostalism" comes from Miller and Yamamori who argue that Pentecostalism replaces Liberation theology.[26] The authors see Pentecostals, at least in some sectors, occupying a space for social justice once held by the Social Gospel movement and later by Liberation Theology. Progressive Pentecostalism, they argue, is very different from these movements but shares some commonalities. Progressive Pentecostalism refers to "Christians who claim to be inspired by the Holy Spirit and the life of Jesus and seek to holistically address the spiritual, physical, and social needs of people in their community. Typically, they are distinguished by their warm and expressive worship, their focus on lay-oriented ministry, their compassionate service to others, and their attention, both as individuals and as a worshiping community, to what they perceive to be the leading of the Holy Spirit."[27] Pentecostals, they argue, have the potential to be agents of social transformation by focusing on the promise of life for those who are oppressed, economic prosperity, and human rights.[28] Progressive Pentecostalism is also different from Liberation Theology as it operates with a different set of guiding principles and tactics.[29]

While Miller and Yamamori focus their attention on the social ministry of Pentecostals in Latin America, Africa, and Asia, whether or not there is any evidence of "progressive Pentecostalism" in North America remains the question to be explored. One possible avenue of research still in its infancy is the work on religion and altruism by Margaret Poloma, Matthew Lee, and Stephen Post. These scholars, funded by Templeton, have begun to establish a new research area focusing on the intersection of divine love and human love among Pentecostals with the outcome of benevolent acts. The research program supports the work of a number of scholars working on these questions with some preliminary research showing a type of "progressive Pentecostalism" or "Godly love" operating in North America and throughout the world.[30]

26. Miller and Yamamori, *Global Pentecostalism*.

27. Ibid., 2–3.

28. Ibid., 32–34.

29. Ibid., 214–16.

30. See "Flame of Love" website for details of the research project including current findings: www3.uakron.edu/sociology/flameweb/index. Also, see the book *Blood and Fire* by Poloma and Hood for a discussion of "Godly love."

"WHERE THE SPIRIT OF THE LORD IS, THERE IS FREEDOM"

The authors of this book accept the assumption that Progressive Pentecostalism has a social orientation and that it can make a contribution to North American Pentecostalism. The Apostle Paul declares that, "where the Spirit of the Lord is, there is freedom" (2 Cor 3:17). But, what is the nature of the freedom of the Spirit and from what and to what does the Spirit set us free? Traditional North American Pentecostalism has often understood the freedom of the Spirit in personal terms. The Spirit brought freedom for Charismatic expression in contrast to the perceived stifled worship of the evangelical, mainline Protestant, and Catholic churches. It included freedom from the usual collection of personal sins, such as smoking and drinking. It also emphasized freedom from physical illness through divine healing.[31] Traditional North American Pentecostalism also has close ties with Evangelicalism. Like Evangelicals, Pentecostals have tended to associate social activism with the Social Gospel of the mainline churches and in contrast have emphasized that the essence of Christianity is a personal relationship with Jesus Christ.[32]

Although Pentecostals correctly maintain that the Holy Spirit saves and liberates individuals, Allan Anderson notes one danger of this theological focus "is that an emphasis on personal piety can become a sop for a lack of social conscience."[33] To put it explicitly, Pentecostalism has not had a strong propensity toward social engagement. Indeed, some scholars have even suggested that Pentecostal experience fosters social detachment and passivity rather than a proactive effort to engage and transcend social marginalization.[34] The exception to this in North America is the tendency of Pentecostals, especially in the last two decades of the twentieth century, to support conservative political positions and candidates. However, the Pentecostal movement is not without resources to develop a vision of redemption that encompasses both the personal and social dimensions of human life. The following discussion outlines two resources for developing a Progressive Pentecostalism; these resources are biblical and historical (which includes both the early Pentecostal experience at the Azusa Street Mission and even implicitly its emphasis on personal redemption

31. Opp, *Lord for the Body*.

32. See Blumhofer, Spittler, and Wacker, *Pentecostal Currents in American Protestantism*.

33. Anderson, *Introduction to Pentecostalism*, 263.

34. E.g., Anderson, *Vision of the Disinherited*.

and empowerment). By drawing on these two categories Pentecostals can pursue a theology of the freedom of the Spirit that applies both to the personal and to the social dimensions of human life.

BIBLICAL RESOURCES

Scripture gives an indication of the broad scope of the Spirit's work of liberation. In Genesis, the Spirit hovers over the cosmic chaos and is active in its transformation from chaos to Eden. The Spirit empowers Judges to liberate the tribes of Israel from their oppression. Although the methods used by the Judges may seem problematic to twenty-first century North Americans, they are portrayed as enabled by the Spirit and they are engaged in activities that bring social, political, and economic liberation to the oppressed. Isaiah describes the Messianic figure as one whom the Spirit will empower "to preach good news to the poor . . . to bind up the broken-hearted, to proclaim freedom for the captives and release for the prisoners . . . and to comfort all who mourn" (Isa 61:1–2). In Luke 4, Jesus announces that he is the fulfillment of these messianic expectations.

The Gospel of Matthew also draws on Isaiah to identify Jesus as the Spirit-anointed Messiah. In Matthew 12, Jesus first heals a man with a shriveled hand and then delivers a demon-possessed man. In order to interpret these healings, the Gospel applies Isa 42:1–4 to Jesus, which says, "Here is my servant whom I have chosen . . . I will put my Spirit on him and he will proclaim justice to the nations." The Gospel of Matthew thus announces that Jesus Christ is the messiah promised in the Isaiah passage; he is the servant who bears the Spirit and who will bring justice to the nations.

But how does Jesus bring justice in the Matthew 12 stories? He does so in at least two ways. First, he brings justice by expressing compassion for the man with the shriveled hand and the demon-possessed man and by rejecting the religious pretensions of the Pharisees. Second, his compassion leads him to redeem the material circumstances of their lives. He heals a physically disabled man and casts out a demon and thereby restores their bodies. Jesus's action toward the man who is physically disabled and the man who is blind and mute correspond to the imagery in Isaiah 42: "a bruised reed he will not break, and a smouldering wick he will not snuff out."

How does this relate to Pentecostalism and the social dimension of the freedom of the Spirit? First, Jesus's performs his acts of physical liberation by virtue of the anointing of the Holy Spirit. As Jesus proclaims to the Pharisees, "if I drive out demons by the Spirit of God, then the kingdom of God has come upon you" (Matt 12:28). Jesus's ministry of liberating people is also the work of the Holy Spirit. Thus, the coming of the kingdom of God needs to be understood in terms of Christology and pneumatology. Second, Jesus did not merely heal a hand and cast out a demon as well as restore sight and speech, but, on a very fundamental level, he transformed their lives. Healing opened up a new horizon of possibilities for their lives. The man healed of the shriveled hand now could live with a fully functioning body. The demon-possessed man could live a life without the debilitating effects of demonic power in his life; he could see and talk. Although the social mobility available to the men in Matthew 12 hardly compares to that of contemporary North Americans, their physical healing no doubt transformed the material and social circumstances of their lives. Thus, Jesus brings justice in the power of the Spirit by being compassionate toward the unattractive, the marginalized, and disenfranchised; by attending to those most of us ignore and relegate to forgotten anonymity; and by fanning the spark of the human spirit that has been nearly smothered by shame, betrayal, offence, and abuse. He does the above precisely by transforming the material aspects of people's lives.[35]

The central Pentecostal passage of Acts 2 and Joel 2 showcase the liberating nature of the outpouring of the Spirit. In Acts 2, Peter interprets the outpouring of the Spirit on the Day of Pentecost as the realization of the promise of Joel 2:28–32, which proclaims, "in the last days . . . I will pour out my Spirit on all people. Your sons and daughters will prophesy, your young men will see visions, your old men will dream dreams. Even on my servants, both men and women, I will pour out my Spirit in those days." Traditional Pentecostalism draws explicitly on the charismatic manifestations foretold in Joel and put on display in Acts 2, but it has not as effectively integrated the social message and liberating work of the Spirit in the Joel text. Yet, the text clearly indicates that the outpouring of the Spirit transcends various categories that human beings routinely use to justify the social marginalization and exploitation of other human beings—race and ethnicity, gender, and social status. Moreover, the implication can be

---

35. Yong makes a similar point under his discussions of material and social salvation. See *Spirit Poured Out on All Flesh*, 93–94.

drawn that the outpouring of the Spirit that transcends social barriers em-powers those who receive the Spirit to become people untrammeled by social prejudices. The outworking of this principle in Acts is the outpour-ing of the Spirit on the Samaritans and the Gentiles.

HISTORICAL RESOURCES

North American Pentecostalism also can draw on its early history for resources to discern ways the Spirit of freedom seeks to liberate human persons from the various forms of social oppression within the North American context. The early Pentecostal movement exhibited an expe-rience of the Spirit that liberated people from social prejudice. Toward the end of the last and beginning of the present centuries, scholars have pointed increasingly to William J. Seymour's and the Azusa Street Mission's experience of the Spirit that fostered ethnic, gender, and ecu-menical transcendent love.[36] For many early Pentecostals Spirit baptism was referred to as a baptism of love. It is this component of divine love that spills over into the social dimensions of life. Edith Blumhofer notes that the "multicultural root of Pentecostalism" thesis reflects more the in-terests of contemporary theology than the historical record of the Azusa Street revivals.[37] Blumhofer's point is a valid one and she may be largely correct that the current interest in multiculturalism and diversity moti-vates the desire to read the Azusa Mission in the above way.

At the same time, our current context may in fact help us to rec-ognize an underappreciated aspect of early Pentecostal experience. In this sense and as Walter J. Hollenweger notes, we are talking about a historical versus a theological discussion.[38] Historically, Spirit baptism and tongues have been the distinguishing doctrines of Pentecostalism, at least in respect to North American Classical Pentecostalism.[39] Yet, from a theological perspective, the multicultural and ecumenical community engendered by the outpouring of the Spirit among the early Pentecostals

36. E.g., Anderson, *Introduction to Pentecostalism*, 270–72; Hollenweger, *Pentecos-talism*, 18–23; Jacobsen, *Thinking in the Spirit*, 63 and 260–61; and Johns, "Pentecostal Spirituality and the Conscientization of Women," 161–65.

37. Blumhofer, "For Pentecostals, a Move Toward Racial Reconciliation," 445–46.

38. Hollenweger makes a similar argument in his critique of Goff's case for Parham as the founder of Pentecostalism instead of Seymour (*Pentecostalism*, 23).

39. E.g., Goff, *Fields White unto Harvest*, 164.

at the Azusa Mission may indicate the theological heart of the movement more so than the doctrines that have tended to characterize it.[40] Moreover, the early Pentecostal experience of the Spirit that overcame the social barriers at play in early-twentieth century North American culture coheres with the socially transcendent activity of the Spirit promised in Joel 2:28–32 and proclaimed as coming to realization on the Day of Pentecost in Acts 2:16–21. Thus, Pentecostal theology needs to recover the social transcending nature of the Spirit's work in order to be true to its biblical and traditional roots.

Ironically, Pentecostalism's traditional emphasis on personal salvation also promises to open up a horizon for a social vision of redemption. North American Pentecostals have tended to reduce the Gospel to a personal and spiritualized salvation. At the same time, and even if it is not made explicit, the traditional Pentecostal stress on personal spirituality and salvation carries with it an implicit message of redemption that entails a broader social emancipation.

Ministries such as Teen Challenge are a case in point.[41] Although its goal of helping people to realize the freedom of the Spirit in respect to the obvious addictions of drug and alcohol abuse reflects the individualism of traditional Pentecostalism, Teen Challenge also entails a broader manifestation of the freedom of the Spirit. The experience of deliverance from various forms of chemical addiction opens up a more expansive liberation for human persons than one limited to the "spiritual" matters of their lives. People who experience redemption from drugs and alcohol addiction suddenly have broader horizons of opportunity available to them. Understood theologically, indeed pneumatologically, these are horizons of the Spirit. For example, many people who have experienced redemption in Pentecostal religious contexts believe they are empowered to pursue higher education, to make a meaningful contribution in this world, and

40. Seymour clearly describes the Azusa Street revival as a multicultural and multiethnic experience. He states, "people of all nations came and got their cup full. Some came from Africa, some came from India, China, Japan, and England." However, he also laments the division that arose along racial lines; maintains that this development grieved the Holy Spirit; and urges the participants to seek unity among the various ethnic groups in order to experience the "greater liberty and freedom of the Holy Spirit" (Jacobsen, *Reader in Pentecostal Theology*, 53).

41. For a detailed analysis of Teen Challenge, see Solomon, *In God We Trust?* For an historical overview of religion and social action, see Schwartz, Warkentin, and Wilkinson, "Faith-Based Social Services in North America." See Wilkinson, "Faith-Based Social Services" for an assessment of Pentecostal social action.

to build healthy families. What is important for the social ramifications of Pentecostalism is that these are ways that people concretely embody the freedom of the Spirit in ways that are inevitably social.

"Where the Spirit of the Lord is, there is freedom" first from evil in its various personal and social forms. The Spirit liberates people, on the one hand, from their participation in personal destructive patterns of life that are self-imposed and/or imposed by others and, on the other hand, from their participation as perpetrators and/or victims in larger exploitive systems of evil. In other words, "where the Spirit of the Lord is, there is freedom" from sin and death in all of the forms that they seek to distort and destroy human lives. Second, the Spirit brings freedom *to* or *for* new ways of living that embrace possibilities that reflect the new creation (2 Cor 5:17) and anticipate in the present the Spirit's eschatological liberation of creation from all dimensions of sin and death (Rom 8:18–25).

PENTECOSTALS AND SOCIAL ACTION

The contributors to this book build on and extend contemporary Pentecostal efforts to engage social issues.[42] The book includes essays under the categories of race and ethnicity, gender, class, and ecology. These four areas represent key issues facing North Americans in the early twenty-first century. We believe that Pentecostalism can make an important contribution to illuminating an appropriate Christian response to these issues. Drawing on multiple disciplines, including theology, history, and sociology, the essays in the volume propose ways that Christians in twenty-first century North America can participate in the freedom of the Spirit that liberates human persons both from perpetrating and suffering social evil.

Section one treats the issue of Pentecostals, race, and ethnicity. It includes essays by Estrelda Alexander, Derrick Rosenior, and Clinton N. Westman. Alexander maintains that a liberation ethos can be found in formulations of some early black Holiness, Pentecostal and quasi-Pentecostal sects. Even though many scholars characterize the African American Pentecostal community as almost totally otherworldly and devoid of a relevant socio-political agenda, she insists that Pentecostals have produced

42 Although a fairly new agenda in Pentecostalism, this volume joins with others who have begun to see the need for Pentecostal scholarship to engage issues of social redemption. For examples, see Johns, "Pentecostal Spirituality and the Conscientization of Women," 153–80; Solivan, *Spirit, Pathos, and Liberation*; Villafañe, *Liberating Spirit*; and Yong, *Theology and Down Syndrome*.

sermons, hymns, essays, and monographs that can be critically mined for a wealth of liberation rhetoric and theology. Much of this rhetoric focuses on giving constituents a different lens through which to view themselves that refuted perceptions by the broader society, rather than engaging and challenging the society itself. Specifically, Pentecostals used four types of prophetic speech that attempted to redefine common theological concepts in a way that addressed the injustices and deficiencies of mainline white Christian theology. These include anthropological, Christological, soteriological, and eschatological redefinitions that enabled black Pentecostals to develop implications of Jesus's offer of abundant life that substantially starts in the here and now and to extrapolate from that abundance to liberation, not just for the person, but also for the community.

In "The Rhetoric of Pentecostal Racial Reconciliation: Looking Back To Move Forward," Rosenior deals with efforts among North American Pentecostals to achieve racial reconciliation. Although Pentecostalism began as an interracial and ecumenical movement, it quickly devolved into a segregated and sectarian one. In a 1994 conference, which became popularly known as the "Memphis Miracle," Pentecostals sought to achieve racial reconciliation. Rosenior argues that in order to achieve this much needed reconciliation, Pentecostals looked back to the narrative of the Azusa Street revival, reexamined their collective memory of the event, and in so doing mythologized the characters and events of that revival with the use of nostalgic rhetoric. He maintains that the interracial character of the Azusa Street revival can serve as a template for racial healing among contemporary Pentecostals.

Westman's essay treats the Pentecostal movement among Canadian Aboriginal peoples. He specifically assesses the degree to which Cree Pentecostalism can be considered as a political movement. Salient questions include whether Pentecostalism is inherently influenced by "right-wing" (that is, pro-development or anti-cultural) values, and whether Pentecostal conversion is characteristically linked to particular (often comparatively marginalized) strata within native society. While outside analysts who have considered these questions often answer them in the affirmative, he considers that such conclusions are simplistic and premature. Pentecostalism's status as a political movement is questionable, but as a religious movement it does have socio-political ramifications, and is situated within the general social context of Aboriginal peoples in Canadian society. In particular, Pentecostal leaders have linkages with a broader political cadre within Aboriginal society that extends from community leaders to the provincial legislature.

The second section explores Pentecostalism and issues of class. Peter Althouse critiques social deprivation interpretations of Pentecostalism while offering a theological appraisal. Deprivation theories based in the church-sect typology have been used by the social sciences to argue that the birth of early Pentecostalism and its practices of glossolalia was a religious sect spawned by poorly educated, lower class, blue collar, and rural workers trying to soothe the misery in their lives. Lack of evidence to support socioeconomic deprivation has forced social theorists to propose relative deprivation as a way of explaining the rise of religious sects, but with the result that they can no longer argue that Pentecostals are from a lower socioeconomic class. However, while willing to admit that Pentecostals today are represented predominantly by the middle class, the prevailing assumption remains that early Pentecostals were uneducated, lower class, and rural workers. Contrary to social deprivation theories, Althouse shows that recent evidence suggests that participants in early Pentecostalism consisted of the full spectrum of socioeconomic class and education, suggesting that perhaps deprivation theories are inherently flawed.

In the next chapter, Adam Stewart engages social deprivation interpretations of Pentecostalism. Many scholars from a variety of disciplines have long regarded Pentecostalism as a religion of the disinherited, the result of wishful thinking on the part of indigent dregs from either rural backwater boondocks or urban industrial cities. They argue that members from the lower classes find something in the Pentecostal tradition, such as closely-knit communal relationships, the promise of a mansion on a hilltop in the life to come, or the ecstatic experience of speaking in tongues, that somehow compensates for either their social, economic, or cultural deprivation. However, this common explanation for Pentecostal belief, practice, and affiliation fails to explain why many members from the upper-middle, and even upper classes, have been drawn to the Pentecostal tradition from the very inception of the movement. After charting examples of social deprivation interpretations of Pentecostalism, Stewart presents historical examples from both the United States and Canada that seriously challenge the conclusions of these scholars. He then proposes a new sociological way to envision the relationship between Pentecostals and social class that does not view Pentecostalism as primarily compensatory, but, rather explains why individuals from a wide array of socio-economic locations have been drawn to the Pentecostal tradition.

The third group of essays engages Pentecostalism and issues of gender. Andrea Hollingsworth and Melissa D. Browning suggest that Pentecostalism has the paradoxical quality of being at once limiting and liberating for women in their ongoing struggle for equality and empowerment. Their essay examines gender dynamics in two North American Pentecostal groups (neopentecostalism and the Sanctified Church), and nuances these analyses by comparing them with experiences of Pentecostal women in the global south. Based on their research, they draw two conclusions. First, where Pentecostalism is *limiting*, the influences of patriarchal European traditions are largely at work, as well as theological emphases on spirit-matter dualism and literalistic biblical interpretation. Second, where Pentecostalism is *liberating*, the ingenuity and courage of Spirit-filled women and men is present, creating a Spirit-space wherein marginalized voices emerge to interpret and proclaim the intuitions of the biblical tradition in the power of the Spirit. They believe that increased freedom and empowerment of Pentecostal women everywhere will require Pentecostal faith communities to work together to better discern the evocative and provocative voice of the liberating Spirit.

Pam Holmes's essay sets forth the case for a feminist-Pentecostal hermeneutic. She joins with an emerging effort among Pentecostal scholars to seek a Pentecostal hermeneutic. She notes that although some Pentecostal scholars are content to carry on evangelical methodologies, many Pentecostal scholars desire a hermeneutic that better represents the ethos and traditions of Pentecostalism. For this latter group, the rationalistic approaches adopted by various evangelical groups are inadequate and what is needed is an approach that recognizes both the Spirit's role and the community's role in the interpretative task. However, except for a few yet significant efforts, within these discussions feminist insights are minimal or absent. This is due to the fact that many Pentecostals tend to be indifferent to feminism or even anti-feminist. Within Pentecostalism, feminism is often viewed as a Western, middle class, academic, humanistic pursuit that neglects or dismisses movements of the Spirit. In order to accomplish her constructive project, she first examines the hermeneutical approaches of two feminists—Elisabeth Schüssler Fiorenza and Phyllis Trible—and then compares their thought with and shows how it contributes to Pentecostal discussions on hermeneutics. As this is a new and unique project, she also draw on her insights and experiences as an ordained Pentecostal clergyperson who was raised within the Pentecostal branch of the Christian church and continues to worship and minister in that context.

The fourth section includes three essays that explore the relationship between Pentecostalism and ecological issues. Michael Wilkinson's essay examines the response of a specific Pentecostal denomination, the Pentecostal Assemblies of Canada, to global problems with a focus on ecological issues. He uses a content analysis of the usage of "global" in the organization's official magazine to examine the frequency and incidence of the term since 1920. Further, an analysis of the specific articles with a focus on ecological concern is offered. The findings show a substantial increase in the usage and incidence of "global" corresponding with Roland Robertson's historical overview of globalization, especially during the "Uncertainty Phase" beginning in the 1960s. However, the particular responses to ecological issues do not fit easily the "liberal" and "conservative" categories typically offered to explain religious responses to social issues. A sociological analysis of religion and globalization is offered to explain the changing character of Pentecostalism and ecological issues in North America.

A. J. Swoboda's "Looking the Wrong Way" offers a survey of theological approaches to ecological theology and points the direction for a Pentecostal theology of the environment. Convinced that ecological issues are some of the most important of our time, he urges Pentecostals to step up to the task of offering a Pentecostal theology that will foster environmental action. Taking on the mantle of this constructive effort he proposes that environmental action is a sign of being Spirit-filled. He advocates that a Spirit-filled creation care can be the Pentecostal movement's contribution to the broader church of the twenty-first century. He believes that a robust and re-invigorated Pentecostal soteriology and pneumatology of creation will play a key role in developing a praxis-centered creation care and a relationality-centered ecological stewardship that will bring Pentecostals into a more effective role in facing the current environmental crisis.

Steven M. Studebaker presents a Pentecostal and theological rationale for seeing creation care as a participation in the redemptive mission of the triune God and, therefore, as a dimension of Christian formation. The foundation of this proposal is a fundamental trinitarian theology that provides a way for Pentecostals to see all of creation as taken up in the redemptive work of the triune God. Romans 8:18–27 promises the liberation of creation from its bondage to decay, Revelation 21 forecasts a new heaven and a new earth, and Revelation 22 portrays the eschaton in the imagery of Eden. Traditional theology readily recognizes that the Spirit is the breath of life in creation, but it often overlooks that the Spirit is at the same time the Spirit of redemption in creation. Since the Spirit who is present within the Christian is the same Spirit present within all of creation and since both are recipients of the promise of redemption, the Spirit's work in both should converge. The Holy Spirit works within human persons and creation at large to draw them toward their eschatological renewal. The result of this comprehensive understanding of the Spirit's work is that all of life is taken up in the eschatological redemption and that all redemptive acts, whether directed toward the traditional "spiritual" dimensions of soul care or more broadly toward creation care, are a participation in the Spirit of redemption. Just as the traditional acts of sanctification and Christian formation can be understood as proleptic experiences of the everlasting kingdom so also creation care is a prolepsis of the eschaton. Creation care is the convergence of the work of the Spirit in the human person and in the broader arena of creation and it is, therefore, a dimension of Christian formation.

It is our hope that this volume will contribute to a sustained research focus on Pentecostals and social issues. There is much work to be done in all of these areas addressed. However, Pentecostals need to continue to assess empirical work along with their theologizing as they address contemporary global issues not explored here including economic exploitation, political activism, sexual orientation, human rights, violence, and many more that affect our common humanity.

BIBLIOGRAPHY

Alexander, Paul. *Peace to War: Shifting Allegiances in the Assemblies of God*. Telford, PA: Cascadia, 2009.

Alves, Rubem. *A Theology of Human Hope*. Meinard, IN: Abbey, 1969.

Anderson, Allan. *An Introduction to Pentecostalism: Global Charismatic Christianity*. Cambridge: Cambridge University Press, 2004.

Anderson, Robert Mapes. *Vision of the Disinherited: The Making of American Pentecostalism*. Oxford: Oxford University Press, 1979.

Assmann, Hugo. *Theology for a Nomad Church*. Translated by Paul Burns. Maryknoll, NY: Orbis, 1976.

Baum, Gregory. *Religion and Alienation: A Theological Reading of Sociology*. New York: Paulist, 1975.

Berryman, Phillip. *Liberation Theology: The Essential Facts about the Revolutionary Movement in Latin America and Beyond*. Bloomington, IN: Meyer-Stone, 1987.

Beyer, Peter. "Defining Religion in Cross-National Perspective: Identity and Difference in Official Conceptions." In *Defining Religion: Investigating the Boundaries Between the Sacred and Secular*, edited by Arthur Greil and David G. Bromley, 163–88. New York: Elsevier, 2003.

———. "Movements, Markets, and Social Contexts: Canadian Pentecostalism in Global Perspective." In *Canadian Pentecostalism: Transition and Transformation*, edited by Michael Wilkinson, 264–76. Montreal: McGill-Queen's University Press, 2009.

Blumhofer, Edith. "For Pentecostals, A Move toward Racial Reconciliation." *Christian Century* 27 (1994) 445–46.

Blumhofer, Edith L., Russell P. Spittler, and Grant A. Wacker, editors. *Pentecostal Currents in American Protestantism*. Chicago: University of Illinois Press, 1999.

Boff, Leonardo. *Jesus Christ, Liberator: A Critical Christology for Our Times*. Translated by Patrick Hughes. Maryknoll, NY: Orbis, 1978.

Boesak, Allan. *Black and Reformed: Apartheid, Liberation, and the Calvinist Tradition*. Maryknoll, NY: Orbis, 1984.

Cox, Harvey. *Fire from Heaven: The Rise of Pentecostal Spirituality and the Reshaping of Religion in the Twenty-first Century*. Reading, MA: Addison-Wesley, 1995.

Dempster, Murray A., Byron D. Klaus, and Douglas Petersen, editors. *Called & Empowered: Global Mission in Pentecostal Perspective*. Peabody, MA: Hendrickson, 1991.

Ferm, Deane William. *Third World Liberation Theologies: An Introductory Survey*. Maryknoll, NY: Orbis, 1986.

Goff, James R., Jr. *Fields White unto Harvest: Charles F. Parham and the Missionary Origins of Pentecostalism*. Fayetteville: University of Arkansas Press, 1988.

Gutiérrez, Gustavo. *A Theology of Liberation: History, Politics, and Salvation*. Translated by Sister Caridad Inda and John Eagleson. Maryknoll, NY: Orbis, 1973.

Hollenweger, Walter J. *Pentecostalism: Origins and Developments Worldwide*. Peabody, MA: Hendrickson, 1997.

Jacobsen, Douglas, editor. *A Reader in Pentecostal Theology: Voices from the First Generation*. Bloomington: Indiana University Press, 2006.

———. *Thinking in the Spirit: Theologies of the Early Pentecostal Movement*. Bloomington: Indiana University Press, 2003.

Johns, Cheryl Bridges. *Pentecostal Formation: A Pedagogy among the Oppressed*. Journal of Pentecostal Theology Supplement Series 2. Sheffield, UK: Sheffield Academic, 1993.

———. "Pentecostal Spirituality and the Conscientization of Women." In *All Together in One Place: Theological Papers from the Brighton Conference on World Evangelization*, edited by Harold D. Hunter and Peter D. Hocken, 161–65. Sheffield, UK: Sheffield Academic, 1993.

Kofi, Appiah-Kubi, and Sergio Torres, editors. *African Theology En Route*. Maryknoll, NY: Orbis, 1979.

Koyama, Kosuke. *Waterbuffalo Theology: A Thailand Theological Notebook*. Maryknoll, NY: Orbis, 1974.

Martin, David. *Tongues of Fire: The Explosion of Protestantism in Latin America*. Oxford: Blackwell, 1990.

Mbiti, John. *Concepts of God in Africa*. London: SPCK, 1970.

McCloud, Sean. *Divine Hierarchies: Class in American Religion and Religious Studies*. Chapel Hill: University of North Carolina Press, 2007.

Miller, Donald E., and Tetsunao Yamamori. *Global Pentecostalism: The New Face of Christian Social Engagement*. Berkeley: University of California Press, 2007.

Miranda, José. *Marx and the Bible: A Critique of the Philosophy of Oppression*. Translated by John Eagleson. 1974. Reprinted, Eugene, OR: Wipf & Stock, 2004.

Opp, James. *The Lord for the Body: Religion, Medicine, and Protestant Faith Healing in Canada, 1880–1930*. Montreal & Kingston: McGill-Queen's University Press, 2005.

Poloma, Margaret, and Ralph Hood. *Fire and Blood: Godly Love in a Pentecostal Emerging Church*. New York: New York University Press, 2008.

Robertson, Roland. *Globalization: Social Theory and Global Culture*. London: Sage, 1992.

Schwartz, Kelly Dean, Buetta Warkentin, and Michael Wilkinson. "Faith-Based Social Services in North America: A Comparison of American and Canadian Religious History and Initiative." *Social Work and Christianity* 35 (2008) 123–47.

Segundo, Jaun Luis. *The Liberation of Theology*. Translated by John Drury. 1976. Reprinted, Eugene, OR: Wipf & Stock, 2002.

Shaull, Richard, and Waldo A. Cesar. *Pentecostalism and the Future of the Christian Churches: Promises, Limitations, and Challenges*. Grand Rapids: Eerdmans, 2000.

Sobrino, Jon. *Christology at the Crossroads: A Latin American Approach*. Translated by John Drury. 1978. Reprinted, Eugene, OR: Wipf & Stock, 2002.

Solivan, Samuel. *The Spirit, Pathos, and Liberation: Toward an Hispanic Pentecostal Theology*. Sheffield, UK: Sheffield, 1998.

Solomon, Lewis D. *In God We Trust? Faith-Based Organizations and the Quest to Solve America's Social Ills*. Lanham, MD: Lexington, 2003.

Song, C. S. *Third-Eye Theology*. 1979. Reprinted, Eugene, OR: Wipf & Stock, 2002.

Stoll, David. *Is Latin America Turning Protestant? The Politics of Evangelical Growth*. Berkeley: University of California Press, 1990.

Villafañe, Eldin. *The Liberating Spirit: Towards an Hispanic American Pentecostal Social Ethic*. Grand Rapids: Eerdmans, 1993.

Wallerstein, Immanuel. *The Modern World System: Capitalist Agriculture and the Origins of European World-Economy in the Sixteenth Century*. New York: Academic, 1974.

Wilkinson, Michael. "Faith-Based Social Services: Some Observations for Assessing Pentecostal Social Action." *Transformation* 24 (2007) 71–79.

Wilkinson, Michael, and Steven M. Studebaker. "A Liberating Spirit: Liberation Theology and the Pentecostal Movement." *Ecumenist* 45 (2008) 1–7.

Yong, Amos. *The Spirit Poured Out on All Flesh: Pentecostalism and the Possibility of Global Theology*. Grand Rapids: Baker, 2005.

———. *Theology and Down Syndrome: Reimagining Disability in Late Modernity*. Waco, TX: Baylor University Press, 2007.

Yong-Bok, Kim, editor. *Minjung Theology: People as the Subjects of History*. Maryknoll, NY: Orbis, 1983.

PART ONE

Issues of Race and Ethnicity

2

Recovering Black Theological Thought in the Writings of Early African-American Holiness-Pentecostal Leaders

Liberation Motifs in Early African-American Pentecostalism

Estrelda Alexander

INTRODUCTION

The insistence by liberation theologian James Cone that God is black as well as the affirmation by womanist theologian, Jacqueline Grant, that the Jesus of black women (and by inference the black community) is diametrically different than white women's Christ are not completely new concepts.[1] In the 1960s and 1970s, black theologians such as Major Jones traced the spiritual heritage that affirmed the ecumenical doctrines of

---

1. Cone, *Black Theology of Liberation* and Grant, *White Women's Christ and Black Women's Jesus.*

the Trinity, Christology, soteriology, and pneumatology for African Americans from sub-Saharan Africa. In every instance, Jones insisted one must ask, "What does this mean for Black people?"[2]

At first glance, much of this conversation seems strangely out of place when one speaks of a particular segment of the black church—the African American Pentecostal community. The accusation that Pentecostalism, particularly African American Pentecostalism, is primarily otherworldly and devoid of a relevant socio-political agenda has found common script among contemporary religion scholars. Because a concept is often repeated, however, does not give it total legitimacy, no matter who contributes to its promulgation. Despite what Amos Yong refers to as the "typical apolitical orientation of much of classical Pentecostalism" and J. Deotis Roberts's contention that the movement is "notoriously short on social conscience and social sins" and that "there is little concern for social transformation," an Africentric, liberative ethos can be found in various forms of formulation in some early Pentecostal and quasi-Pentecostal sects.[3]

The further assumptions that the Pentecostal church is an almost totally oral expression, and lacks the presence of leaders with either the intellectual acuity or ethical interest to craft either a systematic or constructive theological framework representative of the movement are also not entirely true. While the second assumption is, on the surface, somewhat more valid, in that no cogent body of systematic theology has been developed within the tradition, it does not take into consideration the substantial body of work Pentecostals have produced over the life of the movement—not only in sermons, doctrinal statements, and hymns, but in essays and monographs—that take on a variety of subjects. These have been largely overlooked by many both within and outside of the movement, primarily because they have not been marketed as systematic tomes, but have been developed in response to existential necessity. Though much of this work remains unpublished, or has been published by small personal or denominational presses, it needs to be critically engaged to mine from it the wealth of theology that does exist.

It is also a popular mischaracterization of Pentecostals that they are entirely captivated by the fundamentalist or "Christian Right" movement.

---

2. Jones, *Color of God*, 84.

3. Yong, "Justice Deprived, Justice Demanded," 130 and Roberts, *Black Theology in Dialog*, 59.

In truth, Pentecostals, who align themselves squarely in the evangelical camp, have never been an integral part of the fundamentalist wing of Evangelicalism, and for the most part have shied away from the fundamentalist-liberal controversy for a number of reasons. First, fundamentalists generally denounce Pentecostal theological offerings along with those of liberals and Catholics. Second, while fundamentalism primarily falls into the Calvinist camp, Pentecostal doctrine is generally Arminian. Further, the close alliance that has developed over the years between Evangelicals and Pentecostals came about only as Evangelicals began to distance themselves from the fundamentalist camp following World War II.[4]

It is fairly easy to attempt to refute myths, without producing any solid evidence that the reality of a situation is to the contrary. But if one is to escape the charge of simply being revisionist, argumentation for a different reality must involve exposing not just isolated incidences that prove the exception, but must also bring a level of interrogation that shows a different and sustained pattern of engagement that had previously been overlooked. Such a pattern is evident when one takes the time and energy to unearth the voice of protest that has been an integral part of the Afro-Pentecostal movement from its inception.

Surely there is a real sense in which the voice of Afro-Pentecostal leaders was not as clearly communicated to the broader society as were those from other sectors of the black church—especially those considered more liberal. Much of the rhetoric developed within the Pentecostal movement addressed its own constituents and focused on giving its adherents a different lens through which to view themselves while refuting perceptions that were forced on them by the broader society, rather than engaging and challenging that society. Yet upon closer inspection, four types of prophetic speech can be detected in the writings of early black Pentecostals. Each has a different focus, but each redefines common theological concepts in a manner that attempts to address existing social realities as well as deficiencies of mainline white Christian theology.

Anthropological redefinitions provided black Pentecostals with a sense of self not rooted in the dominant society's unbiblical definitions of what it meant to be human, but upheld an understanding of the full humanity and dignity of each person. Christological redefinitions posited a description of Jesus that aligned him with the suffering African American community and lifted up themes of liberation and Christ as

---

4. See Hunter, *American Evangelicalism*, 42–46.

liberator. Soteriological redefinitions broadened the understanding of sin to encompass more than just failures of personal piety, but also to include the failure of individuals and institutions to faithfully live out the mandate for justice. Eschatological redefinitions posited a different future for African Americans than the present reality that held them hostage to injustice and deprivation.

This chapter attempts to correct the common misconception that early Holiness-Pentecostalism was a movement devoid of a liberative social ethic by looking at evidence of social protest within three distinctive eras: the Wesleyan Holiness movement that was the theological and intellectual precursor to Pentecostalism, the engagement of Pentecostals in the Civil Rights movement, and contemporary Pentecostal thought. The expressions we examine represent a little known tradition of liberative discourse that has existed since the inception of the movement, but has been overlooked by scholars who have paid closer attention to its more sectarian elements. They allow us to see that without developing a full-fledged liberation theology, early African American Holiness and Pentecostal leaders and later Pentecostal scholars were outspoken critics of the inequities of American race politics and crafted biblical objections to understandings of racial inferiority or the injustice of social, political, and economic inequity.

WESLEYAN-HOLINESS ROOTS OF BLACK PENTECOSTAL LIBERATION THOUGHT

Black Pentecostal leaders inherited a tradition of religious protest against social injustice from the antecedent Wesleyan Holiness movement on which it depended for much of its doctrinal and ethical foundations. Over Pentecostalism's more than one hundred year history, Pentecostals incorporated the Wesleyan Holiness heritage into formulations that appeared in their preaching, teaching, hymnody, and writing in response to a myriad of issues that faced not only their local congregations, but their surrounding communities and the entire race as well.

The Wesleyan Holiness movement was noted for its radical equality and openness to a degree of racial inclusiveness unprecedented in most of the rest of American society. This heritage stood against slavery and racial inequality as well as upheld a radically different view of the quality of women and men before God and in relationship to each other.

This inclusiveness, however, was not without limitation and women and black Holiness leaders responded by formulating theological positions that called into question the racial and gender politics of whites and men within the movement, as well as the failure of white Holiness leaders to take a more active and visible role in assisting their black brothers and sisters to gain full enfranchisement within American society.

Itinerant Holiness women preachers such as Jarena Lee, Zilpha Elaw, and Amanda Berry Smith used the language of sanctification as a synonym for liberation and insisted that the blood of Jesus liberated them not only from personal sin, but from a less than adequate estimate of their divine worth rendered by whites and men. Tying their personal salvation to their own social liberation, they took for themselves a more aggressive attitude toward mistreatment than they would have claimed prior to their sanctification. Amanda Berry Smith's nearly six hundred page autobiography is laced with social critique of both the sexism and racism she noted within the church and broader society. At one point, she insisted that "I think some people would understand the quintessence of sanctifying grace if they could be black about twenty-four hours."[5] These women railed against both the racism they found in the larger Christian context and the sexism they experienced at the hands of their black brethren that essentially kept them from the possibility of assuming viable pastorates and forced them into itinerancy. Significantly, their liberative legacy would later be picked up by two black Pentecostal matriarchs: Mary Magdalena Lewis Tate and Ida Bell Robinson.

The Holiness leader, William Christian, born in Mississippi in 1856, was a slave during the earliest years of his life. He came of age during the period of Reconstruction. Because of this, he was acutely aware of the racial dynamic of his Southern environment and intentionally set out to address racial inequality. He also had been Baptist before coming into the Holiness movement. From its inception, his denomination, the Church of the Living God (Christian Workers for Fellowship), took on the mantle of combating racist teachings, particularly the claims of some Baptist preachers in the latter part of the nineteenth century that Negroes were not men, but the outcome of a human father and a female beast.[6] To refute this philosophy, Christian developed an early Black theology

5. Smith, *Autobiography*, 116–17.
6. Hollenweger, "Black Pentecostal Concept," 16–19.

asserting that "the saints of the Bible belonged to the black race."[7] The CWFF's statement of faith explicitly states: "We believe in the Fatherhood of God and the Brotherhood of man" and "We believe that all men are born free and equal."[8]

Christian grounded his anthropology within a reworking of Christology, teaching that since Jesus had no earthly father, he belongs to all people and is therefore "colorless."[9] Further, to Christian, because his lineage came through that of Abraham and David, Jesus was black, as were many other saints of the Bible. An excerpt from the catechism of the Church of the Living God gives evidence that Christian employed a liberative hermeneutic that allowed him not only to claim racial affinity with Jesus, but with other biblical characters as well:

> Question: Was Jesus a member of the black race?
> Answer: Yes. Matthew 1.
> Question: How do you know?
> Answer: Because He was in the line of Abraham and David the king.
> Question: Is this assertion sufficient proof that Christ came of the black generation?
> Answer: Yes.
> Question: Why?
> Answer: Because David said he became like a bottle in the smoke (Ps 119:83).
> Question: What color was Job?
> Answer: He was black (Job 30:30).
> Question: Who was Moses's wife?
> Answer: An Ethiopian (or black) woman (Num 12:1).
> Question: What color was Jeremiah?
> Answer: He said he was black (Jer 8:21).
> Question: Should we make a difference in people because they are black?
> Answer: No (Jer 13:23).
> Question: Why?
> Answer: Because it is as natural to be black as the leopard to be spotted (Jer 13:23).[10]

7. Ibid., 18–19.

8. Articles of Faith, Church of the Living God (Christian Workers for Fellowship).

9. Ibid.

10. A Catechism: The Church of the Living God."

The last question must not be understood as one that asks if people should be treated differently because of their race. Rather it is asking whether black people should be discriminated against or denied dignity and respect because of their blackness.

Another Holiness leader, Charles Price Jones, who with Charles Harrison Mason founded the body that became the Church of Christ Holiness, was vitally concerned with the social implications of the race dilemma in America, and sought to bring solace and encouragement to his black brothers and sisters. In his *Appeal to the Sons of Africa*, Jones was cognizant of the hardships their social situation caused and did not fail to deal with the issue of racial prejudice and segregation.[11] But he employed a more accommodationist approach to addressing these issues. He implored blacks not to respond to white oppression by engaging in immoral or unethical behavior, but to do all they could to lift themselves and then trust God for ultimate deliverance. Yet even such an accommodationist stance cannot be dismissed as totally otherworldly. For Jones was as concerned about the temporal welfare of the blacks he led as about their eternal state. He was particularly concerned that blacks should respect and honor each other in the face of dishonor from the white community. But he also envisioned a different future for which blacks should prepare themselves.

In his namesake poem "An Appeal to the Sons of Africa," Jones declared that:

> I know we have a noble race
> Of curled hair and ebon face,
> And princes have from Egypt come;
> God has in Ethiop's breast a home
> Some of the noblest of men
> Have of the Afric descent been[12]

Along with poetry, Jones used prose to spur blacks to live out Christian convictions despite unchristian treatment by whites. In another poem, "Little Black Boy" in the same volume, he envisioned a different temporal future for which blacks should prepare themselves as much as they prepared for heaven:

11. C. P. Jones, *Appeal to the Sons of Africa*, 95–98.
12. Ibid., 17–18.

... As I looked in the depth of the little black eye
And studied the soul that behind it did lie
I wondered, "whatever on earth will he be?"
No telling, no telling, the living will see
He may be a governor, a president, or
He may be a colonel or general in war
He may be a minister, faithful to God
He may be a doctor, or lawyer—or fraud.[13]

EARLY PENTECOSTALS

The legacy of these black Holiness and proto-Pentecostal leaders such as Christian and Jones and the itinerant women informed the radical egalitarian nature of early Pentecostal meetings and rhetoric, even while evidence of race prejudice was subtly or blatantly demonstrated by some white Pentecostal leaders. As leader of the extraordinary Azusa Street Revival that unfolded in 1906, William Seymour promoted racial unity among black, white, Latino, and other believers. Yet Seymour was not oblivious to the racial realities of the culture in which he found himself, and ultimately, after several disastrous encounters with fellow white leaders, determined that the health of his local congregation could best be served by limiting its leadership to blacks, while not breaking fellowship with whites.

Within the popular imagination, the revival which Seymour led was most noted for its ecstatic worship, and particularly for its emphasis on Holy Spirit baptism with outbursts of speaking in tongues. But recent scholarship on the revival, which lasted for more than seven years, highlights its unprecedented racial mixing and gender equality, and the remarkable absence of class distinction. While many of those in attendance were poor or working class, several were from the middle and upper class. More importantly, these distinctions were eliminated in leadership decisions. Clerical distinctions were irrelevant as whoever the Spirit moved upon was allowed to exhort, preach, or pray.

Though Seymour was largely ignored by early white scholars of Pentecostalism, his rediscovery has sparked new interest in the race politics within the nascent movement. Raised in post-Reconstruction Louisiana,

13. Ibid., 47.

Seymour had witnessed first-hand the racial atrocities perpetrated against blacks in that state. Escaping to the relative freedom of the North, he was again subjected to discrimination even at the hands of fellow religionists. But it was when he found himself in the South that he was to suffer perhaps one of his most egregious indignities. As a student at Parham's Bible school in Houston, Texas, he was forced to sit outside the classroom to listen to the lectures instead of being seated in the room with white classmates.

Seymour came to believe that blacks and whites worshipping together was a more authentic sign of God's blessing and the Spirit's healing presence than speaking in tongues. He was concerned that his white brothers and sisters would be liberated from the sin of racism, and traveled throughout the United States, fervently preaching against intolerance. Yet Seymour's efforts were largely unsuccessful in staving off the seemingly inevitable racial division that occurred in the movement within a few years.

Seymour's final exasperation with the race issue was evident in an item in the *Doctrines and Disciplines of the Apostolic Faith Mission*, published in 1915—fifty years after the Emancipation Proclamation declared slavery illegal. Seymour's parents had been slaves before his birth, though he had never been a slave. But the memory of the deplorable conditions left in slavery's aftermath in Louisiana appear to have been fresh on his mind, even fifty years after freedom came. In a section entitled, "Concerning the Institution of Slavery," Seymour wrote:

> We are as much as ever convinced of the great evil of slavery. We believe that the buying, selling, or holding of human beings, to be used as chattels, is contrary to the laws of God and nature, and inconsistent with the golden rule, and with that rule in our discipline which requires all who desire to continue among us to "do no harm," and to "avoid evil of every kind." We therefore affectionately admonish all our ministers and people to keep themselves pure from this great evil, and to seek its extirpation by all lawful and Christian means.[14]

Seymour did not generally offer a sophisticated systematic theological argument. The only other definitive statement Seymour seems to have made concerning racial justice is a terse remark he made on the subject. Seymour asserted, "Christ is neither black, nor white, He is neither

14. Seymour, *Doctrines and Disciplines*, 83.

Chinese, nor Hindu, nor Japanese—but God, and God is a Spirit."[15] But he was quick to point out that at the revival held at his Azusa Street Mission, "people from all nations got their cup full. Some came from Africa . . . , from India, China, Japan, and England."[16]

Seymour's project was not so much about liberating the black race from the effects of racism within society as it was to liberate all men and women from the demoralizing effects of race prejudice within the Church. For Seymour insisted that the lack of unity was as unfortunate for whites as for blacks because it robbed them of the unity that Christ had intended for his Church. Even here, he did not offer a sophisticated systematic theological argument. Rather, he attempted to live out a vision of a Spirit-empowered mutuality and simply stated: "The colored brethren must love the white brethren and respect them in the truth so that the Word of God may have its free course, and our white brethren must love our colored brethren and respect them in the truth so that the Holy Spirit will not be grieved."[17] Part of Seymour's spiritual nurture came at the hands of the Evening Light Saints, a radically egalitarian Holiness group that denounced all forms of racial, gender, and cultural discrimination as thoroughly unbiblical. During his tenure with them, Seymour gained an appreciation for the possibility of people of various cultures being in Christian fellowship and working together without regard for the restrictions that characterized the rest of society.

As pastor of the Azusa Street Mission in Los Angeles, Seymour was as much concerned with the liberation of his black brothers and sisters from unjust discrimination as he was for their eternal wellbeing. The interracial aspects of the movement in Los Angeles were a striking contrast to the racism and segregation of the times. The phenomenon of blacks and whites worshipping together under a Black pastor seemed incredible to many observers. The ethos of the meeting was captured by Frank Bartleman, a White Azusa participant, when he said of Azusa Street, "The color line was washed away in the blood." Indeed, people from all the ethnic minorities of Los Angeles, a city that Bartleman called "the American Jerusalem," were represented at Azusa Street.[18]

---

15. Ibid., 13.

16. Ibid., 10.

17. Ibid.

18. Bartleman, *How Azusa came to Los Angeles*, 54.

Elias Dempsey Smith, founder of Triumph the Church and Kingdom of God, made a distinction between the "church militant of whites and the peace loving church of blacks." Dempsey joined forces with Charles Harrison Mason shortly after his group was founded in 1904. But while Mason was open to interracial cooperation and fellowship, his racial ethics were too conciliatory for Smith. After World War I, the generally elusive Smith became involved in the Back to Africa movement and Ethiopianism. In 1919 he hosted Marcus Garvey, head of the Universal Negro Improvement Association at the denomination's national convention. In 1920, Smith made a pilgrimage to Ethiopia, where he was given the reception of a king, including a lavish banquet. He died the next day.

Smith's foundation for establishing his denomination rested on what he saw as a God-given vision, in which an eagle, lion, and "brown skin damsel," dressed as a bride adorned for her husband, whom he married. According to Smith, the vision symbolized that through the strength God would provide, as represented by the lion, the black church and the entire black world would have the ability to birth all its needs.[19] The national anthem of the Triumph the Church declares its focus on Ethiopia as the center of civilization and God's redemptive plan for humanity:

> Onward, onward Ethiopia (3x)
> In this great triumphant church.
>
> God is calling Ethiopia (3x)
> To this great triumphant church.
>
> Gather yourselves together Ethiopians (3x)
> In this great triumphant church.
>
> They are coming from the north. They are coming from the south.
> They are coming from the east. They are coming from the west.
> They are coming from all nations to the fountain to be blest.
> In this great triumphant church.
>
> Come and get your blessings Ethiopians (3x)
> In this great triumphant church.[20]

19. Triumph the Church and Kingdom of God in Christ Constitution, n.l., n.p, n.d. 11.

20. Triumph National Anthem. Triumph the Church and Kingdom of God in Christ: http://www.triumphthechurchnatl.org/creed%20and%20Anthem.htm#Creed/ Anthem.

Smith called upon his followers to "take a definite stand against prejudice and segregation in church, society and state."[21] According to the denomination's official history, he further cautioned, "Don't be looking for a white Jesus coming down on a cloud, nor don't you expect to go up on one. Understand what the Scriptures say."[22]

Even today, the church that Smith established has imbibed his theology and carried it even further, espousing an afro-centric approach that incorporates elements of ecclesiology, anthropology, and eschatology into its theology. For example, its general catechism teaches that, "for God's everlasting kingdom, there is an original language that God gave man in the Garden of Eden when he created Adam and Eve . . . for . . . the Holy Ghost will teach a language that the kingdoms of this world will not be able to learn unless they are filled with that Spirit."[23] Further, it insists that, "God will return every earthly kingdom to the people that came from beyond the rivers of Ethiopia. Many nations and kingdoms all over the world have been built by the blood, sweat and slavery of Ethiopian descendants. The DNA of Ethiopia is everywhere on this earth." The catechism further asserts that "God has [en]trusted the Jews with a dispensation, and . . . the Gentiles [i.e., non-Blacks] with a dispensation, but God is now calling Ethiopia (the black race). God will turn every kingdom of this world over to us, but we must become the royal priesthood and holy nation that he has called us to be."[24]

Dempsey's and Jones's one time collaborator, Charles Harrison Mason, took a different stance regarding issues of race. While more conciliatory than Dempsey, unlike Jones, Mason was dedicated to recovering the influence of Africa, preserving the cultural expression of slaves within the black church. He incorporated Africanisms including shouting (or dancing) and healing ritual into the ministry of the Church of God in Christ and took pains to ensure that such expression was not only allowed, but celebrated.

Though the majority of his rhetoric dealt with more eternal matters, Mason took a definite stand on two temporal issues that had important consequences for his black constituents: pacifism and lynching. Mason's

21. McKinney, "Azusa Street Revival."

22. "Church Covenant," Triumph the Church and Kingdom of God in Christ, Sixth Episcopal District: http://www.triumphthechurchnatl.org/creed%20and%20Anthem. htm#Creed/Anthem.

23. McKinney, "Azusa Street Revival."

24. Ibid.

outspoken pacifist convictions were so strong that they kept him under surveillance by the Federal Bureau of Investigation (FBI) and led to his incarceration on at least two occasions. During World War I, Mason's pacifist stance made him one of the earliest Pentecostal political activists and incurred the suspicion of the federal government.[25] Mason was jailed in 1918 for explicitly preaching against "trusting in the power of the United States" and its allies instead of "trusting in God."[26] But though some accused him of being a German sympathizer, later that year he preached a sermon condemning treason.[27] For Mason, the shedding of blood and taking of life was contrary to the teaching of Jesus. In its earliest days, COGIC was opposed to military engagement in all its forms and did not differentiate between just and unjust war. Mason articulated a practical liberation theology in which he saw God on the side of the widow, orphan, and the downtrodden. For him, lynchings were being carried out because "the preachers are leading people away from the reproof of God and not to the glory of God. They are cowards until they are baptized with Jesus' baptism."[28]

Bishop Ida Robinson founded the Mt. Sinai Holy Church of America to liberate women from the dominance of hierarchical and exclusionary leadership structures within black Pentecostalism. She developed her organization's newsletter, *The Latter Day Messenger* to deal with a variety of social, ethical, and religious issues. Articles, sermon excerpts, testimonials, and praise reports from the various congregations, constituent letters, and items showed the breadth of Robinson's and her congregation's concerns. Amid birth announcements or coverage of weddings, issues such

25. For a discussion of Mason's activist activities see, Kornweibel, "I Thank my God for the Persecution," 149–63.

26. Kornweibel, "Bishop C. H. Mason and the Church of God during World War I," 277.

27. Ibid., 265.

28. This quote is from a sermon Mason preached on Sunday at Convocation, December 7, 1919. The statement raises a question of what cowardly preachers Mason was talking about. White or black, present or absent preachers? Given the lack of political voice of black men, and their constant life-risk in the South, it seems unlikely (though possible) that Mason would have been making this evaluation of them. The vast majority of the nation's preachers were white men and the voices of white men (including preachers who had been abolitionists) were all but silent against lynching (Blum, *Reforging the White Republic*). It seems likely that he was directing it to whomever "the shoe fit," and however it fit. See Mason, *History and Life Work of Elder C. H. Mason*, 49.

as racial and economic discrimination, race relations, and women's roles in the church stood side by side with doctrinal discussions.

While like the majority of Pentecostals, she was theologically conservative, holding to such doctrines as the inerrancy of Scripture, the Virgin birth, and a literal heaven and hell, Robinson was genuinely concerned with the material welfare of her congregations and the entire African American community in the here and now. For despite holding conservative views of personal piety including strictures on social activity, dress, and family relations, Robinson was socially progressive. Not only was she interested in providing spiritual, but also moral leadership for her denomination. Robinson was not afraid to take unpopular stands on controversial issues and, therefore, was not without controversy within the circle of people who knew of her. One organization that knew of her and kept her activities under scrutiny was the United States government—the FBI.

A series of factors kept Robinson under FBI surveillance in the 1930s and 1940s. First, her congregation was racially mixed at a time when segregation, even in the North, was at its height. Among the whites who were a part of her congregation was her secretary, a German woman, married to an Italian man. During the war, they were suspected of sympathizing with the enemy—a situation that brought Robinson's congregation under suspicion of harboring enemy sympathizers.[29]

Robinson was furthermore an outspoken pacifist. Members of Mount Sinai could serve in the armed forces, but only as conscientious objectors. She used her radio broadcast to take stands on her moral convictions, including her stance against supporting the war effort. This action brought severe consequences from the federal government. Twice in 1942 she was placed on the FBI list of suspected agitators for remarks allegedly supporting Japanese victories during the early war years.[30] Whether Robinson made the alleged remarks is under contention; and her name was later dropped from the FBI list.

As an example of Robinson's moral courage and ability to tackle issues beyond the specific spiritual needs of her constituency is an unsigned article entitled "The Economic Persecution," that is attributed to her in

29. Interview with Harold Trulear, June 20, 2001.

30. Federal Bureau of Investigation. Foreign Inspired Agitation among the American Negroes in Philadelphia Division. File No. 100–135–37–2, Section 39497 July, 1942 and File No. 100–135–37–9, September, 1942. This document is available under the Freedom of Information Act. Though significant information is blocked, a list of those under surveillance is attached; Robinson's name is clearly identified.

The Latter Day Messenger. In it, Robinson prominently attacked racial discrimination in America and compared the lynching of Blacks in the Southern United States with the persecution of Christians under pagan emperors of the early centuries.[31] She also attacked the hypocrisy of the Southern white church for not taking a stand against the hideous occurrences she graphically depicts or standing against racism in general:

> Our people in certain southern states are killed, their bodies dismembered and thrown to vultures. This, of course[,] is a common occurrence, and unfortunately where "Christianity" is more prevalent than any part of our union. For in this section of the country, laws are made to uphold Christianity in their states, and to prevent any teachings in their institutions of learning that tend to distort, minimize or otherwise change the principle of the doctrine of Christianity as taught in the Bible; . . . anyone found guilty of teaching doctrine contrary to Christianity in any [state] supported school . . . [that person] shall be punished to the extent of the law. . . . But these same people . . . will toss their own laws to the four winds and trample under feet the laws of Christianity and utterly ignore the words of the sacred "Book" they pretend to love so dearly, and esteem so highly. . . . So let us Saints pray that the Constantine of our day . . . sends a letter to the modern pagans in the polluted southland in the form of "Anti-Lynching" legislation that is now pending in Congress. We can overcome and we will overcome, right here in this present world, the persecution we ar[e] made to suffer by our unjust brethren. It is written, the Ethiopians shall stretch forth their hands in righteousness to God, and by the help of God and the agencies He has so gloriously provided, we shall overcome.[32]

These early Pentecostal leaders were neither completely unlearned nor oblivious to the social realities which constricted the freedom of their people to live out the full dignity of their humanity. Though they were not systematically trained theologians, they took the biblical witness of the equality of all people before God and what they saw as the ungodly treatment of their fellow black as a mandate to simply speak the truth to the evil systems that surrounded them.

---

31. Robinson, "Economic Persecution," 2. Collier-Thomas cites this work as a sermon of Robinson's in *Daughters of Thunder*, 203–5.

32. Robinson, "Economic Persecution," 2.

STRAINS OF LIBERATIVE THEMES IN ONENESS PENTECOSTAL THOUGHT

In 1915, Holiness minister William T. Phillips left his Mobile, Alabama, Methodist Episcopal Church to found the Ethiopian Overcoming Holy Church of God and embrace oneness Pentecostal doctrine. Phillips used the term "Ethiopian" to emphasize the African heritage of black people in America. Though Phillip's "first inclination was to make this church strictly a Black religious movement," he came to realize "the inadequacy of any spirituality that was defined and controlled by "racialistic denominationalism," and determined that "holiness is not racial, it is Biblical."[33] So in 1927, he changed the term Ethiopian to Apostolic to make the church more racially inclusive and more clearly identifiable as an Apostolic denomination, and changed the wording of the statement of faith to declare that, in the Apostolic Overcoming Holy Church of God, "We believe, in the equality of all mankind and that every man's duty toward God is the same."[34]

Garfield T. Haywood is one of the most well-known figures in early black oneness Pentecostalism.[35] As a leader and later presiding bishop of the Pentecostal Assemblies of the World (PAW), Haywood would write hundreds of sermons and hymns and a number of books that have become standards among African American Pentecostals. He also published a periodical, *Voice in the Wilderness*, until his death in 1931. His writing principally dealt with doctrinal issues relating primarily to the dogmatic defense of oneness theology, yet he did not completely ignore the racial realities of his constituencies. Further, the continued existence of PAW as an integrated religious body with congregations in both the South and North was a testimony to lived protest of the racial mores of early twentieth century American society. As long as Haywood served at the head of the denomination, he struggled to maintain that multi-racial presence within the denomination.

As a young man, Garfield T. Haywood worked as a writer and cartoonist for two secular African American newspapers in Indianapolis—

33. Ayers, "Apostolic Movement."

34. "What We Believe." The Official Website of the Apostolic Overcoming Holy Church.

35. The most distinguishing marks of the oneness (or "Jesus only" or Apostolic) movement is its insistence on the necessity of baptism "in the name of Jesus" rather than with the Trinitarian formula and the oneness belief in a modalistic understanding of the Godhead.

the *Freedmen* and the *Recorder*. His caricatures depicted concern with race issues. Both newspapers commented regularly on discrimination within the Indianapolis community and throughout the nation. However, since the majority of the articles in these periodicals were unsigned it is difficult to determine Haywood's specific contribution.[36] From the beginning of Haywood's ministry, his Indianapolis congregation was interracial, even while the state of Indiana maintained a heavy Ku Klux Klan presence. And, though his writings on race and social issues were not prolific, his dedication to maintaining an interracial body in the midst of rampant racism even from within demonstrated a commitment never repeated in Pentecostalism.

Robert Lawson, another important figure within African American oneness Pentecostalism,[37] founded the Church of Our Lord Jesus Christ of the Apostolic Faith in 1918. This body has been the parent—or grandparent—denomination of several major oneness denominations, and during the mid-twentieth century oneness leaders generally paid homage to Lawson and Haywood as being progenitors. Like Haywood, Lawson was a prolific songwriter, author, businessman, and community leader, as well as pastor of one of the most influential congregations within the black Oneness movement. While like most other Pentecostals of his day Lawson espoused a strict personal moral code and a hopeful eschatological vision of ultimate justice, he was also an outspoken opponent of segregation who led his denomination in manning a sustained effort to fight discrimination. He represents one of the most unrelenting Pentecostal challenges to the status quo of mid-twentieth century American racial politics. Speaking to the church in particular, Lawson contended that: "The church should set the example of democracy and no man or woman should be denied the right to worship his God in any church in the country. There should be no segregated episcopal districts where whites are set apart from Negroes when they are supposed to be worshipping the same God. . . . It is the church's job not to foster, aid[,] or abet white supremacy through segregation[,] but to eliminate it."[38]

36. Two of his cartoons appear in Garrett's biography, *Man Ahead of his Times*, 40–42.

37. For an overview of African American Oneness Pentecostalism, see Richardson, *With Water and Spirit*. Also see Reed, *In Jesus' Name*.

38. Lawson, *Open Letter to a Southern White Minister on Prejudice*, 20.

Lawson shared with his predecessor, Seymour, the unrealized hope that, "the Pentecostal movement could have been the church which should redeem Christendom [sic] from the virus and plague of race prejudice and segregation."[39] He insisted that, "a Christian's moral judgment should never represent the prejudice of the community."[40] He went on to lament that, "[w]e have white Pentecostal churches and colored Pentecostal churches, white bishops and colored bishops. We have Jim Crowed the Lord's table which is an effrontery to God."[41] Further, Lawson insisted that racism within a Christian community is sin—a violation of the very gospel entrusted to it, and a "spiritual monstrosity, not just a question of one's preference or a spot on the garment of faith."[42]

Obviously, Lawson was writing for a broader audience than the black church. He was intent on challenging misguided conceptions of black inferiority held by white Christians, and berated the abuse of the truth of the history of black people, insisting that "the only thing to kill race prejudice is to give truth, knowledge, and understanding to races that are prejudiced against each other."[43] But Lawson's critique was not even confined to the broader church. He was aware of the negative implications of racism in America for the spread of the Gospel throughout the world, and insisted: "The status of race relations is not only affecting international affairs, but also the status of Christianity before the world . . . because of color prejudice . . . the darker races have reached a point where they will not graciously accept a gospel of love and brotherhood when the denial of their essential manhood by Christian peoples negates the tenets that they are asked to accept."[44] Lawson did not accept passivity toward the issue of race that simply waited for God to make all things right in the Eschaton. Rather, he was an activist in a time when many Pentecostals were not and asserted, "it is time to protest."[45] Further, he cautioned with prophetic fervor: "If the white brethren don't preach the fatherhood of God and brotherhood of man irrespective of color or

---

39. Lawson, "Greatest Evil in the World is Race Prejudice," 248.

40. Ibid.

41. Ibid.

42. Gerloff, "Inner Dynamics of the Pentecostal Oneness (Apostolic) Movement from North America to the Caribbean."

43. Lawson, *Anthropology of Jesus Christ our Kinsman Redeemer*, 6–11.

44. Ibid., 6.

45. Ibid., 7.

nationality, and exemplify the true spirit of brotherhood to all, their civilization is doomed."[46] For Lawson, Christology and soteriology were keys to understanding and dismantling racial prejudice. He proposed what he called the "Hamitic contribution to the anthropological development of Jesus"[47] in which he contended that, "it was necessary in the plan of God to develop the most perfect man of the human race, to mingle and intermingle the blood of the three branches [of the human race] to produce the best and most perfect man."[48] Further, he declared that: "God disrobed himself of his glory and overshadowed the Virgin Mary . . . in whose veins flowed the blood of Japheth, and of Shem, and of Ham. For so had been the purpose and work of God in mixing the bloods of all three branches of the human race, that upon the basis of kinship, He might have the right to redeem all men."[49]

Echoing a theme later heard in James Cone's theology, Lawson boldly made the audacious assertion that Jesus had "Negro blood" in his veins.[50] Though his assertion was more anthropological than philosophical, the similar implications for the oppressed black community cannot be overlooked. For Lawson, "[i]f any race have whereof to boast . . . relative to our Lord Jesus Christ, the colored race has more[,] for they gave the two mothers of the tribe of Judah—out of which Christ came."[51] For Lawson attributed part of Jesus's blackness to two women—Rahab the Jerichoian harlot who helped the advancing Israelites and Bathsheba, the wife of Uriah the Hittite, whom David seduced and married subsequent to his murder of her husband. Solomon, the son born to David and Bathsheba, was of mixed parentage and it is out of this line, he insisted, that Jesus comes.

Lawson made the extraordinary proposal concerning racism that "every other ill that afflicts humanity comes out of this evil in the heart."[52] He expressed disappointment that Pentecostals had joined Baptists and Methodists before them in dividing their churches along racial lines,[53]

46. Ibid.
47. Ibid., 27.
48. Ibid.
49. Ibid., 40.
50. Ibid., 28.
51. Ibid., 29.
52. Ibid., 34.
53. Ibid., 33.

since according to him: "The Lord, through mixing our human natures by the process of miscegenation . . . forever abolished the basis and principle of race prejudice. Therefore if God is a kinsman to all having their blood in his veins, then whosoever hateth his brother, hateth his Lord. And whatever race one chooses to hate, remember, our Lord is of that race—whether Semitic, Hamitic, or Japhetic."[54] To further illustrate his point, Lawson continued: "Although our savior isn't wholly any race . . . he is a relative of all. . . . He is our savior. Not a Jewish savior, not a Negro savior, not an Anglo-Saxon savior. Jesus Christ is a human, universal savior (our kinsman) by virtue of the fact that the blood of Shem, Ham and Japheth, who are representatives of the entire human race, flows through his veins."[55]

Lawson's influence among Oneness Pentecostals cannot be underestimated, since a number of Oneness bodies were founded by leaders who had been a part of the Church of the Lord Jesus Christ. During their tenure with COOLJC, they would imbibe Lawson's thought, venerate his wisdom, and incorporate both his strategies and his arguments into their own ministries. Once they left the organization, many would continue the tradition of pragmatic and articulate protest against American race politics.

Perhaps the best example of a person who inherited Lawson's sustained pattern of protest was Smallwood E. Williams. Williams was a protégé of Lawson, who broke with his leaders in 1957 to form Bible Way Church of Our Lord Jesus Christ World-Wide, setting up his headquarters in Washington, DC. From this strategic vantage point, Williams used his worship services, radio broadcast, and writings to become a local and national political force with which to be reckoned. In the 1950s, he led the first sit-in and legal battle against Washington's segregated public schools, helped found Citizens Against Police Brutality, headed the local chapter of the NAACP and served as vice chair of the Democratic Central Committee.

Williams's sermons regularly decried race prejudice and segregation, and castigated American leaders for their role in perpetuating the dual evils, while calling on them to remedy the situation. He was not afraid to identify, by name, both the friends and enemies of the African American community, and to commend friends for their support, while chiding enemies for their specific unjust actions. In 1953, for example,

54. Ibid., 47.
55. Ibid.

he took the occasion of the death of Theodore Bilbo, a notoriously segregationist Senator from Mississippi, to lambast the treatment blacks had received in that state.

Earlier in 1945 when President Franklin Roosevelt died, he praised him for the work he had done to assist the African American community. In one sermon, entitled, "Let my people go," Williams was explicit that God was not only interested in human salvation but also in human freedom and that: "God is not indifferent to the welfare of human beings, for He has created every human being in His own image, giving him the capacity of intelligence, knowledge, and the capabilities to reach [the] top of the ladder of human achievement, regardless to the color of his skin."[56] As if to put to rest the assertion that Pentecostalism is totally otherworldly, Williams further asserted that, "anyone who tells you that God is not interested in human freedom, does not know God. Anyone who says that God is not interested in the physical as well as the spiritual condition of humanity is ignorant theologically of God's interest in the human family."[57] Williams was adamant that government leaders at the state level and in Congress who upheld racist policies were in rebellion against God. Williams continued Lawson's liberative project of refutation of the interpretation of the Hamatic curse which Williams called a "theological misconception."[58]

Williams was an ardent supporter of Martin Luther King, and called his death by assassination, "a loss . . . beyond human estimation."[59] On the one year memorial of King's death, Williams called for American leaders to make King's birthday a national holiday and to:

> Permit no further hesitation or procrastination in the prompt elimination of all vestiges of racial discrimination in our total national life, promptly eliminate ghetto environmental conditions of people and places with accompanying problems of crime, violence, delinquency, and alienation of our youth; and provide adequate solutions to the problems of hunger, poverty, and privation of the under-privileged black and white people, with dignity, using the almost un-limited wealth of this Nation properly, instead of its dissipation in foreign wars.[60]

56. Williams, *Significant Sermons*, 146.
57. Ibid., 147.
58. Ibid., 150.
59. Ibid., 118.
60. Ibid., 120.

Smallwood Williams's outspoken approach would gain for himself, his congregation, and his movement, a political capital that would allow him to wield a degree of power that few black preachers in the nation's capitol had held up to that time, and parlay it into a number of concessions from the white power structure.

CONTEMPORARY LIBERATIVE EXPRESSIONS

Within the contemporary context more classically trained Afro-Pentecostal scholars, notably James Tinney, James A. Forbes, Jr., Bennie Goodwin, Herbert Daughtry, George McKinney, Leonard Lovett, and Robert Franklin raise a solid socio-political critique of the American church and society. Within this critique, they have continued to seriously consider the intersection of Pentecostal spirituality and the myriad problems still facing the African American community. Lodged in the middle of an era that was rife with the black struggle for social justice, they implicated both the white church and the broader society for their role in perpetuating injustice.

James Tinney targeted a good portion of his socio-political critique at two areas: 1) the racism of white Pentecostalism in continually negating the contribution of Seymour as the founder of the movement and 2) the homophobic tendency of the Pentecostal movement. His championing of the latter cause would marginalize him more than that of the former, but Tinney provided an invaluable service in raising issues within the movement that ultimately could not be ignored, although many of these have not been completely resolved to the satisfaction of either Tinney's critics or supporters.

The theological work of James Forbes, former pastor of Manhattan's Riverside Church, was informed by his early years as the son of a United Holy Church bishop. James A. Forbes has continued to raise solid critique from his now more mainline position, and was one of the scholars contending that the opportunity that the Azusa Street revival provided for a prophetic witness on the racial crisis in America was lost.[61] Forbes asserted that "there was such intense seeking of God . . . that the color and bank book questions were forgotten." And insisting that, "had this continued and spilled out into the larger society, it might have revolution-

---

61. See for example, Forbes, "Christian Ethics and the Sit-In," 272; "Shall We Call This Dream Progressive Pentecostalism," 7–14; *Holy Spirit and Preaching*; and "To keep the Nation from losing its Soul," 24–25.

ized [that] society. He finally laments, however, that "alas, in a few years, it had fallen into the race and class groves."[62]

Bennie Goodwin's pneumatology placed him in direct dialogue with black theology. Though the main focus of his work was on development of leadership within the African American church, in many of these, like Albert Cleage, he probed the tie between the Holy Spirit and liberation.[63] He questioned how the "tremendous power released and transferred in Pentecostal worship" could inform liberative praxis and how ecclesial structures could be altered to allow that power to effectively solve the social problems that continue to plague the African American community.[64] For Goodwin:

> The times in which we live demand more than people jumping around in the church, lifting their hands and saying, "Praise the Lord' in an unknown tongue. The times demand that we speak with power to the powerful in a known tongue. The times demand that we discover where the power is trying to express itself in us, and that we develop that expression. We must take our places among the powerful and devote the God-given Pentecostal power in us to the liberation of the poor, the broken-hearted, the oppressed, the blind and the bruised.[65]

Goodwin's contribution has probably been one of the least known and appreciated among black Pentecostal liberationists. Yet, his work is hardly known outside of a handful of likeminded black Pentecostal scholars. Nevertheless, his critique was often on target, showing sharp critical sensitivity and an appreciation for the church and the academy, as necessary political action required to bring about liberation of the African American community.

Herbert Daughtry, who since 1960 has served as pastor of Brooklyn's House of the Lord Pentecostal Church and presiding bishop of the denomination by the same name that his father founded, combines Pentecostal rhetoric and liberal activism. This activism involved him in the struggle for integration in the 1950s and community control of schools in the late 1960s. In the 1980s his efforts led to the founding of the National Black

62. Forbes, "Shall We Call This Dream Progressive Pentecostalism," 10.

63. See Cleage, *Black Messiah*.

64. See for example, Goodwin, "Speak Up Black Man"; "Education as liberation," 89–99; and *Reflections on Education*.

65. Goodwin, "Social Implications of Pentecostal Power," 31–35.

United Front. Daughtry demonstrated that one did not have to forsake Pentecostal spirituality to involve oneself in radical social protest. In 1982, he founded the African People's Christian Organization expressly as a movement that combined an Africentric, biblical Christianity with a willingness to engage in the struggle for self-determination. In 1997, after the unprovoked killing of fifteen-year-old Randolph Evans by a New York City police officer, Daughtry was instrumental in organizing the Coalition of Concerned Leaders and Citizens to Save our Youth and leading the group in using economic boycotts to win jobs and services for Blacks from merchants in the community. Daughtry, a prolific writer, has authored several volumes and writes a semi-weekly newspaper column.[66] His work has consistently and strongly confronted the issue of racial disparity and lack of social justice in America.

David Daniels categorizes Leonard Lovett's contribution in pneumatological terms. Despite ongoing racism in the movement from its earliest stages, Lovett holds that Pentecostalism is a trans-cultural, trans-denominational, and trans-social phenomenon morally capable of addressing societal issues. He proposes a theology of 'conditional liberation' that replaces liberation theology's dependence on a Marxist framework with one that identifies the spiritual roots of racism and other socio-political problems and demands a spiritual solution. For him, the Pentecostal experience can awaken a political consciousness to mobilize adherents into liberation movements and free them to authentically confront oppression. Thus for him, personal liberation precedes social and political liberation.[67] Moreover, for Lovett, the racist trajectory that divided the twentieth century Pentecostal movement was a missed Kairos moment, in that the movement "originated from the womb of the black religious experience [and went from] . . . the ghetto on Azusa Street in Los Angeles to the world. . . . Once again God used a "saving moment" from the ranks of the despised and oppressed people of the earth to inject new life and power into the church universal.[68] In the end, Lovett contends that, "[a]uthentic Pentecostal encounter cannot occur unless liberation becomes

---

66. See for example, Daughtry, *No Monopoly on Suffering*; *My Beloved Community Sermons*; and *Jesus Christ*.

67. Daniels, "Response to William C. Turner," 17.

68. Lovett, "Perspectives on Black Origins of the Contemporary Pentecostal Movement," 42.

the consequence . . ." for "no man [or woman] can experience the fullness of the Spirit and be a racist."[69]

George McKinney, a scholar and ecclesiastical leader in the Church of God in Christ, also interprets the early Pentecostal movement as a missed pneumatological opportunity, in which the Holy Spirit was attempting to forge a new paradigm for the church in America through an unlikely source. Since, while holding an earned doctorate of philosophy degree, McKinney is primarily a pastor and denominational leader, his work has found even less exposure in academic discussions than has other Pentecostal scholars. But McKinney, like Lovett, sees the racism that has plagued the Pentecostal movement as a missed opportunity. He maintains:

> Segregation laws prohibited Blacks, Whites and Hispanics from social or spiritual mixing. The laws . . . throughout the south said Blacks and Whites could not worship together. In 1914, . . . [i]n that historic meeting in Hot Springs, White and Black brothers in Christ failed to understand the burden of history and the opportunity to speak Biblical truth to the powers of racism and segregation. It was a Kairos moment when the course of U.S. history could have been changed. A fatal choice was made to conform to the racist laws rather than to resist. God had spoken, he had manifested His power. He had revealed his will for a united church. For a moment just suppose the White, Brown, and Black brethren had appropriated the Holy Ghost power they had received to oppose the evils of segregation and racism. From 1906 to 1914, the Church of God in Christ was racially mixed. Just suppose that the whole Pentecostal/Holiness movement, that is today more than four hundred million strong, had mustered the courage of Martin Luther or Dietrich Bonheoffer, Martin Niemüller, and Martin Luther King, and declared to the powers in each state, "We are brothers and sisters. We are in covenant, we will not be separated by your laws. We are members of the family of God. We will worship and minister and fellowship together or we will go to jail together or we will die together. Here we stand, so help us God." Without doubt such a position would have resulted in lynchings and martyrdom, but God's truth would have won in the end. Then the Civil Rights movement would have been fought on spiritual grounds and the church would have fulfilled Christ's mandate to be salt in a tasteless society and light in

69. Ibid., 48.

that darkness. God visited America in the Azusa Revival in an unlikely place, a former stable. He used unlikely servants including the sons and daughters of slaves. This movement had the full potential of being God's solution to the American dilemma of racism, sexism, and classism.[70]

A new cadre of academically trained Pentecostal leaders used their educational advantage to keep before the church and the American public the continuing reality of racial prejudice and inequity. They coupled their exposure to mainline black and liberation theology with Pentecostal spirituality to supply a more nuanced theological framework for engaging the ongoing struggle for racial justice that built upon the contribution of earlier leaders yet broadened the discourse to take the systematic cause of racial injustice seriously.

CONCLUSION

The consensus among prophetic black Pentecostal leaders is that early white leaders within the movement who had experienced the "miracle at Azusa Street" missed the opportunity to lead our nation in the Godly resolution of the American dilemma of racism. The central focus of Pentecostal preaching is the offer of eternal life through appropriation of the atoning work of Christ in the Crucifixion, but contrary to popular characterizations, for black Pentecostals that offer is not rigidly couched in pie-in-the-sky, white robe and golden slipper escapism. Rather, at times, that offer has been more broadly expressed as socially, as well as spiritually, liberative. Some have taken the personal implications of Jesus's offer of abundant life that starts in the here and now seriously, and in more progressive understandings have extrapolated that abundance to refer to liberation, not just for the person, but for the community.

Black religionists within the mainline churches displayed class elitism in dismissing the contribution of African American Pentecostal clergy in the struggle for racial justice in the United States. Across the country in large and small Pentecostal congregations, pastors lifted up the plight of their people as an affront to God and called on the powers that be to give relief. It is a problematic, therefore, to mistake the theological conservatism of black Pentecostals for social and political accommodation.

70. McKinney, "Azusa Street Revival." In speaking of the 1914 meeting, he was referring to the founding of the Assemblies of God as an essentially white denomination.

Indeed it is that very theological conservatism, the penchant to engage the Word of God as authoritative warrant for the living of life, which drives the social and political agendas of African American Pentecostalism. While these black Pentecostal leaders rarely used the explicit language of liberation in their rhetoric, they implicitly understood and found ways to communicate to their congregations that what happened to them in their Pentecostal experience had implications that went beyond ecstatic expression in a highly emotive worship service. They knew that somehow the God who had so powerfully visited them and invested himself in them in that worship was as concerned with their temporal reality as with their eternal welfare and had a different assessment of their identity than found in the common script of American race politics. In the Pentecostal experience, they had found what Ithiel Clemmons contends is a "spirituality of deliverance."[71]

For early and contemporary black Pentecostals, Jones's questions continue to resonate. What does the experience of Pentecostalism mean for the present situation of black people? What does it mean that Jesus is the Christ? What does it mean that we are saved? What does it mean that we claim a supernatural measure of God's empowerment? How does that empowerment enable us to negotiate the oppressive terrain that does not grant us complete dignity as being fully created in the same image of God as those within the dominant culture? How does Pentecostal empowerment allow them to reject the white racist God that capriciously discriminates against one branch of his creation?

Despite all their attempts, Black Pentecostals have not always been clear and effective in communicating the answers to these questions to their constituents or the broader context. Yet even with his broad critique of the social consciousness of the Pentecostal movement in general, J. Deotis Roberts concedes:

> Black Pentecostals have been formulating a black theology for a long time. They have relied on oral traditions, African cultural retentions, and the like. Blacks join African, Latin American, and Asian tongues groups in rejecting the definition of whites. In essence . . . black Pentecostals have called attention to the racism that has splintered the Pentecostal ranks. It has provided a very perceptive critique of the authenticity of the fellowship, theology and practice of white Pentecostalism. The fruit of the

71. Clemmons, *Charles Harrison Mason and the Roots of Church of God in Christ*, 68.

Spirit are absent in regard to humanity of blacks and the poor.
. . . This critique of this movement by black theologians may be
a service to the entire church after all.[72]

BIBLIOGRAPHY

Articles of Faith, Church of the Living God (Christian Workers for Fellowship). Online:
  http://www.ctlgcwff.org/articles.htm.
Ayers, George W. "The Apostolic Movement." Online: http://www.aohchurch.com/
  about_u/shtml.
Bartleman, Frank. *How Azusa came to Los Angeles*. Los Angles: n.p., 1925.
Blum, Edward. *Reforging the White Republic: Race, Religion, and American Nationalism,
  1865–1898*. Baton Rouge: Louisiana State University Press, 2005.
"A Catechism: The Church of the Living God." Online: http://www.mc.maricopa.edu/
  ~kefir/club/ african_american/index.html.
"Church Covenant." Triumph the Church and Kingdom of God in Christ, Sixth Episcopal
  District. Online: http://www.triumphthechurch6thdistrict.org/ChurchCovenant7
  .htm.
Cleage, Albert B. *The Black Messiah*. New York: Sheed & Ward, 1968.
Clemmons, Ithiel. *Charles Harrison Mason and the Roots of the Church of God in Christ*.
  Los Angeles: Pneuma Life, 1996.
Cone, James H. *A Black Theology of Liberation*. Philadelphia: Lippincott, 1970.
Daniels, David D., III. "Doing All the Good We Can." In *New Day Begun: African
  American Churches and Civic Culture in Post-Civil Rights America*, edited by R.
  Drew Smith, 164–82. Durham: Duke University Press, 2003.
———. "A Response to William C. Turner Jr." *Journal of Pentecostal Theology* 14 (2005)
  17–21.
Daughtry, Herbert. *From Magnificence to Wretchedness: The Sad Saga of Black Human-
  ity: A Special Message to Men of African Ancestry*. New York: House of the Lord
  Church, 1981.
———. *Jesus Christ: African in Origin, Revolutionary and Redeeming in Action*. New
  York: House of the Lord Church, 1981.
———. *My Beloved Community: Sermons, Lectures, and Speeches of Rev. Daughtry*.
  Trenton, NJ: Africa World, 2001.
———. *No Monopoly on Suffering: Blacks and Jews in Crown Heights and Elsewhere*.
  Trenton, NJ: Africa World, 1997.
Forbes, James A., Jr. *Christian Ethics and the Sit-In*, by Paul Ramsey. *Union Seminary
  Quarterly Review* 17 (1962) 272.
———. *The Holy Spirit and Preaching*. Nashville: Abingdon, 1989.
———. "To Keep the Nation from Losing Its Soul." *Sojourners* 20 (1991) 24–25.
———. "Shall We Call This Dream Progressive Pentecostalism." *Spirit* 3 (1979) 7–14.

72. Roberts, *Black Theology in Dialog*, 62.

Garrett, Gary W. *A Man Ahead of his Times: The Life and Legacy of Bishop Garfield Thomas Haywood.* Springfield, MO: Apostolic Christian, 2002.

Gerloff, Roswith. "Inner Dynamics of the Pentecostal Oneness (Apostolic) Movement from North America to the Caribbean." Paper presented to the Annual Meeting of the Society for Pentecostal Studies, Assemblies of God Theological, Springfield, MO, November 12–14, 1992.

———. *A Plea for British Black Theologies: The Black Church in Britain in its Transatlantic, Cultural and Theological Interaction with Special References to the Pentecostal Oneness (Apostolic) and Sabbatarian Movements.* Frankfurt: Lang, 1992.

Goodwin, Bennie E. *Reflections on Education: a Christian Scholar Looks at King, Freire and Jesus as Social and Religious Educators.* East Orange, NJ: Goodpatrick, 1978.

———. "Social Implications of Pentecostal Power." *Spirit* 1 (1977) 31–35.

———. "Speak Up Black Man" [n.l.: n.p.], 1972.

———. "Education as Liberation: An Analysis of Paulo Freire" *Journal of the Interdenominational Theological Center* 2 (1975) 89–99.

Grant, Jacqueline. *White Women's Christ and Black Women's Jesus: Feminist Christology and Womanist Response.* Atlanta: Scholars, 1989.

Hollenweger, Walter J. "Black Pentecostal Concept." *Concept* 30 (1970) 3–71.

Hunter, James D. *American Evangelicalism: Conservative Religion and the Quandary of Modernity.* New Brunswick, NJ: Rutgers University Press, 1983.

Jones, Charles Price. *An Appeal to the Sons of Africa.* Jackson, MI: Truth, 1902.

Jones, Major J. *The Color of God: The Concept of God in Afro-American Thought.* Macon, GA: Mercer University Press, 1987.

Kornweibel, Theodore, Jr. "'I Thank My God for the Persecution': The Church of God in Christ under Attack." In *Investigate Everything: Federal Efforts to Compel Black Loyalty during World War I,* 149–63. Bloomington: Indiana University Press, 2002.

———. "Bishop C. H. Mason and the Church of God during World War I: The Perils of Conscientious Objection." *Southern States: An Interdisciplinary Journal of the South* 26 (1987) 261–81.

Lawson, Robert C. *An Open Letter to a Southern White Minister on Prejudice: The Eating Cancer of the Soul.* Rev. Ed. 1949. Piqua, OH: Ohio Ministries, 1995.

———. *The Anthropology of Jesus Christ our Kinsman.* Piqua, OH: Ohio Ministries, 1925.

———. "The Greatest Evil in the World Is Race Prejudice." In *For the Defense of the Gospel: The Writings of Bishop R. C. Lawson,* edited by Robert C. Lawson and Arthur M. Anderson, 248–56. New York: Church of Our Lord Jesus Christ of the Apostolic Faith, 1971.

Lovett, Leonard. "Perspectives on Black Origins of the Contemporary Pentecostal Movement." *Journal of the Interdenominational Theological Center* 1 (1973) 36–49.

Mason, Mary. *The History and Life Work of Elder C. H. Mason and His Co-Laborers.* Memphis: The Church of God in Christ, 1924.

McKinney, George. "The Azusa Street Revival." A lecture presented at Beeson Divinity School, Sanford University in Birmingham, Alabama on October 3, 2001.

Patterson, James Oglethorpe. *History and Formative Years of the Church of God in Christ; with Excerpts from the Life and Works of Its Founder, Bishop C. H. Mason.* Memphis: Church of God in Christ, 1969.

Reed, David A. *In Jesus' Name: The History and Beliefs of Oneness Pentecostals.* Blandford Forum, UK: Deo, 2008.

Richardson, James C. *With Water and Spirit: A History of Black Apostolic Denominations in the U.S.* Washington, DC: Spirit, 1980.

Roberts, J. Deotis. *Black Theology in Dialog.* Philadelphia: Westminster, 1987.

Robinson, Ida. "The Economic Persecution." *The Latter Day Messenger* (May 23, 1935) 2. Cited in Bettye Collier-Thomas, *Daughters of Thunder: Black Women and Their Sermons: 1850–1979*, 203–5. San Francisco: Jossey-Bass, 1998.

Seymour, William J. *The Doctrines and Disciplines of the Azusa Street Apostolic Faith Mission of Los Angeles California.* Los Angeles: The Apostolic Faith Mission, 1915.

Smith, Amanda Berry. *An Autobiography: The Story of the Lord's Dealings with Mrs. Amanda Smith, the Colored Evangelist: Containing an Account of Her Life Work of Faith, and Her Travels in America, England, Ireland, Scotland, India, and Africa as an Independent Missionary.* Chicago: Meyer & Brother, 1893.

Triumph National Anthem. Triumph the Church and Kingdom of God in Christ. Online: http://www.triumphthechurchnatl.org/Creed%20and%20Anthem.htm.

Triumph the Church and Kingdom of God in Christ Constitution, s.l, s.n. s.d, 11. Cited at Triumph the Church and Kingdom of God in Christ, Sixth Episcopal District, History. Online: http://www.triumphthechurch6thdistrict.org/ChurchHistory1 .htm.

"What We Believe." The Official Website of the Apostolic Overcoming Holy Church. Online: http://www.aohchurch.com/articles_church2.shtml.

Williams, Smallwood E. *Significant Sermons.* Washington, DC: Bibleway Church, 1970.

Yong, Amos. "Justice Deprived, Justice Demanded: Afropentecostalisms and the Task of World Pentecostal Theology Today." *Journal of Pentecostal Theology* 15 (2006) 127–47.

3

The Rhetoric of
Pentecostal Racial Reconciliation

Looking Back To Move Forward

Derrick R. Rosenior

INTRODUCTION

In many of his speeches and sermons, Dr. Martin Luther King Jr. often referred to eleven o'clock on Sunday morning as "the most segregated hour in America."[1] Over forty years after his death, even the most integration-minded churches still struggle to cross the cultural divide that keeps Christians in America worshipping apart. Ten year ago, a team of journalists from *The New York Times* set out in an attempt to answer the question "What are race relations [in America] like today?" They traveled to fifteen communities talking with a wide range of people about their experiences. Their investigation of this question resulted in the book *How*

---

1. This is a statement that is generally attributed to Dr. King. He often made it in many of his speeches and sermons.

Race is Lived in America: Pulling Together, Pulling Apart,[2] which captured the perspectives, experiences, and stories of the individuals within its pages like only a well written narrative can. It presents its readers with a much deeper, more complex, human, and personalized approach to the issue of race relations in America than most other previous works on the subject. Others have presented statistical, analytical, and theoretical approaches to the subject while this book, on the other hand, presents an approach to the topic that is not often seen. This approach was filled with raw human emotions, struggles, and a candid personal and human discourse on the issue of race.

One of the several stories told in the book is the account of a Pentecostal church in Decatur, Georgia, that has been transformed from a predominantly white congregation to an interracial one. The story chronicles the experiences and perspectives of two families, one white the other black. They both attend the Assembly of God Tabernacle as they struggle with the history of racism in the south, present day race relations, and interracial worship at their church. The church was founded in 1916 as a white only church in downtown Atlanta that had now moved out to the suburbs and had become in the words of the Pastor's mission statement a "multiracial, multicultural, maturing body of believers."[3] Fifty-five percent of the members are white, forty-three percent are black and the rest are Asian or racially mixed. The members of the church not only worship together on Sundays but also "visit each other in the hospital, share motel rooms at retreats and attend potluck dinners at one another's homes."[4]

In spite of this image of interracial perfection, there are indications that just like the Pentecostal church mentioned above, the Pentecostal movement as a whole, like the rest of American society, has not moved past the issue of race but deals with it on a regular basis. In this chapter, I examine the rhetoric of racial reconciliation used by Pentecostals, specifically at the 1994 "Memphis Miracle" event, and make the case that this was primarily rhetoric of collective memory, myth making, and nostalgia with the Azusa Street revival as its primary focus. When one examines the type of rhetoric used, it can be reasonably established that based on racial differences, black and white Pentecostals have created divergent collective memories of the events, characters, and circumstances surrounding

2. Correspondents of the *New York Times, How Race Is Lived in America.*

3. Ibid., 5.

4. Ibid., 6.

the Azusa Street revival and early Pentecostalism. Nevertheless, in the process of the racial reconciliation dialogue, it is evident that both groups had come to mythologize the characters and events of the Azusa Street revival and relied on the rhetoric of nostalgia as a rhetorical tool to bring about racial reconciliation.

In order to make my case, I will first discuss the link between Pentecostalism and American culture, specifically African American culture, and the historical development of Pentecostalism in America with regard to issues of race which led up to the racial reconciliation event in Memphis. I will then take a look at the rhetoric of racial reconciliation based on the issues of collective memory, myth, and nostalgia. The effectiveness of this rhetoric can also be analyzed based on post 1994 efforts made toward racial reconciliation. Finally, both denominational and grassroots efforts toward building racial unity in American Pentecostalism will be discussed.

PENTECOSTALISM AND (AFRICAN) AMERICAN CULTURE

Race and racism has played a significant role in the history of the church in America. The issues of race, racism, discrimination, prejudice, and racial stereotyping have long dominated the American cultural psyche. The history of racism and the church in America can be traced back to the time when the first Africans were brought to the shores of the "New World" as slaves. Albert Raboteau presents a graphic and realistic description of the experience of slavery that reveals its inherent racist and dehumanizing characteristic:

> Weakened by the voyage, disoriented, and frightened, the captives began to groan and weep; some cried aloud to God. Others struck their faces with their hands and threw themselves to the ground. Several sang the funeral songs of their home-lands. Many became frantic as the captors began to divide the crowd into smaller groups, separating, in the process, parents from children, husbands from wives, relatives from relatives, friends from friends. Children, dragged from parents, struggled free to run back to them; mothers shielded their children with their bodies and were beaten for hindering the separation; husbands clung desperately to wives. The sight of such misery moved some spectators unexpectedly to tears. Eventually, the partition completed, the captives came face to face with their fate of slavery for life.[5]

5. Raboteau, *Canaan Land*, 4.

Although most of the black Africans who were brought as slaves from sub-Saharan West Africa to the New World had been influenced by non-African religions such as Islam and Christianity, the majority adhered to the indigenous African religious beliefs which they took with them into slavery. According to Iain MacRobert, these indigenous African religions were not religions with creeds, written liturgies, or holy books. African religion was passed down from generation to generation through oral tradition. "It was in narratives—myths, legends and folk tales—riddles, songs, proverbs, and other aphorisms that African theology was enshrined and codified. They were a means of preserving and transmitting knowledge, values, attitudes, morals, ethics, sacred rituals, dogma, history, and the wisdom of the ancestors." [6] This reliance on narrative and the creation of myth for the transmission of religious values would later be seen in how Pentecostals, especially black Pentecostals, passed on their history and tradition from one generation to another. They later used this as common ground for racial reconciliation with white Pentecostals, as will be posited in this chapter.

Other traditional characteristics of black Pentecostalism today (or even of Pentecostalism as a whole) can be traced back to the African primal religions. MacRobert makes the claim that "African primal religion was danced and sung, beaten out in the rhythms and tones of 'talking' drums, the swaying of bodies and the stomping of feet . . ."[7] For the people of West Africa, drumming, singing, dancing, and other forms of expressive worship were associated with religious rituals in which the devotees would be 'possessed' by various spirits. Raboteau states: "So essential are music and dance to West African religious expression that it is no exaggeration to call them 'danced religions.'" [8] The preservation of this Afrocentric form of worship was very important to the black founders and leaders of the Pentecostal movement such as Bishops William J. Seymour and Charles H. Mason. Bishop Mason in particular made it a point to preserve in Pentecostalism the "slave religion" that the ancestors of African Americans had brought with them from Africa. For Mason, Seymour, and generations of other black Pentecostals, religion was primarily about experiencing God through dance, worship, and the "moving of the Spirit." They felt a need to experience God in a very real and

6. MacRobert, *Black Roots and White Racism of Early Pentecostalism*, 12.

7. Ibid.

8. Raboteau, *Slave Religion*, 15.

tangible way. It was primarily a religion of the Spirit and secondarily a religion of the Book. Because the Bible was used by many slave holders and white preachers as a means to justify slavery and the subjugation of blacks, many slaves were often very skeptical of it. And so the God they served in their secret meetings was a God who filled them with His Spirit and liberated them in ecstatic worship.

American Pentecostalism can arguably be described as a uniquely indigenous religious movement with distinctly African (American) characteristics and roots. Having been birthed out of the Christian renewal and restorationist movements of the late nineteenth and early twentieth centuries, such as the holiness movement of the late 1800's, the "Topeka, Kansas Outpouring" of 1901 and the Azusa Street revival of 1906–1909 in Los Angeles, Pentecostalism has grown into a global phenomenon. The globalization of Pentecostalism can be understood in a number of ways as is evident in the works of Michael Wilkinson, Donald E. Miller, and Tetsunao Yamamori.[9] As it has become more internationalized, it has inevitably assumed and taken on the various national and regional cultures within which it exists. Nevertheless, the international Pentecostal movement has retained some of the characteristics of its American and even more specifically its African American roots. Characteristic expressions of Pentecostal worship and preaching that are seen universally regardless of the national culture, such as rhythmic hand clapping, expressive dancing, and charismatic and highly energetic preaching can be traced back to the "Africanization" of American Christianity. Wilmore, in summarizing the underlying African elements in the black religious community in America, argues that it consisted of "the imaginative and creative use of rhythm—singing and dancing—in the celebration of life and the worship of God . . . these aspects of African religions were found in some form, however attenuated, in the black religion of the eighteenth and nineteenth centuries and were absorbed into black Christianity in the Caribbean, South America and the United States."[10] Melville Herskovits also supports this argument and posits that it was "spirit possession by the Holy Ghost" which inspired "motor behavior that is not European but African, rhythmic hand clapping, the antiphonal participation of the

9. Wilkinson, *Spirit Said Go*; Wilkinson, "What's 'Global' about Global Pentecostalism?"; and Miller and Yamamori, *Global Pentecostalism*.

10. Wilmore, *Black Religion*, 301–4.

congregation in the sermon, the immediacy of God in the services and baptism by immersion, are all survivals of Africanisms."[11]

The church has always played a critical and dominant role in black society and culture.[12] It can be argued that practically every aspect of black life in America has been centered on religion from the various forms of artistic expression to political activism, education, and recreation. Booker T. Washington, in 1909, declared that "The Negro Church represents the Masses of the Negro people. It was the first institution to develop out the life of the Negro masses and it still remains the strongest hold upon them."[13] In the early decades of the twentieth century, racism and racist ideologies were rampant in America. Racist views and ideologies such as Social Darwinism and other forms of scientific racism were common place. As many white Americans continued to discount the merits and values of African and African-American culture as backwards and "uncivilized" many established black churches began to seek mainstream acceptance by banning and/or discouraging certain African elements of their past in their worship such as shouting, dancing, and ecstatic expression. They replaced these Africanized forms of worship with more formal, refined, and civilized forms of worship such as sedate hymns, canticles, and anthems.

The black Holiness-Pentecostal church was the antithesis of this mindset as it kept alive and preserved the Africanisms of black religious expression. Folklorist and anthropologist Zora Neale Hurston, in her groundbreaking 1923 work entitled *The Sanctified Church,* discussed the role of the "sanctified" or "holiness" church (as some black Pentecostal churches have been and still are known) in African-American culture and society. According to Hurston "The Sanctified church is a protest against the high-brow tendency in Negro protestant congregations as the Negro gains more education and wealth."[14] Hurston mentions further that,

> The Saints, or the Sanctified church is a revitalizing element in Negro music and religion. It is putting back into Negro religion those elements which were brought over from Africa and grafted onto Christianity as soon as the Negro came into contact with it, but which are being rooted out as the American Negro

11. Herskovits, *Myth of the Negro Past*, 232–35.
12. Youngblood and Winn, "Shout Glory," 355–70.
13. Washington, *Story of the Negro*, 3–4.
14. Hurston, *Sanctified Church*, 103.

approaches White concepts. The people who make up the sanctified groups, while admiring the white brother in many ways thinks him ridiculous in church.[15]

Bishop Charles Harrison Mason, the founder of the Church of God in Christ (COGIC), a son of former slaves, born in 1866 immediately following the American civil war which brought the slaves their freedom, often as a boy prayed with his mother and would pray that "above all things for God to give him a religion like the one he had heard about from the old slaves and he had seen demonstrated in their lives."[16] Preserving this "slave religion" became an important goal for him when he founded COGIC. African elements of worship such as the "ring shout," which eventually became the "shout," were integral components to black Pentecostal (COGIC) worship. Even today when COGIC members worship by dancing it is referred to as "getting to shouting."

COGIC and the other Holiness-Pentecostal churches also took the preservation of African elements of rhythm and music seriously. This could be seen in the prominence of "hand clapping and foot stomping," but also in the numerous instruments often associated with secular music during the early 1900s. Pentecostals both black and white were the first to popularize the use of these "secular" instruments such as drums, guitars, trumpets, steel triangle tambourines, and other percussion instruments in sacred worship. It was not uncommon for those early Pentecostal churches, even the white churches, to have music bands which they referred to as "orchestras," which they would often set up on street corners, parks, and other public places and use as an attention getting, crowd gathering tool so that they could then evangelize and proselytize. Clemmons also makes mention of the fact that "The Saints were recognizable in the black communities with their tambourines and Bibles."[17] For most of the twentieth century Pentecostal churches were the only settings where such instruments were part of sacred worship. Of course, today, these instruments are now used in worship in a wide range of Christian churches. These traditionally characteristic Pentecostal forms of worship have now been adopted by non-Pentecostal churches. Furthermore, Clemmons points out that it was not until the rise of gospel music after World War

15. Ibid., 104.

16. Clemmons, *Bishop C. H. Mason*, 4.

17. Ibid., 33.

II that black Baptists and Methodists began to introduce drums into their churches. He also asserts that until the social revolution of the 1960s the Baptist and Methodist churches experienced much tension over the use of drums. "Elderly members angrily protested, 'This is not a holy roller church!' Younger members did not see a problem."[18]

Another aspect of the African slave past quite visible in black Pentecostalism is the concept of "call and response." Call and response was seen in the singing and preaching of black Pentecostals. In singing the leader would sing a line of a song followed by the second line which was sung by another person or the congregation. In preaching, the preacher would make a point and instinctively someone or a group of people in the congregation would respond with an "Amen!" "Yes Sir!" or "Preach it, Preacher!" The sermon therefore becomes more or less a dialogue between the minister and the congregation, which is dominated by the minister and supported by the congregation. This interaction and response by the audience is an affirmation that his listeners agree with him and he is not boring them. Hurston says that members call this response to the preacher "bearing him up."[19] On some occasions where the minister is not receiving the reaction that he or she desires he or she may humorously interject something such as "Can I get a witness" or "Ya'll don't hear me." This cyclical rhetorical devise is very Afrocentric and is quite the opposite of the more linear approach to rhetoric that is practiced in a Eurocentric context. Black Pentecostalism has obviously made significant contributions to American culture and society. Its contribution to black America is immeasurable. Long before expressions such as "Black Power" were popularized or before the Afrocentrism of the 1960s and 70s, black Pentecostals such as COGIC were reaching back into their African and slave past and forming a connection and a bridge between the past and the future of black America and changing African-American society and culture while doing so.

WILLIAM J. SEYMOUR AND INTERRACIAL BEGINNINGS AT AZUSA STREET

The history of the Pentecostal movement is not that far removed from the history of race relations in the United States. Two names stand out in

18. Ibid., 183.

19. Hurston, *Sanctified Church*, 104.

Pentecostal history: Charles Fox Parham and William Joseph Seymour.[20] According to John Hardon "Parham was white and Seymour a Negro, which partly explains the interracial character of most Pentecostal churches."[21] Vinson Synan builds a good case for the interracial origins for the modern Pentecostal movement.[22] He posits that Parham and Seymour share roughly equal positions as founders of modern American Pentecostalism. According to Synan, Parham laid the doctrinal foundation of the movement, while Seymour served as the agent for popularization. He further makes the case that "the early Pentecostal movement could be classified as neither 'black' nor 'white' but as interracial."[23] However, as the movement grew, the races were soon divided. Few white Pentecostals, according to Lovett, although they acknowledge their debt to Seymour, are willing to recognize him as the founder of the movement. African-American Pentecostals on the other hand, refer to Seymour as the "apostle and pioneer" of the movement and insist that the movement began as a black phenomenon later accepted by whites.

As the narrative is told, the spiritual roots of about 500 million Pentecostal people, nearly one-quarter of all Christians in the world according to David Barrett go back to a spiritual renewal that began in 1906 that was housed in an old converted warehouse on 312 Azusa Street, in the heart of Los Angeles, California.[24] William Joseph Seymour, the leader of the revival, was the son of Louisiana slaves.[25] He had been asked to come to Los Angeles by the "colored people of the city" who had been "led by the Spirit" to invite him to "give them some Bible teaching."[26] At the time of the request, Seymour was in Houston, Texas, attending a Bible School led by early Pentecostal leader, Charles Fox Parham.

Parham taught that speaking in tongues (glossolalia) was the 'Bible' evidence of one receiving the baptism in the Holy Spirit and a sign of the nearness of the end of the world and the second advent of Jesus Christ. Seymour accepted this teaching but did not yet himself receive 'the baptism in the Holy Spirit' or experience glossolalia. He was soon invited by

20. Lovett, "Black Origins of the Pentecostal Movement," 123–41.

21. Hardon, *Protestant Churches of America*, 170.

22. Synan, *Holiness-Pentecostal Movement*.

23. Ibid., 170.

24. Barrett, *Signs and Wonders*.

25. Martin, *Life and Ministry of William J. Seymour*.

26. Seymour, *Doctrines and Disciplines*, 2.

a small black Holiness congregation in Los Angeles to come out and be their pastor. William J. Seymour left Houston, Texas and arrived in Los Angeles on February 22, 1906, and began his ministry two days later at a church associated with the Southern California Holiness Association, a black Holiness church. In his first sermon at his new church, Seymour preached on Acts 2:4, announcing the necessity of speaking in other tongues as evidence of the Pentecostal experience. According to Synan, as a result of this new teaching, Seymour was promptly locked out of the facility.[27] Seymour, however, was not rejected by everyone. He was immediately invited to the home of two working class African-American believers, Ruth and Richard Asberry, at 214 North Bonnie Brae Street.[28] Soon, several people under Seymour's leadership began to gather there for prayer and Bible study. For the next two months Seymour conducted evening prayer meetings and Bible studies. While the small congregation was predominantly black, Cecil M. Robeck notes that "blacks and whites mingled freely."[29]

On Friday April 6, 1906, they began a ten-day fast. Three days later, on April 9th one of the participants by the name of Edward S. Lee in whose home Seymour had originally stayed when he arrived in Los Angeles, asked him to come by his home and pray for him to recover from illness so that he would be able to attend the evening meeting at Bonnie Brae Street. According to MacRobert, after anointing him with oil and prayer, Lee felt better and requested Seymour pray for him to receive the Holy Spirit with the sign of tongues.[30] As he prayed Lee burst forth into rhapsodical utterance in a new tongue.[31] The two men then walked over to the meeting at Bonnie Brae where Seymour proceeded in his usual pattern to preach on Acts 2:4. However, this time in his sermon he recounts the events which had occurred earlier that evening when he had prayed for Lee. However, he could not finish the story for as he was telling it, Lee lifted up his hands and began to speak in other tongues.[32] Nelson describes what followed:

27. Synan, "William Joseph Seymour," 778–81.

28. This home still exists at what is now 216 North Bonnie Brae and is now a designated historic site according to the *Christianity Today/Christian History* Web site.

29. Robeck, "Azusa Street Revival," 32.

30. MacRobert, *Black Roots and White Racism of Early Pentecostalism*.

31. Nelson, *For Such a Time as This*.

32. MacRobert, *Black Roots and White Racism of Early Pentecostalism*.

> The entire company was immediately swept to its knees as by some tremendous power. At least seven—and perhaps more—lifted their voices in an awesome harmony of strange new tongues. Jennie Evans Moore, falling to her knees from the piano seat, became the first woman thus to speak. Some rushed out to the front porch, yard and street, shouting and speaking in tongues for all the neighborhood to hear. . . . Teenager Bud Trayer stood on the front porch prophesying and preaching. Jennie Evans Moore returned to the piano and began singing in her beautiful voice what was thought to be a series of six languages with interpretations.[33]

Larry Martin notes that some in the group were in trances for up to five hours, while others were baptized in the Holy Spirit in a few minutes.[34] According to MacRobert the group was made up exclusively of black people who were washer women and others who held low paying unskilled menial jobs and believed that God had visited them and that this was the restoration of Pentecost as foretold in the Bible. MacRobert mentions further that not only were all the participants black, the Asberry home at Bonnie Brae Street was in a black residential district of Los Angeles. Nevertheless, as crowds began to gather over the next three days, whites began to come as more and more people continued to manifest glossolalia, fall into trances, and receive miraculous healings.

On April 12, 1906, Seymour received the baptism in the Holy Spirit and experienced glossolalia for the first time. Nelson gives a vivid description of what happened to Seymour:

> He kept on, alone, and in response to his last prayer, a sphere of white hot brilliance seemed to appear, draw near, and fall upon him. Divine love melted his heart; he sank to the floor seemingly unconscious. . . . As from a great distance he heard unutterable words being uttered—was it angelic adoration and praise? Slowly he realizes the indescribably lovely language belonged to him, pouring from his innermost being. A broad smile wreathed his face. At last, he arose and happily embraced those around him.[35]

The personal accounts from these early months of Seymour's ministry serve to indicate that the Pentecostal experience resulted in desegrega-

---

33. Nelson, *For Such a Time as This*, 191.

34. Martin, *Life and Ministry of William J. Seymour.*

35. Nelson, *For Such a Time as This*, 192.

tion, which was an uncommon occurrence in the United States in the early twentieth century. MacRobert noted that the fact that black and white worshipped together without segregation was in itself unusual in the United States at that time, and that it happened under the leadership of a black minister was truly remarkable. Frank Bartleman, a white man who was later to become one of several significant figures in the emerging Pentecostal movement, visited the house on Bonnie Brae Street on March 26, 1906. He found that "both white and colored saints were meeting there for prayer."[36] Bartleman recalls that on April 9 the power of God came upon Seymour and seven others who had gathered together. Bartleman relates:

> As though hit by a bolt of lightning, the entire company was knocked from their chairs to the floor. Seven began to speak in diverse kinds of tongues and to magnify God. The shouts were so fervent-and so loud!—that a crowd gathered outside, wondering, "What meaneth this?" Soon it was noised over the city that God was pouring out His Spirit. White people joined the colored saints, and also joined the ranks of those filled with the Holy Ghost, Lydia Anderson being one of the first white recipients. Seymour received the experience of Acts 2:4 which he had been preaching on April 12. The home on Bonnie Brae Street could not begin to accommodate the congregation which spilled into the street.[37]

As reported by this eye-witness account, the small home at Bonnie Brae soon could not contain the crowds that were showing up to witness this spectacle. In fact, at one point so great was the gathering and the rush on the house that the porch gave way and collapsed under the weight of the crowd. The group began to seek for a facility that would be large enough to house the fledgling revival movement. They found such a place at 312 Azusa Street in a run-down dilapidated part of town. The facility, a two story wooden chapel built in 1888, had originally belonged to the Stephens African Methodist Episcopal Church (now First A.M.E). After the church had vacated the premises, it had been used as a stable and at the time the group found it, it was being used to store construction materials. The congregation immediately began to renovate the building, and services were moved to this location. The building was cleared, sawdust

36. Bartleman, *Azusa Street*, 45.

37. Brumback, *Suddenly From Heaven*, 3.

scattered on the floor and seating was fabricated by laying planks across nail kegs, boxes, and old chairs. The pulpit was constructed from two wooden crates covered with cloth.

According to Martin, the first service in their new location was probably held on Saturday April 14, 1906, the day before Easter.[38] Early eye-witness accounts report that soon after the mission was opened as many as 1300 attended services and up to 800 crowded into the small building with the rest standing on the sidewalk outside observing through the low windows and open doors. *The Los Angeles Daily Times* reported "The room was crowded almost to suffocation. Many were seated in the windows and scores who could not enter crowded around the lobby and struggled for a view."[39] Another article entitled "Weird Babel of Tongues" appeared in the Wednesday morning April 18, 1906 issue of *The Los Angeles Daily Times* breaking the news to the world of this "newest religious sect" reporting that there was a "wild scene last night at Azusa Street" and described the congregation as a group of "colored people" with a "sprinkling of whites."[40]

From its inception, the Azusa Street mission was an interracial congregation, pastored by an African-American with a racially integrated staff and board.[41] Synan notes that "this striking interracial phenomenon occurred in the very years of America's most racist period, between 1890 and 1920."[42] Synan points out further that "in an age of Social Darwinism, Jim Crowism, and general white supremacy, the fact that Pentecostal blacks and whites worshipped together in virtual equality was a significant exception to the prevailing attitudes and practices. Even more significant is the fact that this interracial harmony occurred among the very groups that have traditionally been the most at odds—the poor whites and the poor blacks."[43]

According to Lawrence Catley, a participant in the revival, "There was no difference in race or color; everybody was somebody . . . Azusa Street itself started out with mostly black folks, and then the white folks began to come in from all over." Another 1906 eye-witness at the

38. Martin, *Life and Ministry of William J. Seymour*.

39. *Los Angeles Daily Times* (September 3, 1906) 11.

40. Ibid., 1.

41. Robeck, *Past*, 15.

42. Synan, *Holiness-Pentecostal Tradition*, 167.

43. Ibid.

Azusa Street church noted that "In Los Angeles . . . everybody went to the altar together. White and colored, no discrimination seemed to be among them." A visiting Anglican clergy man from England recorded his thoughts:

> It was something very extraordinary, that white pastors from the South were eagerly prepared to go to Los Angeles to the Negroes, to have fellowship with them and to receive through their prayers and intercessions the blessings of the Spirit. And it was still more wonderful that these [same] white pastors went back to the South and reported to the members of their congregations that they had been together with Negroes that they had prayed in one Spirit and received the same blessings as they. [44]

A white lady reported that at Azusa, "Everybody was just the same; it did not matter if you were black, white, green, or grizzly. There was a wonderful spirit. Germans and Jews, black and whites, ate together in the little cottage at the rear. Nobody ever thought of color."[45] Based on this eye-witness account, it is clear that this interaction between the races did not only occur during the church service times, but that the fellowship existed beyond those times. Catley asserts that Azusa Street was truly an interracial assembly. Not merely whites and blacks sitting together, but experiencing real unity. It is reported that even as late as 1910 the two groups could be found eating, sitting, and praying together.

Seymour himself seemed to be the one who encouraged this mixing of the races. In his periodical *The Apostolic Faith,* he made the claim that, "No instrument that God can use is rejected on account of color or dress or lack of education." Seymour further stated that if the revival "had started in a fine church, poor colored people and Spanish people would not have got it" and added "but praise God it started here."[46] He was of the firm belief that the breaking down of the racial barriers was a "sign" of the renewal of Pentecost and of the second coming of Christ. In the above mentioned article he wrote "One token of the Lord's coming is that He is melting all races and nations together, and they are filled with the power and the glory of God. He is baptizing by one spirit into one body and making up a people that will be ready to meet Him when he

44. MacRobert, *Black Roots and White Racism of Early Pentecostalism,* 55–56.

45. Ibid.

46. Seymour, *Apostolic Faith,* 1.

comes."[47] Synan asserts that "There can be no doubt that in its early stages the Pentecostal movement was completely interracial. The Azusa Street meeting was conducted on the basis of complete racial equality."[48]

CHARLES HARRISON MASON AND THE ROLE OF THE COGIC

During the latter half of 1906 another African-American preacher was to become instrumental in the furtherance of the interracial nature of early Pentecostalism. Charles Harrison Mason, who along with another Holiness preacher, Charles Price Jones, had founded the Church of God in Christ in Memphis, Tennessee in 1897. Mason received reports of the Pentecostal revival in Los Angeles. In early 1907 Mason, along with his colleagues J. A. Jeter and D. J. Young, traveled to California.[49] Under the ministry of William J. Seymour, all three received the Baptism in the Holy Spirit and experienced glossolalia.

This experience radically revolutionized Mason's major emphasis in ministry and brought a new spiritual vitality. Prior to his Azusa Street experience, his main concern was the preservation of the "slave religion" of African-Americans. Although Mason continued to maintain this emphasis in his ministry and in the growth and development of the Church of God in Christ, after his Azusa Street experience, he became more concerned with the "baptism experience" as an instrument of social change, affecting both black and white disenfranchised. Clemmons states that "Seymour and Mason envisioned the transformation of society through the experience of the Holy Spirit. They saw the potential for correcting a theological gap and building a respectable heritage for the poor and oppressed black and white in racist America."[50] Sydney Ahlstrom adds that Azusa Street became "a process by which black piety exerted its greatest direct influence on American religious history, for the gift of tongues came during those years to black and white alike."[51]

One aspect of Mason's ministry became particularly important to the history of Pentecostalism. At the time of his "conversion" to the Pentecostal message, and subsequent leadership of the Church of God

47. Seymour, *Apostolic Faith*, 1.

48. Synan, *Holiness-Pentecostal Tradition*, 170.

49. Martin, *Life and Ministry of William J. Seymour*, 215.

50. Clemmons, *Racial and Spiritual Unity*, 29.

51. Ahlstrom, *Religious History of the American People*, 1063.

in Christ, Mason, an African-American, was the only minister who led a legally incorporated church body within the young Pentecostal movement, and thus could ordain ministers whose status would be recognized by government authorities. Such recognition allowed the newly ordained Pentecostal ministers to perform legal marriages and carry out other ministerial functions. It also allowed them to receive a railroad discount, which was very important for early Pentecostal evangelists as they traveled throughout the country spreading the Pentecostal gospel. Synan makes note of the fact that during the period from 1907 to 1914 the only organized Pentecostal denominations were the Church of God in Christ, the Church of God (Cleveland, Tennessee), The United Holy Church, and the Pentecostal Holiness Church, none of which with the exception of Mason's COGIC were legally incorporated. COGIC was legally incorporated in Memphis when it had been initially founded in 1897.[52]

As a result of Mason's Church of God in Christ's legal status, many white Pentecostal ministers sought ordination from Mason. Large numbers of white ministers obtained credentials carrying the name, "Church of God in Christ." According to Clemmons, in the years 1909–1913, there were as many white Churches of God in Christ as there were black all carrying Mason's credentials and incorporation.[53] Synan posits that, "So great was Mason's prestige that many white Pentecostal ministers accepted ordination at his hands. From 1907 to 1914 the church was interracial, and many whites joined it."[54] Mason even referred to the white ministers who carried COGIC credentials as the "White work of the Church."

RACIAL SEPARATION AND THE FORMATION OF THE ASSEMBLIES OF GOD

The Church of God in Christ and the Pentecostal movement as a whole was not to remain interracial for long, however. As the Pentecostal movement became "established" it began to fall victim to some of the social pressures of the greater American culture of the time, and soon began to reflect the racial separatism of the day. The color line that had been in the words of Frank Bartleman, "washed away in the blood [of Jesus]" began to reappear in denominational Pentecostalism.

52. Synan, *Holiness-Pentecostal Tradition.*
53. Clemmons, *Racial and Spiritual Unity in the Body of Christ.*
54. Synan, *Holiness-Pentecostal Tradition,* 125.

Vinson Synan makes the point that white ministers in COGIC, led by H. A. Goss, D. C. O. Opperman, H. G. Rodgers, and A. P. Collins (all of whom were to be among the founding leaders of the new Assemblies of God), were becoming increasingly dissatisfied with the denomination.[55] Many of them perceived the organization as "frail" and "inadequate" in its ability to provide leadership for its growing membership. In addition, there were reports of violent acts being committed against white leaders within COGIC. The spring 1987 issue of the *Assemblies of God Heritage* magazine reports incidents of white church members leaving their black congregations and being accosted on the way home. Events such as these made the interracial make-up of Pentecostal congregations extremely difficult to maintain, especially in the Southern states.

The growing dissatisfaction of the white ministers within COGIC, in addition to racially motivated violence from those outside the church, ultimately resulted in an overt attempt by the white faction to separate. According to Edith Blumhofer on December 20, 1913, white COGIC elders E. N. Bell and H. A. Goss issued a call to convene a general council of "all Pentecostal saints and Churches of God in Christ."[56] The call read in part: "This call is to all the Churches of God in Christ, to all Pentecostal or Apostolic Faith Assemblies who desire with united purpose to cooperate in love and peace to push the interests of the kingdom of God everywhere. This is, however, only for saints who believe in the baptism of the Holy Ghost with the signs following."[57] While the invitation was technically issued to "all" Churches of God in Christ, it was, however, issued in E. N. Bell's periodical *Word and Witness* which was circulated only among white members of COGIC.

The General Council meeting was held at the Grand Opera House on Central Avenue in Hot Springs, Arkansas in the "chilly early spring of 1914."[58] Robeck posits that:

> The poignant significance of this break is that it gave rise to two conflicting views of the historic relationship between the Assemblies of God and the Church of God in Christ. In blessing their departure, even if the departure was made because of white dissatisfaction with black leadership Mason can be seen as

55. Ibid.

56. Blumhofer, *Assemblies of God.*

57. *Word and Witness*, December 20, 1913.

58. Blumhofer, *Assemblies of God*, 197.

giving birth to a new offspring, the Assemblies of God. On the other hand, those who formed the Assemblies of God tended to emphasize the relative independence they had experienced when they carried the Church of God in Christ name claiming the relationship to be merely a business necessity.[59]

There is no existing literature to ascertain how Charles Mason felt about the division of his denomination. However, he did nothing to hinder the occurrence. In fact, Mason traveled to the Hot Springs convention to invoke God's blessing on the newly formed General Council of the Assemblies of God (AG).[60] This was the first of only two "official" interactions that C. H. Mason had with the Assemblies of God, the other was when he once again addressed another of the AG's general councils, this time the 1937 council in Memphis.[61] In the 1914 formative general council of the AG, Mason brought along a gospel choir from Memphis and preached on Thursday night to more than four hundred white Pentecostal preachers. Only one of the delegates there was black, G. T. Haywood of Indianapolis.[62] According to Clemmons, "Mason bid the white leaders a warm farewell and gave them leave to void their Church of God in Christ credentials in order to switch to those of their new denomination."[63] Since the doctrine of the two factions remained basically the same, the argument cannot be made that the separation was doctrinal.[64] This April, 1914 formation of the General Council of the AG marked the beginning of the end of the interracial homogeneity of Pentecostalism that had been a hallmark of its earliest years.

Other Pentecostal denominations followed suit. For example, according to Richardson, Oneness (Apostolic) Pentecostals, like their holiness counterparts, also experienced the unfortunate effects of racism.[65] The Pentecostal Assemblies of the World, the oldest Oneness groups, started as an integrated church. Synan notes that for nine years this organization operated as a completely interracial church with roughly equal

59. Robeck, "Azusa Street Revival," 33.

60. *Assemblies of God Heritage*, Spring 1987.

61. Kenyon, *Bishop Mason and the Sisterhood Myth*, 12.

62. *Assemblies of God Heritage*, Spring 1987.

63. Clemmons, *Bishop C. H. Mason*, 587.

64. Richardson, *Why Black and White Pentecostals are Separated*.

65. Ibid.

numbers of black and whites serving as both officials and members.[66] However, by 1924, the majority of whites in this body split to form their own church. Two other major Southern white Pentecostal denominations, the Church of God and the Pentecostal Holiness Church, also began as interracial organizations. By 1926 the Church of God had become segregated with the black constituency maintaining their own General Assembly, although by law of the church, the General Overseer of this assembly was to be a white man. This according to Synan was the polity of the Church of God until 1966.[67]

THE PENTECOSTAL FELLOWSHIP OF NORTH AMERICA

Before 1948 when the Pentecostal Fellowship of North America (PFNA) was founded, there was little interaction among the various white Pentecostal denominations and groups. Of course interaction between white and black Pentecostals was basically non-existent at this point or minimal at best. However, according to Warner it took the formation of the National Association of Evangelicals (NAE) in 1942 and the creation of the Pentecostal World Conference in Zürich, Switzerland in 1947 to bring white North American Pentecostals together.[68]

On May 7, 1948, following the annual meeting of the NAE, twenty-four leaders of eight Pentecostal groups met to explore the possibility of forming a fellowship for the purpose of unity. A second exploratory meeting was held in Chicago later that same year and was attended by twenty seven leaders of twelve denominations. An important component of this second meeting was the appointment of a committee to draw up articles of the fellowship. As a result of these meetings the PFNA was organized at Des Moines, Iowa on October 26–28, 1948. Of significant note is that no black Pentecostal denomination or group was invited to be a part of this new body. West states that "this non-invitation to a ministerial fraternity dedicated to spiritual unity has stood as a symbolic racistic offense between black and white Pentecostals."[69] It is ironic that among the four objectives adopted for the founding of the fellowship in 1948, the second reads as follows: "To demonstrate to the world the essential unity

66. Synan, *Holiness-Pentecostal Tradition*.
67. Ibid.
68. Warner, *Pentecostal Fellowship of North America*.
69. West, *That His People May Be One*, 88.

of Spirit-baptized believers, fulfilling the prayer of the Lord Jesus 'that they all may be one' (John 17:21)."[70]

Not only were black Pentecostals not invited to be part of this "unifying fellowship" but both black and white non-Trinitarian Pentecostals (also known as Oneness, United, or Apostolic Pentecostals) were excluded from this fellowship when it adopted a doctrinal statement that included a Trinitarian paragraph. The PFNA remained an all white body until October 1994.

THE "MIRACLE IN MEMPHIS"

From October 17–19, 1994, over a thousand pastors, bishops, denominational executives, scholars, and various other Pentecostal leaders gathered in Memphis, Tennessee, for a historic conference called *Pentecostal Partners: A Reconciliation Strategy for Twenty-first Century Ministry*. Upon arrival in Memphis on October 17, there was a sense of expectation among the delegates that something historically significant was about to happen. The evening sessions of the conference were held in the Dixon-Meyers Hall of the Cook Convention Center in downtown Memphis and attended by over 3,000 people. The significance of the Memphis location must have been evident to all as this city had played an important role in the unfolding civil rights events of the 1960s. It was here that Dr. Martin Luther King Jr. had given his famous last speech known as the "Mountaintop speech" at the famed Mason Temple, headquarters of COGIC. It was in this city that Dr. King had been assassinated in 1968. Here, it was hoped, that the city would be remembered for a great racial healing rather than racial strife. The late Bishop Ithiel Clemmons, at that time a member of the Presidium of COGIC, and Bishop Bernard E. Underwood, then Presiding Bishop of the International Pentecostal Holiness Church and Chairman of the Pentecostal Fellowship of North America, served as co-chairmen of the steering committee and as co-moderators for the conference. The late Bishop Gilbert E. Patterson, former Pastor of the Temple of Deliverance COGIC and former Presiding Bishop of COGIC, and Rev. Samuel Middlebrook, former Pastor of Raleigh Assembly of God, both of Memphis, Tennessee, also provided leadership.

The Memphis meeting had been the result of a few years of preliminary meetings and talks between black and white Pentecostal lead-

70. Minutes, PFNA Board of Administration & Annual Meetings, 1948.

ers. The process had been initiated by the late Bishop Ithiel Clemmons of COGIC, and Bishop Bernard E. Underwood of the International Pentecostal Holiness Church—a predominantly white Pentecostal denomination. These men had met while serving on the planning board of a conference in 1987 and through their discussions and interactions began laying the groundwork for racial reconciliation among American Pentecostals. When Bishop Underwood was elected chair of the all white Pentecostal Fellowship of North America (PFNA) in 1991 he was determined to use his leadership to bring an end to the racial division among Pentecostals. On March 6, 1992 the Board of Administration of the PFNA voted unanimously to "pursue the possibility of reconciliation with our African-American brethren."[71] This opened the door for four pre-Memphis meetings. The first was on July 31, 1992 in Dallas, Texas, where PFNA leaders got to meet and hear from COGIC Bishop O. T. Jones Jr. The second was in Phoenix, Arizona, on January 4–5, 1993. The third meeting was held during the PFNA annual meeting in Atlanta, Georgia, where Dr. Jack Hayford of the International Church of the Foursquare Gospel and the late Bishop G. E. Patterson of the COGIC brought strong support and affirmation for the reconciliation plan. The fourth and final meeting leading up to the "Memphis Miracle" meeting was held in January 1994 and became known as the "20/20 Meeting" because twenty whites and twenty blacks met to plan the final conference to be held in Memphis in October of that year.

During the morning sessions at the Memphis conference, presentations were made by a team of leading Pentecostal scholars. Responses to these presentations were given by various Pentecostal leaders and scholars. The history of separation, racism, and prejudice in Pentecostalism played a key role in the narrative that was presented to those assembled. These narratives brought to life the reality of past injustices and the absolute need for racial reconciliation. Not only was the historical narrative of the racial separation and racism of the past given prominence, but even more importantly, the narrative of the interracial birth and beginnings of the Pentecostal movement served as a rallying point for the present racial reconciliation effort. The presentations were in four parts. The first was *The Past: Historical Roots of Racial Unity and Division in American Pentecostalism* by Dr. Cecil M. Robeck Jr. with responses by Dr. Oliver

71. See the *Pentecostal/Charismatic Churches of North America* Web site. Online: http://www.pccna.org.

J. Haney Jr. and Dr. Lamar Vest. The second, *The Present: The Problem of Racism in the Contemporary Pentecostal Movement*, was presented by Dr. Leonard Lovett with responses by Rev. Thomas E. Trask and Dr. Robert Michael Franklin. The third presentation by Dr. Vinson Synan was titled *The Future: A Strategy for Reconciliation* with responses provided by Clifton E. Buckrham Sr. and Bishop Charles E. Blake. The final presentation was *The Ideal: The Biblical Pattern of Unity, Endeavoring to Keep the Spirit's Unity*, by Dr. William Turner with responses by Dr. Ray H. Hughes and Bishop Barbara Amos. The bulk of my rhetorical analysis focuses on the first presentation and responses that dealt with the past, but also includes the second and third presentations since they too made several references to the history of racism and prejudice within American Pentecostalism. The first presentation by Dr. Robeck, focusing on the past, was by far the most extensive, both in length and depth.

These presentations precipitated the climactic moment of the conference, when the white Pentecostal leaders repented for a history of prejudice and racism. This act of repentance culminated in an on-stage, spontaneous, and extemporaneous "foot-washing" with a white Assemblies of God pastor washing the feet of a black Pentecostal church leader. The white pastor explained that he had felt called of God to wash the feet of a black leader as a sign of repentance and humility. In a moment of tearful contrition, he washed the feet of the late Bishop Ithiel Clemmons, while begging forgiveness for the sins of the whites against their black brothers and sisters. In an emotional speech the next day, Dr. Paul Walker, a white Pentecostal leader called the event, "the Miracle in Memphis," a name that stuck and made headlines around the world. It was called the "Memphis Miracle" by those gathered in Memphis as well as the press, which hailed the historic importance of the event.[72]

It was called a miracle because it ended decades of formal separation between the predominantly black and white Pentecostal churches in America. The white delegates at this meeting representing the racially exclusive PFNA organization voted to dissolve the organization for the formation of a new more inclusive one. On October 19, 1994, the PFNA ceased to exist, and a new organization, the Pentecostal/Charismatic Churches of North America (PCCNA) was born. A constitution and a Racial Reconciliation Manifesto were drawn up by which the new organization would be guided.

72. *Christian Century* April 27, 1994; *Christianity Today*, December 12, 1994.

THE RHETORIC OF RACIAL RECONCILIATION

The New Merriam-Webster Dictionary defines reconciliation as "to cause to be friendly or harmonious again."[73] This definition carries with it the implication that those who seek out reconciliation had at one time been harmonious and friendly, and had lost that through differences, conflict, or other reasons. This definition accurately describes the American Pentecostal movement having been once founded as an interracial movement with both blacks and whites playing significant roles in its inception and development, yet going their separate ways due to racial attitudes and pressures. Their reconciliatory rhetoric, therefore, sought to return to the harmonious and friendly interaction they had once enjoyed but had lost to racism. In achieving this goal, one could say that the Pentecostal movement was successful through the use of the rhetoric of nostalgia, myth, and collective memory that it employed. However, this dictionary further defines reconciliation as the ability to "adjust, or settle differences."[74] In this regard, I will argue that the Pentecostal movement is not as successful. The rhetoric of reconciliation employed by the leaders of the Pentecostal movement during the Memphis racial reconciliation conference, and at other occasions, has not proven to be as successful in "adjusting or settling" those differences that exist between black and white Pentecostals.

COLLECTIVE MEMORY

The argument can be made that the collective memory of American Pentecostalism centers on the narrative of the Azusa Street revival. This collective memory of the Azusa Street narrative goes beyond the mere historical recounting of the events of that revival; it also focuses on the subjectivity of the historical narrative. Traditionally, historical studies have focused on the assumption of objectivity, accuracy of memory, and factual information, with little consideration for subjectivity in the accounts.[75] However, the issue of subjectivity as emphasized by scholars of collective memory has brought about a dialectic between traditional history and collective memory studies, although some traditional historians

73. *New Merriam-Webster Dictionary*, 609.

74. Ibid.

75. Thelen, "Memory and American History."

such as Jan Vansina are coming to the conclusion that collective memories sometimes constitute the most authentic recollection of the past.[76]

The subjectivity of the memory of the Pentecostal narrative was brought to the fore through the discussion of the various eye witness accounts and narratives of the events at the Azusa Street Mission. These accounts are usually told from the racial and cultural point of view of the narrator. Both black and white Pentecostal rhetors have varying narratives and interpretations of the historical events that are clearly shaped by their racial and cultural differences. These differences included varying narratives regarding the person who should ultimately be called "founder" or leader of the Pentecostal movement. White Pentecostals have traditionally leaned toward the position of "no human leadership," emphasizing instead that it was the Holy Spirit who gave birth to and led the early Pentecostal movement while giving minimal attention to the role of blacks such as William J. Seymour, Charles H. Mason, and others in the founding and leading of the movement. Black Pentecostals have not necessarily discounted the significance of the Holy Spirit in the founding of the movement, but have however emphasized the important role of the African-American roots of Pentecostalism including the black leader of the Azusa Street revival, William Joseph Seymour. White Pentecostals on the other hand, have tended to consider the role of Charles F. Parham (who was white), despite his racial and moral failings, as more important in the founding of the movement than was Seymour. Another example of racial and cultural difference in the collective memory of the Pentecostal narrative is the divergent collective memories of white and black Pentecostals centering on the accounts of the racial division itself. While white Pentecostal historians (particularly in the AG) maintain that the relationship with Charles H. Mason's Church of God in Christ was merely a "marriage of convenience," and "an association mainly for the purpose of business," black Pentecostals in COGIC maintain that it was an opportunity for an integrated fellowship made up of both blacks and whites. They saw the reason for whites leaving COGIC and forming their own fellowship (AG), as purely racial, while those white COGIC ministers who left to form the AG argue that it was not racial.

76. Hasian and Frank, *Rhetoric, History, and Collective Memory*; Vansina, *Oral Tradition*; Zelizer, *Reading the Past Against the Grain*; Lloyd, *Collective Memory, Commemoration, Memory, and History*.

Traditionally, historical accounts and narratives have favored the dominant group. Barbie Zelizer asks the questions "Who remembers? And for whom is remembering being accomplished?"[77] Most often these questions can be answered that remembering is the domain of dominant societies to determine, and that their history and their accounts of the past should be the accepted account and should shape the narratives of all other communities and the way these minority communities see themselves within the context of history. However, collective memory, with its inherent subjectivity, brings with it the opportunity for these minority communities who have long been "footnotes" in history to reclaim their voice and tell the narratives of history from their vantage point and perspective. Zelizer emphasizes that a community's collective memory is shaped and underscored by their past experiences, narratives, culture, etc.[78]

Collective memory in this case thus becomes important to the rhetoric of racial reconciliation in American Pentecostalism, because it emphasizes and brings to light the point of separation between black and white Pentecostals. Although arguably the reasons for the racial separation in American Pentecostalism may be numerous, and the accounts presented here may not be exhaustive, these divergent narratives underscore the differences that exist between black and white Pentecostals. They also serve as an appropriate starting point for a discussion on the rhetoric of racial reconciliation. This is so because for any two parties to engage in reconciliation rhetoric, they must first investigate and bring to the dialogue those things that either have caused division or continue to keep them apart. Therefore, these varying collective memories, from a rhetorical standpoint, serve as a means of discussing those differences that keep black and white Pentecostals apart.

MYTH MAKING

Myths, like collective memory, are a product not of any one individual, but of a community of people.[79] Also like collective memory, myths depend on the formation and development of narratives. The American Pentecostal community, in the telling and retelling of the narrative of the

77. Zelizer, *Reading the Past against the Grain*, 214.

78. Zelizer, *Covering the Body*.

79. Braden, *Myths in a Rhetorical Context*; Marx, *Machine in the Garden*; Smith, *Virgin Land*.

Azusa Street revival, and the rhetoric of reconciliation, has mythologized the characters and events of the early Pentecostal movement. The argument can be made that the mythologization of these persons and events of early Pentecostalism serve as a moral compass for future racial reconciliation efforts. In their mythic rhetoric, Pentecostal leaders at the Memphis Miracle conference reexamined the characters and personalities of the early Pentecostal movement, and in so doing, were able to guide the dialogue toward racial healing and reconciliation by using the characters of the early Pentecostal pioneers as examples for present day Pentecostals to emulate or to avoid. As Roderick P. Hart states, myths become "master stories describing exceptional people doing exceptional things and serving as moral guides to proper action."[80] Through the use of cosmological mythic narratives, Pentecostal rhetors could look back at the heroic actions of pioneers such as Seymour and Mason who stood for racial justice and unity, and call present day Pentecostals back to that same spirit. This "myth of return" as described by Mircea Eliade could enable Pentecostals to achieve racial reconciliation. Thus myths become those narratives that "symbolically solve the problem facing the society."[81]

From a mythic perspective, while the heroic actions of certain early Pentecostal pioneers such as W. J. Seymour and C. H. Mason are to be applauded and emulated, no mythic narrative is complete with just heroes and no "villains." One could point to the fact that contrary to the heroic actions of Seymour, Mason, and others who stood for racial unity and justice, the "villainous" actions of certain Pentecostal pioneers such as Parham and other white Pentecostal leaders of the day need to be identified, repudiated, and avoided. Parham and others who verbally attacked Seymour and the attendees of the Azusa Street Mission and made several (unsuccessful) attempts to wrestle control of the Azusa Street Mission from him, and the actions of Clara Lum and Florence Crawford who absconded with the Mission's mailing lists, or the white Pentecostal leaders who used Bishop Mason's kindness and generosity for their own gain, only to break fellowship with him as soon as it became convenient, are not to be applauded, but are to be called out for what they really were and rejected. The mythic narrative thus becomes invaluable to the rhetoric of reconciliation among American Pentecostals, because it begins to identify

80. Hart, *Modern Rhetorical Criticism*, 234.

81. Eliade, *Myth of the Eternal Return*; *Myth and Reality*; Rowland, *On Mythic Criticism*, 103.

some of the injustices, prejudices, and hurtful actions caused by some of the early white Pentecostal leaders that eventually led to racial separation and a strained relationship between black and white Pentecostals.

NOSTALGIA

The rhetoric of the myth of return tends to lead naturally to a nostalgic rhetoric. In the case of the rhetoric of reconciliation in American Pentecostalism, this is no different. The longing for a past, a yearning for yesterday, becomes a means through which communities engage in a kind of rhetoric they can hold onto while reaffirming their identity through their past in spite of any havoc, hurt, or insecurities that may have taken place in the course of time.[82] In the case of American Pentecostalism, this is very true following the pain caused by racial prejudice, discrimination, and segregation in the movement. Nostalgia thus becomes a powerfully effective means for rhetors to connect their audiences emotionally and psychologically with the "good old days" before the hurt and turmoil occurred. The rhetoric of nostalgia may not be effective or necessary in every reconciliationary dialogue as the parties involved may never have had a time when they were united in peace, friendship, and harmony before there was a breach of trust and hurt was caused by one or both parties involved. However, by definition, reconciliation implies that at one time the parties involved had been together and had separated for some reason and are now attempting to restore the lost relationship. Therefore, it may be difficult to use the term for dialogue that involves parties that never once had a prior relationship. Nevertheless, for American Pentecostals, the term is very appropriate as both black and white Pentecostals at one time had a relationship and had interacted during the formation of the movement at the Azusa Street revival.

This event thus becomes the focal point of the rhetoric of nostalgia as employed by Pentecostal rhetors during the racial reconciliation dialogue. The Azusa Street revival and the interracial beginnings of the Pentecostal movement thus become this "perfect example" of racial unity and cooperation, regardless of whether or not it was "perfect" in the true sense of the word. Whether or not it was truly perfect, nostalgia acts as a means of "distort[ing] the past for the sake of effect" so that the past becomes a

---

82. Davis, *Yearning for Yesterday*; Tannock, *Nostalgia Critique*; and Davis, "Nostalgia, Identity, and the Current Nostalgia Wave."

perfect example of how one should live their life today.[83] Nostalgic rhetoric sometimes downplays the failures of the past, and paints a glowing image of a more perfect past. In the case of racial reconciliation rhetoric in American Pentecostalism however, although the interracial spirit of Azusa Street was talked about in glowing terms, the failures and hurtful behavior of the past was discussed, not as an example to return to and for Pentecostals to emulate, but as a warning for what Pentecostals today need to look out for and avoid. Vinson Synan, Cecil M. Robeck Jr., and other Pentecostal rhetors called the movement back to unity of diversity and the spirit of interracial togetherness that once held sway at the Azusa Street revival.[84]

Even one of the culminating events of the racial reconciliation conference—the spontaneous foot washing of Bishop Ithiel Clemmons by Don Evans—made use of the rhetoric of nostalgia. As he washed Bishop Clemmons's feet, Evans, a white AG Pentecostal minister, sought to "wash away the offenses of the past" thus removing the stain of racism, discrimination, prejudice, and bigotry that had plagued the Pentecostal movement for all these years and returning it to the spirit of perfect unity and interracial worship that once prevailed at Azusa Street before it was interrupted by the stain and sin of racism. As he washed Bishop Clemmons's feet, Evans mentioned by name Charles F. Parham, who as a significant historical figure and leader in the Pentecostal movement, stood as a representation of the many white Pentecostals who were responsible for creating the hurt and "offense" through racism against their African-American brethren. Evans further mentioned by name Bishops William J. Seymour, pastor of the Azusa Street Apostolic Faith Gospel Mission, and Charles H. Mason, founder of the Church of God in Christ, men who as (black) leaders and founders of the Pentecostal movement had experienced racism and bigotry from their white counterparts. In doing so, this foot washing by Don Evans becomes a nostalgic rhetorical act, calling the movement back to a time when interracial "perfection" existed in American Pentecostalism. Nostalgia thus becomes an indispensable rhetorical tool in the Pentecostals' rhetoric of racial reconciliation.

83. Parry-Giles and Parry-Giles, "Collective Memory, Political Nostalgia, and the Rhetorical Presidency," 241.

84. Synan, *The Future* and Robeck, *The Past*.

POST 1994 EFFORTS TOWARD RACIAL RECONCILIATION

Finally, efforts toward racial reconciliation in the years following the 1994 "Memphis Miracle" reconciliation conference should be discussed. The importance of this aspect of the rhetoric of reconciliation in American Pentecostalism speaks to whether or not any real change in the attitudes and behavior of Pentecostals was brought about as a result of the reconciliationary dialogue of the 1990s.

While the 1994 conference was hailed as a "miracle" by insiders as well as the press after the conference, some leading Pentecostal clergy and scholars are of the opinion that there has been precious little achieved by way of actual tangible actions toward racial reunification and reconciliation in the movement in the years since then. This attitude is more prevalent among African-American Pentecostal scholars. On the other hand, some black and white Pentecostal leaders continue to encourage interracial dialogue, emphasizing the fact that given the long history of racial disunity in the movement, one must not expect instantaneous change. Some white Pentecostal leaders such as Rev. Scott Temple, Intercultural Ministries Director for the Assemblies of God, and a participant at the 1996 "Memphis Miracle Revisited" conference, are urging their fellow white Pentecostals (and ultimately all Pentecostals) to "redeem this time for reconciliation" and "move beyond good rhetoric to good working relationships."[85] One can also point to examples of denominational and grassroots/local church actions toward racial reconciliation following the 1994 Memphis conference. It must be emphasized however, that although these steps toward racial interaction and unity between black and white Pentecostals are applaudable, there is still much work to be done for one to say that the rhetoric of reconciliation has truly become effective in the American Pentecostal movement.

CONCLUSION

On April 25–29, 2006, thousands of Pentecostal believers from all over the world gathered in Los Angeles, CA for the centennial anniversary celebration of the Azusa Street revival. This event, with its many speeches, sermons, and significant highlights served as one large rhetorical tool of collective memory, myth making, and nostalgic longing for the

---

85. Temple, *King of Reconciliation* and Temple, *Memphis Miracle Revisited*.

past. Pentecostals have always looked to the past, such as the birth of the Christian Church on the day of Pentecost when the Holy Spirit descended, as an example of racial and ethnic unity (Acts 2:5 records that there were people gathered there from many different nationalities). They have also looked nostalgically at the multi-ethnic and interracial Azusa Street revival as a template for present-day racial healing and reconciliation. As Pentecostals enter their second century of existence, it is a certainty that their collective memory, myth, and nostalgic longings for the "good old days" of Azusa Street will continue to evolve. Furthermore, it is also a certainty that Pentecostals will continue to employ and rely on these aforementioned rhetorical instruments to guide them, and enable them to negotiate not only racial reconciliation, but any other issues they may face in the future.

BIBLIOGRAPHY

Ahlstrom, Sydney. *A Religious History of the American People*. New Haven: Yale University Press, 1972.

Barrett, David. B. "Signs and Wonders and Statistics in the World of Today." In *Pentecost, Mission and Ecumenism: Festschrift in Honor of Professor Walter J. Hollenweger*, edited by J. A. B. Jongeneel, 64–88. Frankfort: Lang, 1972.

Bartleman, Frank. *Azusa Street: The Roots of Modern-Day Pentecost*. 1925. Reprint, Gainesville, FL: Bridge-Logos, 1980.

———. *Another Wave Rolls In!* Northridge, CA: Voice, 1970.

Blumhofer, Edith L. *The Assemblies of God: A Chapter in the Story of American Pentecostalism*. 2 vols. Springfield, MO: Gospel, 1989.

Braden, Waldo W. "Myths in a Rhetorical Context." *The Southern Speech Communication Association Journal* 40 (1975) 113–26.

Brumback, Carl. *Suddenly—from Heaven: A History of the Assemblies of God*. Springfield, MO: Gospel, 1961.

Clemmons, Ithiel C. *Bishop C. H. Mason and the Roots of the Church of God in Christ*. Bakersfield, CA: Pneuma Life, 1996.

———. "Racial and Spiritual Unity in the Body of Christ: An Interview with the Chairman of the Newly Formed Pentecostal/Charismatic Churches of North America." Interview by Wayne Goodall. *Advance* (Fall 1995) 66–68.

Correspondents of the *New York Times*. *How Race Is Lived in America: Pulling Together, Pulling Apart*. Online: http://www.nytimes.com/library/national/race.

Davis, Fred. "Nostalgia, Identity, and the Current Nostalgia Wave." *Journal of Popular Culture* 1 (1977) 422.

———. *Yearning for Yesterday: A Sociology of Nostalgia*. New York: Free, 1979.

Eliade, Mircea. *Myth and Reality*. Translated by Willard R. Trask. New York: Harper, 1963.

————. *The Myth of the Eternal Return or Cosmos and History*. Princeton, NJ: Princeton University Press, 1954.

Hardon, John A. *The Protestant Churches of America*. Westminster, MD: Newman, 1957.

Hasian, Marouf, Jr., and Robert E. Frank. "Rhetoric, History, and Collective Memory: Decoding the Goldhagen Debates." *Western Journal of Communication* 63 (1999) 95–114.

Hart, Roderick P. *Modern Rhetorical Criticism*. Boston: Allyn & Bacon, 1997.

Herskovits, Melville J. *The Myth of the Negro Past*. Boston: Beacon, 1958.

Hurston, Zora Neale. *The Sanctified Church: The Folklore Writings of Zora Neale Hurston*. Berkeley, CA: Turtle Island, 1923 [1981].

Kenyon, Howard N. "Bishop Mason and the Sisterhood Myth." *Assemblies of God Heritage* 7 (1987) 12.

————. "Black Ministers in the Assemblies of God: Ellsworth S. Thomas First Black Minister Credentialed in 1915." *Assemblies of God Heritage* 7 (1987) 10–13, 20.

Lloyd, Jennifer M. "Collective Memory, Commemoration, Memory and History: Or William O'Brian, the Bible Christians, and Me." *Biography: An Interdisciplinary Quarterly* 25 (2002) 46–58.

Lovett, Leonard. "Black Origins of the Pentecostal Movement." In *Aspects of Pentecostal-Charismatic Origins*, edited by V. Synan, 123–41. Plainfield, NJ: Logos, 1975.

————. "The Present: The Problem of Racism in the Contemporary Pentecostal Movement." Unpublished paper presented at Pentecostal Partners: A Reconciliation Strategy for Twenty-first Century Ministry. Memphis, TN, 1994.

MacRobert, Iain. *The Black Roots and White Racism of Early Pentecostalism in the USA*. London: Macmillan, 1988.

Martin, Larry. *The Life and Ministry of William J. Seymour*. Joplin, MO: Christian Life, 1999.

Marx, Leo. *The Machine in the Garden: Technology and the Pastoral Ideal in America*. New York: Oxford University Press, 1964.

Miller, Donald E., and Tetsunao Yamamori. *Global Pentecostalism: The New Face of Christian Social Engagement*. Los Angeles: University of California Press, 2007.

Nelson, Douglas J. "For Such a Time as This: The Story of Bishop William J. Seymour and the Azusa Street Revival." PhD diss., University of Birmingham, 1981.

Parry-Giles, Shawn J., and Trevor Parry-Giles. "Collective Memory, Political Nostalgia, and the Rhetorical Presidency: Bill Clinton's Commemoration of the March on Washington, August 28, 1998." *Quarterly Journal of Speech* 86 (2000) 417–37.

Raboteau, Albert J. *Slave Religion: The Invisible Institution in the Antebellum South*. New York: Oxford University Press, 1978.

————. *Canaan Land: A Religious History of African Americans*. New York: Oxford University Press, 2001.

Richardson, J. C. "Why Black and White Pentecostals Are Separated." *Logos* (1980).

Robeck, Cecil M. "Azusa Street Revival." In *Dictionary of Pentecostal and Charismatic Movements*, edited by Stanley M. Burgess and Gary B. McGee, 31–36. Grand Rapid: Zondervan, 1988.

————. "The Past: Historical Roots of Racial Unity and Division in American Pentecostalism." Unpublished paper presented at Pentecostal Partners: A Reconciliation Strategy for Twenty-first Century Ministry. Memphis, TN, 1994.

Rowland, Robert C. "On Mythic Criticism." *Communication Studies* 41 (1990) 101–16.

Seymour, William J. *The Doctrines and Disciplines of the Azusa Street Apostolic Faith Mission of Los Angeles, California*. Los Angeles: Published by the author, 1915.

Smith, Henry Nash. *Virgin Land: The American West as Symbol and Myth.* Cambridge: Harvard University Press, 1950.

Synan, Vinson. *The Holiness-Pentecostal Movement in the United States.* Grand Rapids: Eerdmans, 1971.

———. "William Joseph Seymour." In *Dictionary of Pentecostal and Charismatic Movements*, edited by Stanley M. Burgess, Gary B. McGee, and P. H. Alexander, 778–81. Grand Rapids: Zondervan, 1988.

———. *The Holiness-Pentecostal Tradition: Charismatic Movements in the Twentieth Century.* Grand Rapids: Eerdmans, 1997.

———. "The Future: A Strategy for Reconciliation." Unpublished paper presented at Pentecostal Partners: A Reconciliation Strategy for Twenty-first Century Ministry. Memphis, TN, 1994.

Tannock, Stuart. "Nostalgia Critique." *Cultural Studies* 9 (1995) 453–64.

Temple, Scott. "The King of Reconciliation." Sermon, 1996.

———. "The Memphis Miracle Revisited." Sermon presented to the Assemblies of God's New Jersey District Committee for Reconciliation, 1996.

The New Merriam-Webster Dictionary. Springfield, MA: Merriam-Webster, 1989.

Thelen, David. "Memory and American History." *Journal of American History* 75 (1989) 1117–29.

Vansina, Jan. *Oral Tradition: A Study in Historical Methodology.* London: Routledge & Kegan Paul, 1965.

Warner, Wayne E. "Pentecostal Fellowship of North America." In *The New International Dictionary of Pentecostal and Charismatic Movements*, edited by Stanley M. Burgess and Eduard M. Van der Mass, 968–69. Grand Rapids: Zondervan, 2002.

Washington, Booker T. "The Story of the Negro." In *African American Religious History: A Documentary Witness*, edited by Milton C. Sernett. Durham: Duke University Press, 1999.

West, Russell W. "That His People May Be One: An Interpretive Study of the Pentecostal Leadership's Quest for Racial Unity." PhD diss., Regent University, 1997.

Wilkinson, Michael. *The Spirit Said Go: Pentecostal Immigrants in Canada.* New York: Peter Lang, 2006.

———. "What's 'Global' about Global Pentecostalism?" *Journal of Pentecostal Theology* 17 (2008) 96–109.

Wilmore, Gayraud S. *Black Religion and Black Radicalism.* New York: Doubleday, 1972.

Youngblood, John D., and J. Emmet Winn. "Shout Glory: Competing Communication Codes Experienced by the Members of the African American Pentecostal Genuine Deliverance Holiness Church." *Journal of Communication* (2004) 355–70.

Zelizer, Barbie. *Covering the Body: The Kennedy Assassination, the Media, and the Shaping of Collective Memory.* Chicago: University of Chicago Press, 1992.

———. "Reading the Past Against the Grain: The Shape of Memory Studies." *Critical Studies in Mass Communication* 12 (1995) 214–39.

4

Pentecostalism among Canadian Aboriginal People

A Political Movement?

Clinton N. Westman

INTRODUCTION

In many Aboriginal communities in Canada, particularly across the north, the predominant religious grouping is neither tribal traditionalism, neo-traditional intertribal spirituality, nor the Catholic or Anglican creeds propagated by well-resourced and government-backed missionaries for over a century. Rather, Pentecostal churches, generally established over the last forty years and increasingly led by local people, are frequently a focal point of community life. In some regions, over fifty percent of local residents may claim Pentecostal commitments.[1] Overall, Pentecostalism is proportionately three times as strong among Aboriginal people

1. Burkinshaw, "Native Pentecostalism in British Columbia,"153; Dorais, *Quaqtaq*, 70; and Prince, "Psychiatry Among the James Bay Cree," 25.

relative to the national level of identification.[2] One might expect that any religious movement with such a large membership would have a corresponding impact on the local political scene. This is certainly the case with Pentecostalism, which inspires both its devotees and opponents to political action within Aboriginal communities. Pentecostals themselves are active on a wide range of issues, with some leaders representing Aboriginal people nationally and lobbying for justice at the highest levels. As I shall show here, this reality is inconsistent with prominent scholarly views about Pentecostalism and its meaning in northern Aboriginal contexts. In this chapter, I provide new data from northern Alberta, and summarize the findings of other scholars nationally and internationally, to demonstrate some of the complexity I see in Aboriginal Pentecostal politics.

Pentecostalism is the most important social and religious movement in the communities where I have carried out ethnographic fieldwork since 1996. Yet, as a graduate student, I was able to find little scholarly information on this movement. Robert Burkinshaw confirms that, in spite of their numbers, Pentecostals in Aboriginal communities are under-studied.[3] This scholarly lacuna has enabled some prejudicial misconceptions to flourish relatively unchallenged. Notwithstanding the diverse stands taken by Aboriginal Pentecostal leaders, many analysts have concluded, somewhat simplistically, that the politics of Pentecostalism promote among Aboriginal adherents a negative attitude towards their traditional culture and spirituality.[4] Correspondingly, scholars read into this a reluctance to support land claims or oppose development projects on tribal traditional territory. Looking at the data, I consider that such conclusions are simplistic and premature, often based on generalizations from insufficient fieldwork. Indeed, when one looks beyond stereotypes and rigid theoretical models, one discovers diversity and ambiguity in what remains, nevertheless, a political and a politicizing movement.

What is the relationship of Pentecostalism to other political, social, and economic phenomena in the region, including land claims, inequality and other social problems, and resource development? To answer this question satisfactorily we must move beyond stock analyses that see religious conversion (particularly to Protestantism) as closely linked to given economic and political changes. The general inadequacy of such models

2. Burkinshaw, "Native Pentecostalism in British Columbia," 153.

3. Ibid., 142.

4. Guenther, "Ethnicity and Evangelical Christians in Canada," 390–91.

is compounded by the small scale of Aboriginal community politics. In a recent international panel discussion on conversion and social cohesion in the circumpolar north, Chris Southcott affirmed that Pentecostals constitute an important social movement, beyond the level of ritual practice, and are major players in the social economy throughout Canada's north, in effect operating as an informal resource sharing network.[5] As a movement of localized political networks, Pentecostals take diverse stances on various issues from time to time and place to place.

Like other analyses that see Pentecostalism both as a means to accept and reject elements of Euro-Canadian culture, Southcott's remarks capture some of the complexity of this movement, which defies deterministic analytical models inspired by an opposition between secular modernity and the American fundamentalist religious right.[6] While some Aboriginal Pentecostals may become active on key issues for Christians nationally (such as gay rights including marriage, to use an example provided by Laugrand and Oosten[7] as having mobilized Christians in Nunavut), in other cases the issues animating political and theological debates are pre-eminently local or even ethnic. In such cases, Pentecostal leaders are able to speak for Aboriginal people, who might otherwise lack the ability to communicate effectively with the broader Evangelical Christian electorate. That is, religious/political cleavages may break differently in Aboriginal communities than nationally, but coalitions can be built.[8] In light of this, prima facie generalizations about the political character or meaning of conversion in different cultural and social contexts are unhelpful.

Observations in this chapter flow out of secondary reading, and primary ethnographic research (conducted mainly in Trout Lake and Peerless Lake, Alberta, between 2004 and 2008). As such, I will begin by providing some background information about the field setting. Trout Lake has a population of between 350 and 400 residents, while Peerless Lake is slightly larger; these two semi-isolated communities are 25 km apart, over 250 km from the nearest town, and feature only the most basic services. In

5. Southcott, "Remarks in a Panel Discussion on Conversion and Community Cohesion."

6. Laugrand and Oosten, "Reconnecting People and Healing the Land" and Preston, "Belief in the context of Rapid Change." Also see Pelkmans et al., "Christian Conversion in a Changing World" and Westman, "Faith in God's Temple," "Understanding Cree Religious Discourse."

7. Laugrand and Oosten, "Reconnecting People and Healing the Land," 238.

8. Smith, *Native Americans and the Christian Right*.

both communities, education levels, employment, labor market participation and other key indicators are well below provincial levels. These trends are more notable in Trout Lake than Peerless Lake.[9] Trout Lake also has a higher proportion of Pentecostals, according to the Census. This certainly supports an argument that Aboriginal people in general convert to Pentecostalism because of economic and attendant insecurity. However, a great deal of research would be required to determine the degree to which differing levels of Pentecostal identification *within* the region are related to varying levels of economic prosperity.[10] Any such study would have to contend with the existence of otherwise similar communities, both in the region and nationally, having few to no Pentecostals.

The region's population was divided historically between Indians and Métis; today, however, nearly all residents are considered Status Indians. Most are members of the Bigstone Cree Nation (BCN), headquartered at Wabasca-Desmarais, some 300 km away by road. BCN is one of the largest First Nations in Canada, in terms of population, largely due to the "stragglers" or "late adherents" at places such as Trout Lake and Peerless Lake, who were arbitrarily linked to the band after 1900. Wabasca was the center for regional trade, missionary activity, reserve creation, and education efforts during the early to middle twentieth century. Consequently, at Trout Lake and Peerless Lake, there are no reserves and no local representatives on the BCN council. A patchwork of health and social services are mainly delivered by provincial agencies with little Aboriginal-specific programming, since BCN is only funded by Ottawa to deliver programs to residents of its reserves.

Negotiations are under way for a land base and new band for these communities. According to an Agreement in Principle concluded in 2007, a separate First Nation with considerable new infrastructure and reserve lands is to be created at Trout Lake/Peerless Lake. This 'band split' will represent the fulfillment of long-standing local aspirations, based on a negotiated agreement with BCN in the context of the land claim. As a means to obtain land, money, jobs, community infrastructure, education and housing, the land claim is the pre-eminent local political issue. More so than other political issues, it is also raised in worship and ritual contexts. Nevertheless, there is no one Pentecostal outlook on the land claim.

9. Canada Census, "Trout Lake/Peerless Lake Aggregated Census Divisions."
10. See Guenther, "Ethnicity and Evangelical Christians in Canada," 393.

Leaders advocate both for and against the claim, according to individual opinion and, sometimes, role.

In Trout Lake, recent census data suggest that a clear majority of locals identify as Pentecostals or "Christians."[11] As such, this group would have the potential to act decisively in local politics. While I suggest that this majority is a questionable figure (partly because it is extrapolated from a 10% sample), even so my data show that active Pentecostal adherence has been at relatively high levels (say 25–30% or more) in both Trout Lake and Peerless Lake since the late 1960s. This is far higher than national or provincial averages. Still, when one takes into account that, at any given service, some of the 20–40 people generally in attendance at church are not from Trout Lake, then my informal attendance counts suggest that far fewer than one third of Trout Lake's 180+ (as identified in Canada 2001) Pentecostals are weekly churchgoers. In spite of the remarkably high proportion of nominal Pentecostals in Trout Lake, then, we can say that ongoing church participation among self-identified Pentecostals is lower than the national average church attendance, of above one third, for that denomination.[12] This suggests that, while many locals may consider themselves Pentecostal for census purposes (perhaps by virtue of coming from a Pentecostal family) they very seldom participate in Pentecostal public ritual.[13] Nevertheless, church remains important for at least several dozen core adherents, even those who may not be among the most regular attendees.[14] Also, at times such as funerals, public feasts, and political meetings, the entire community will be exposed to Pentecostal ideas and participate in Pentecostal rites. In such a way, Pentecostal pastors represent themselves as speaking for the whole community, not just for churchgoers. This in turn facilitates their ability to enter and influence the political arena, both locally and, to a lesser extent, further afield.

SCHOLARLY CONTEXT

Apart from my doctoral thesis on Cree Pentecostalism, I have written a detailed analysis of Cree Pentecostal ritual practice, an analysis of commonalities between Pentecostal, Catholic, traditional and neo-traditional

11. Canada Census, "Trout Lake/Peerless Lake Aggregated Census Divisions."

12. Noll, *History of Christianity in Canada and the United States*, 471.

13. The Canadian Census only measures reported religious identification and not attendance, membership or participation.

14. See Dorais, *Quaqtaq*, 77.

practices, a close analysis of a series of early missionary encounters around Trout Lake, and a general history of the region's political development.[15] I have also published numerous articles, chapters and reports pertaining to Aboriginal and environmental politics. In my research generally, I am striving to combine approaches from symbolic anthropology with analysis of political economy, as suggested by Pauline Turner-Strong for the study of Native North American religious issues.[16] So I am interested in linkages between religion and politics. One line of argument that I am rejecting, based on my data, is that there is a strong relationship between Pentecostalism and either class status (taken as differentiation within the local community, based on production or income) or community activism on land claims, resource development, or Aboriginal rights. On a global level, there is currently not enough evidence to assess conflicting claims that have been presented in this regard, a conflict which reflects classical social science disputes.[17]

While the study of Pentecostalism among Aboriginal people has been slow to develop, even so, of the existing scholarly accounts of Aboriginal Pentecostal social life, many of which consist of brief comments, a relatively large number of analyses focus on political aspects of the religion. Perhaps this is because outside analysts have generally been reluctant to analyze the ritual life of Pentecostals, encountering them mainly at public meetings, so that political life presents itself by default as the main object of study.[18] Studying a minority group (Pentecostals) in a small community means that personal and local contingencies can distort data and lead to faulty generalizations. It is unfortunate that this observation has characterized much academic research on Aboriginal Pentecostals. While comparative analysis of case studies might correct for this problem to some extent, it has rarely been undertaken. This has led to a tendency on the part of outside analysts to lampoon Pentecostals.

15. Westman, "Faith in God's Temple," "Cree Pentecostalism and its Others," "Making of 'Isolated Communities' in Alberta's Lesser Slave Lake Interior," "Missionary Tour North from Wabasca, Alberta, 1907," and "Understanding Cree Religious Discourse."

16. Turner-Strong, "Recent Ethnographic Research on North American Indigenous Peoples," 257.

17. Robbins, "Globalization of Pentecostal and Charismatic Christianity," 131; Also see, Navarro, "Pentecostal Churches and their Relationship to the Mexican State and Political Parties"; Samson, "Maya Evangelical Presence in Guatemala" and "Martyrdom of Manuel Saquic"; and Thompson, Making of the English Working Class.

18. Robbins, "Globalization of Pentecostal and Charismatic Christianity," 126.

Often, Pentecostalism appears as a negative, in opposition to the analyst's favored cultural or political projects, which are portrayed as litmus tests to define ethnic purity.

By studying a community where Pentecostals represent a majority, I have been able to avoid focusing on factional cleavages between Pentecostals and others, which might have resulted in an essentialist or distorted view of the relation between religion and politics. On many theological and political issues discussed in Trout Lake and Peerless Lake, Pentecostals are represented on both sides of the argument. Differences in doctrinal interpretation, strategic goals, tactical plans, family status, and personal interest may be as important as religion in forming individuals' opinions and political groupings. This is contrary to a body of literature in which Pentecostalism appears as authoritarian, doctrinaire, monolithic, and divisive. I will briefly review and assess this literature, and provide examples to the contrary.

Two lines of argument prevail in the Pentecostal literature. The first line of argument, used to justify the conclusion that Pentecostals are opposed to fair land claim settlements, suggests that Pentecostals are less involved in bush activities; therefore they will benefit more from industrial development and do not need their Aboriginal and treaty rights protected by land claims. Interestingly, in this line of argument, land claim settlements appear to be a proxy for a conservative life oriented to Aboriginal culture. The second line of argument, which is contradictory to the first on two levels, suggests that Pentecostal converts tend to be among those who do not benefit from culture projects such as land claims and self-government. This line of argument sees land claim settlements and self-government essentially as modernization processes, creating a bureaucratic elite who use the symbols of tradition to establish dominance over a non-technocratic larger group, who do not benefit as much from bureaucratization or wage labor, but who strive to live more traditionally in economic terms by favoring subsistence activities. This second group is held to be more likely to reject the bureaucratized trappings of Aboriginal culture in favor of Pentecostalism, while continuing to practice traditional activities. Note that both these arguments entail specific theoretical assumptions, not only about Pentecostalism and conversion but also about land claims, politics, modernization, class, and culture. I suggest that each of these arguments offers surprisingly little insight into the lived experience of Aboriginal Pentecostals.

Perhaps the most sophisticated exemplar of the first argument is anthropologist Richard Preston.[19] His work analyzes James Bay Cree Pentecostalism as a cultural response to rapid change, showing signs both of continuity and discontinuity with Cree values. Preston may have been the first analyst to note the essential independence of Pentecostal churches, which, once propagated by outsiders or returned insiders, tend to maintain themselves at a community network level. I too find that this shift to local leadership has been central to developing and maintaining Pentecostal congregations. Crucially, he also considers how Pentecostal conversion may allow people simultaneously to achieve both "white" and "Indian" standards of ideal behavior, competence, and self-reliance (e.g., by not drinking), even while remaining outside of mainstream white society and away from white control over ritual space.[20] Thus, Pentecostalism allows people to regain self-control in some areas, such as over drinking, which are esteemed by whites, while surrendering it in others, such as through ritual, which are generally unseen by whites.[21] Control over self, spirits, and environment is closely linked to political roles in Cree society traditionally, lending force to Preston's analysis.

With these theoretical innovations in mind, it is interesting to note that Preston nevertheless characterized Pentecostalism as a negative aspect of Cree society, seeing many of its early adherents during the 1960s and 1970s as marginal, town- (as opposed to bush) oriented families and individuals, who tended to favor development projects over traditional ways. Recently, he has gone further, revising some of his 1975 findings and providing time depth to his analysis of James Bay Cree Pentecostalism. Consistent with Preston's writing on other topics, he asserts that modification and blending of spiritual practice comprise a search for new types of autonomy, expressing tension between the individual and the social.[22] Again, the emphasis on autonomy itself resembles that seen in traditional Cree hunting culture and religion, but is also strongly relevant to attempts to identify the political "meaning" of Pentecostal conversion. Preston's work on this topic benefits from decades of observation, and a willingness to re-examine earlier conclusions in light of new data.

19. Preston, "Belief in the Context of Rapid Change."

20. See Pelkmans et al., "Christian Conversion in a Changing World."

21. Preston, "Belief in the Context of Rapid Change," 122

22. Ibid.; "Cree Narrative," 14; "Transformations musicales et culturelles chez les Cris de l'Est"; and "Twentieth Century Transformations of East Cree Spirituality in Autonomy."

On a similar note, Adrian Tanner made an early observation that James Bay Cree Pentecostals were more dependent on the bush sector than were non-Pentecostals (as opposed to Preston's observation made in a nearby community at a similar time).[23] However, like Preston, Tanner has subsequently modified his finding to suggest that this is no longer the case, and that Pentecostals are no longer more involved in bush activities than others.[24] The repeated and somewhat contradictory analyses of Tanner and Preston show the difficulty in pointing to one political or economic meaning characterizing a religious phenomenon, even over a relatively long term of study. Their analyses show the specificity in time and place of conversions, socio-economic practices, and their complex political meanings.

As can be seen from such disagreements and revisions, the view that Quebec Cree Pentecostals were opposed to land claims settlements became difficult to sustain as Pentecostals' numbers and engagement with local political issues grew. This has been the case since the late 1980s, given the high profile of Pentecostal leaders among the James Bay Cree. Chief Billy Diamond, an architect of the 1975 James Bay and Northern Quebec Agreement (Canada's first modern land claims settlement), subsequently converted to Pentecostalism, without compromising his stand in favor of land claims and self-government.[25] Another Quebec Cree and Pentecostal, Matthew Coon Come, also went on to become chief of the Grand Council of Crees of Quebec, as well as, later, the Assembly of First Nations (AFN), the national First Nations political organization. During his term at the helm of the AFN, Coon Come took a moralistic, biblically inspired stance on many questions (for instance, castigating chiefs for dancing and drinking), but a politically radical and confrontational stance on others (such as governance and land claims). Throughout his 2000–2003 term, Coon Come felt called to criticize his own constituents, but also to call upon the state for justice, and to threaten civil disobedience in support of political goals as he had in his term as Grand Chief of the Quebec Cree. In the latter role, Coon Come had led his people to work with environmentalists in Canada and internationally, winning the cancellation of a proposed damming project. Clearly, then, Cree Pentecostals

---

23. Tanner, "Bringing Home Animals," 211.

24. Tanner, "Nature of Quebec Cree Animist Practices and Beliefs."

25. MacGregor, *Chief.*

are members of a national movement, with support and potential for flexible strategic engagement in other sectors of society.

It is typical of commentators on Aboriginal Pentecostalism that they do not cite one another, leaving each to repeat the same errors and remake the same discoveries, conveyed in offhand ethnographic references. Thus, the same faulty lines of argument earlier displayed in Quebec were recapitulated in the 1990s in Alberta, by journalists and scholars who had become active in support of the Lubicon Lake First Nation's land claim. The large number of Pentecostals and Evangelicals in Little Buffalo Lake (the main Lubicon community) and surrounding region were thus targeted for re-education. The cultural purity and political solidarity of these people with their neighbors and family members were repeatedly brought into question by outsiders having little familiarity with Cree life.

In his account of the Lubicon Cree First Nation's land claim, John Goddard writes that people in Little Buffalo Lake began turning to Evangelical groups around 1990, as their frustration with land claim politics grew. In fact this is ahistorical, given that Evangelical missionaries had arrived in the 1950s as the first resident missionaries, and converted most local residents. By the 1960s, Little Buffalo Lake was a sending community of Cree Pentecostal missionaries to neighboring communities, including Trout Lake. All this occurred well before the land claim and regional resource development became pressing political issues, drawing Goddard's dependent and independent variables into question.

Again, we see an analysis that privileges land claims as the most important variable, the meaning of which is fixed in relation to other phenomena, such as religious conversion. Goddard suggests that the many rapid conversions damaged solidarity in the community, thus causing a negative influence. Through Goddard's argument, Evangelicals and Pentecostals are made scapegoats for the failure of governments (including the Lubicon leadership) to settle a land claim that had been open for 50 years. Furthermore, Goddard prejudicially compares Evangelicalism to other symptoms of social unease such as drinking and fighting, which diminished the political solidarity of the Lubicon Band.[26] A similar frame of analysis is seen in Mohawk anthropologist Dawn Martin-Hill's more scholarly account of the Lubicon claim during the early 1990s, which puts a premium on traditionalism, solidarity, and political support for the claim and the chief, irrespective of the opinions of Pentecostal com-

26. Goddard, *Last Stand of the Lubicon*, 213.

munity members.[27] Once again, other phenomena are read mainly in relation to the land claim, the settlement of which is closely linked to traditionalist and neo-traditionalist values.

Such analysts do not attempt to hide their favor for traditionalists and current Lubicon leaders, who oppose Pentecostalism. In this and many other ways, they obscure the divisions in the community of Little Buffalo Lake and the region as a whole. As such, these analysts view Pentecostalism as a rival creed/movement in a high stakes political game: the land claim, which spills over into culture and religion. Of course, such analysts would lose their privileged access to the community's leaders and elders if a power shift occurred; this is consistent with their behavior in targeting their patrons' political rivals, including Pentecostals and others, with *ad hominem* attacks.

Overall, I find that proposed linkages between Pentecostalism, land claims, and political solidarity, which have been made to date, are not supported by data. To state otherwise has the effect of discrediting an autonomous, native-led, network: something one might think recent analysts, supporting Aboriginal political advancement, would have been loath to do. In any case, as the Coon Come and Diamond examples show, there is no proof that traditionalists are better or more radical negotiators of land claims than are Pentecostals or, for that matter, atheists. Further such examples could be drawn from many communities surrounding Little Buffalo Lake, communities where Pentecostal chiefs and councilors have negotiated Agreements in Principle and Final Agreements on land claims and other matters, while the Lubicon claim remains mired in acrimony and recrimination.

I now return to my typology of arguments. Moving beyond the local region of my study, perhaps the best-known exemplar of the second line of argument (a line also seen in Tanner's early work, quoted above) is American anthropologist Kirk Dombrowski. Dombrowski's 2001 study of Pentecostalism in southeastern Alaska, *Against Culture: Development, Politics, and Religion in Indian Alaska*, is the only book-length study of Pentecostalism in Native North America. Its major theoretical contribution is Dombrowski's observation that Aboriginal Pentecostals live both within and against their culture. Furthermore, "Pentecostal church membership offers people an institution through which many of their own

27. Martin-Hill, *Lubicon Lake Nation*, 150.

feelings about the failure of current identity projects can be expressed."[28] Dombrowski contends that the Alaska Native Claims Settlement Act (ANCSA) created two classes of local residents, with differential access to jobs, resources, and subsistence rights. He further suggests that poor Alaska Natives, who must hunt for food, are more drawn to Pentecostalism, while their wealthier, bureaucratically employed counterparts are more involved in Native culture and/or more traditional Christian denominations. Dombrowski puts forth surprisingly little data in support of these linkages over the course of his book; nevertheless he relies extensively on these glosses in developing his core argument. As such the book's conclusions are highly problematic.

Dombrowski's hypothesis, linking Pentecostal conversion to internal status differences, at first appears to be supported to some extent by the findings of Dorais, whom Dombrowski does not cite.[29] In spite of their brevity, Dorais's remarks on Pentecostalism display both time depth and substantial attention to kinship and social structure. Dorais shows how some members of kindreds with less sturdy linkages to the Inuit community's largely Anglican power structure were more likely to become Pentecostal. He also demonstrates the degree to which conversion follows family lines. However, Dorais rejects taking this hypothesis too far, in saying that the inherent attractions of the Pentecostal message, and its possible fit with Inuit culture, are stronger explanatory factors for the religion's growth.[30] Demonstrating the complexity in view, Dorais shies away from presenting a single, deterministic, explanatory model. For example, he states that Pentecostals are more likely to hold jobs and seek education than their counterparts, while not seeing this as indicative of an overall stance for modernity or against culture. Like Tanner, then, one cannot link Dorais definitively with either line of argument.

Thus, while the second line of argument, exemplified by Dombrowski's "against culture" analysis, is somewhat more flexible than those represented by the first line of argument I have summarized above, it cannot be sustained when broader regional and circumpolar data are taken into account. This has been pointed out by reviewers and other scholars respecting the application of Dombrowski's theory in Alaska and

28. Dombrowski, *Against Culture*, 14.

29. Dorais, *Quaqtaq*, 76–79.

30. Ibid., 76 and 78–79.

adjacent regions.[31] Moreover, Dombrowski's proposed linkage between relative economic status and conversion does not reflect the complexity I will describe in the region I studied. Overall, it is clear that a deprivation-based argument for conversion is not the whole story: other questions such as cultural fit are also important. In a recent article, Dombrowski steps away from linking conversion primarily to economic status, and addresses some other concerns raised by these reviewers, which appears to be a response to the critiques of Kan, Nadasdy, and Thornton.[32]

Like Dombrowski, my analysis shows the relations between Pentecostalism, traditionalism, land claims, economic change, and "identity projects." I also appreciate his focus on how people live both within and "against" their culture. In my reading, Dombrowski's theory about the failure of current identity projects resembles elements of Preston's proposal that Cree Pentecostals seek to conform to both white and Indian norms of behavior and autonomy. One might also mention Waugh's contention that many Cree in the Trout Lake area rejected an indigenized Catholicism in favor of Pentecostalism, partly because they desired to participate more fully in Canadian society, rather than follow an ethnically based religion, even while they saw in Pentecostalism strong correspondences to Cree spiritual practice.[33] Thus, I suggest that conversions to Pentecostalism draw on a wide range of individual factors and interpretations, the analysis of which should incorporate, but not be subordinate to, consideration of economics and politics.

It can be seen that, in both lines of argument outlined above, land claims and Pentecostalism are each read as proxies for different types of modernization. While they differ in some respects, both lines of argument place Pentecostals irrefutably in opposition to land claims. The problem with such conclusions is that Pentecostalism, which travels relatively easily across cultural boundaries, does not have one pre-inscribed meaning, any more than land claims or other political arrangements do. Trying to analytically fix the relationship between the two objects, according to Weberian, Marxist, or Foucauldian principles, is thus fruitless. Moreover,

31. Kan, "Against Culture"; Nadasdy, "Against Culture"; and Thornton, "Against Culture." Compare with Burkinshaw, "Native Pentecostalism in British Columbia," 154–55; Dorais, *Quaqtaq*, 76; and Laugrand and Oosten, "Reconnecting People and Healing the Land," 242.

32. Dombrowski, "Subsistence Livelihood, Native Identity and Internal Differentiation in Southeast Alaska," 223–24.

33. Waugh, *Dissonant Worlds*, 301.

as I shall show, rather than being hierarchical, authoritarian, and rigid politically, as some analysts would have it, the doctrinal and individual response of Pentecostals to land claims, politics, and other social issues is in fact quite varied and contingent.[34]

ETHNOGRAPHIC DATA

To begin this section in detail it is necessary first to sketch the political structure of the communities. As Trout Lake and Peerless Lake are off-reserve communities, there is no chief or band council. While most residents are members of BCN (nominally under federal jurisdiction), the governments that provided most services in the community were the province and its creations: the Municipal District (MD) of Opportunity, Northlands School District, and Aspen health board. Both Trout Lake and Peerless Lake have elected representatives on these organizations, including the MD council, as well as having limited autonomous government structures. These last include local school committees as well as local community associations (not-for-profit societies with voluntary membership and limited staff). The community associations provide some services such as limited housing and training programs. Also, as part of its ongoing land claim negotiations, BCN maintains a quasi-governmental consultation/negotiation structure: one "chief," two "councilors," and (during my fieldwork) a part-time clerk, in each community. These bodies are meant to function as government-in-waiting, for the time when Trout Lake and Peerless Lake will become a separate First Nation with a land base; however, the interim councils currently have little formal power in the communities. There is thus a diffuse local governance structure, which at the same time is somewhat interlocking, reflecting the small number of local people involved formally in political life.

Accordingly, local people's participation in national and provincial politics is limited. This voter apathy reflects the domination of political life by local elites (who are generally more integrated into larger-scale politics). Although the 2006 federal election featured multiple Aboriginal candidates at the riding level, including one running for an Aboriginal party, I noted little discussion of political issues and no electoral signs

---

34. Legros, "Communautés Amérindiennes contemporaines," 54, and Polson and Spielmann, "Once There Were Two Brothers," 307. Also see Dorais, *Quaqtaq*, 76.

during the campaign. Even the key Christian electoral issue of 2005–2006 (gay marriage) was never raised by any of my consultants.

Provincial politics are closer to home: both provincial constituencies in the region were represented by Aboriginal cabinet ministers during the time of my major fieldwork, creating a conduit for local political leaders to directly voice their concerns about road safety, for example, at the highest provincial levels. (Road safety, also the subject of prayers in church, is more sensitive than it may appear since it potentially touches on important local concerns such as alcohol, access to services, and the pace of resource development, as well as road quality itself, which is undeniably poor.) Signs, posters, and T-shirts demonstrate community support for these Aboriginal legislators, in and out of election season. Even so, brokered accommodation of local Aboriginal leaders in these ridings has not extended to cabinet support for a new highway to Trout Lake, nor for First Nations attempting to charge an access fee to developers working on their traditional lands and to hold companies to environmental standards, nor (one might argue) to the speedier settlement of major land claims and attendant problems in the region. Indeed, it is noteworthy that one of the cabinet ministers at the top of this brokerage system (Mike Cardinal, not a Pentecostal, of Calling Lake) was seen as a fiscal conservative who cut welfare rates as minister responsible for social services in the 1990s: a move disproportionately impacting Aboriginal people, including his own constituents and family members. So it is wrong to see Aboriginal politicians, whether Pentecostal or otherwise, as being inherently inclined to the left or right of the political spectrum. The poor fit of such ideological labels with Aboriginal politics generally is even more evident at the local level. Moreover, political disputes are not necessarily religious in character.

Within the communities, the political cadre of interlocking leaders and committees has religious significance: in its membership one can see a proxy (by means of electoral behavior) for local Pentecostal numeric strength. Though it is not always true that Pentecostals vote for their co-religionists, electoral outcomes provide perhaps a surer measure than Census reporting. In Trout Lake, Peerless Lake and other nearby communities, Pentecostal pastors and adherents form a key network within this political cadre, who may act in a coordinated fashion to achieve spiritual and temporal goals. Dorais also uses electoral standings and community leaders as a proxy for the demographic strength of competing sects, but cautions that the idea of competition should not be taken too literally: most if not all community members are sincerely interested in advancing their community's interests, he writes. This point has been forgotten by some other analysts in northern Alberta and elsewhere, as I pointed out previously.

Pentecostals held approximately one third of political seats in Trout Lake during my fieldwork, somewhat fewer in Peerless Lake. This may be a good indicator of the proportion of active Pentecostals in each community, based on political support for their candidates. In Cree society, political and religious leaders are often one and the same, and this is also true of Pentecostal leaders. This political/ecclesiastical leadership cadre brokers contacts with the outside world, while working closely with a group of unilingual elders (some of whom are former community leaders), who provide advice and legitimacy internally. My identification of such a leadership cadre is a significant contribution to subarctic church and political studies.

It has been well documented that Aboriginal political leaders of the postwar period often benefited from the knowledge, skills (including language skills), and networks they obtained from missionaries or in residential schools. This is somewhat true in my study region, where Evangelical missionaries began establishing day schools in the 1950s. Missionaries also benefited from the collaboration and skills of those who had attended residential schools run by Catholics or Anglicans, and who had been so embittered by the experience that they sought a new spiritual home in Evangelical (and later Pentecostal) congregations.

During the 1950s and 1960s, the willingness of these Evangelical missionaries (who, unlike their more established Catholic and Anglican competitors, generally did not speak Cree) to identify, promote, and ordain indigenous translators as leaders (who could then provide liturgy and counseling in Cree) was to become a major factor in the success of the subsequent development of Evangelical and, later, Pentecostal movements in the region. As these new Cree leaders received the gifts of the spirit in ways not sanctioned by Evangelical doctrine, they formed the nucleus of the local Pentecostal network, swiftly displacing both more established Anglican and Catholic missionaries, as well as their own erstwhile Evangelical allies and patrons. To a lesser extent, the political development of this group of ecclesiastical leaders (who were among the first full generation of bilinguals in the area), has been instrumental in the subsequent development of an effective political leadership cadre since the 1960s.

The 1960s was a time of increasing radicalism among Aboriginal people generally, and this had some impact locally as well. In the late 1960s, poverty, neglect, and increasing development were significant factors in contributing to the increase of political activism in these isolated communities. A number of local individuals such as William Beaver (a Trout Lake resident who had been educated in Wabasca, who later became chief of BCN and an important Pentecostal leader) were salient in these efforts, working through community associations, and with both the Indian Association of Alberta and the Metis (sic) Association of Alberta, to advance local concerns, including treaty, Aboriginal, and Métis rights. Thus, Pentecostals were present at the birth of contemporary political activism in the region, and have continued to play a leading role in local political networks.

By the early 1970s, signs of institutionalization and continuity of leadership could be seen in local Pentecostal life. During this phase, local pastors set up freestanding churches, some of which have endured. Some local leaders took formal training from an outside pastor before returning to the communities to build the church. In Trout Lake, the Pentecostal congregation has formal affiliation to the province wide Aboriginal ministry, JC Ministries, led by Métis evangelist, politician, and leader, Jeannette Calahasen. Both in their linkages and their longevity, these local churches mark the phase (occurring in the early seventies) during which Pentecostalism coalesced from a nascent network into an established (at least in local terms) movement. In each case, local control over congregational affairs seems to have survived the linkage to a larger body. Again we see the importance of autonomy in Cree religion. This may be one element that made Pentecostalism (mainly propagated by independents, some of whom were Aboriginal) more attractive to local people than other missionary denominations. In terms of the local relevance of autonomy and spiritual power, I find it extremely significant that each local pastor is the scion of leading families in Trout Lake and Peerless Lake, and a direct descendant of some of the last "medicine men" in the region.

A major strength of Pastor Johnny Noskiye's network at Trout Lake has been the presence of several credible spokespeople in a strong leadership cadre, who can present a Pentecostal message in Cree or English at various church and community functions, so that Johnny himself may stay in the background. One example of this is the weekly/occasional women's evening service held at the church, led by Johnny's sister. Another example is the consistent presence of church members represented on political bodies such as the community association, interim council, and/or local school committee in Trout Lake. Since the majority of political seats are generally not held by Pentecostals, ensuring effective representation by those Pentecostal politicians holding the minority of seats is of some importance for local Pentecostal electors, and of considerable strategic interest to pastors.

For the Cree, as for many independent missionaries, personal networks and charisma are often more important than denomination. Accordingly, church attendance seems to be mainly organized on family lines. While churches tend to be based around a small number of extended families, it is important that not all patronage accrue to the pastor's family.[35] In the case of large extended families, intra-family rivals may necessitate attempts to create two "family" churches. Thus, existing Cree kinship and political networks have been the major connective tissues supporting widespread and rapid conversion to Pentecostalism and Evangelicalism, and a proliferation of local churches. A priest in Trout Lake during the 1960s described the many conversions to Pentecostalism and Evangelicalism as "above all something territorial and familial;" that is, conversion in part responds to local, rather than external, variables, structures and meanings.

Although I am not proposing a deterministic linkage between religion and economics, it is clear that the religious upheavals of the 1960s must be seen in the context of socio-economic changes in the region. Apart from the culture shock of moving into sedentary communities (which nevertheless had poor to non-existent services, wage economies, and access), there is evidence of declining health and diet standards, poor accommodation, heavy reliance on relief, and increased availability of alcohol during this period. Also, during this period people began to receive formal medical care, in some cases being transferred to Edmonton for long- or short-term attention. This contributed to a growing number of people in the region who had been institutionalized outside the immediate region (through the medical or educational systems, or both) and were thus exposed to facets of white society in depth. As Ronald Niezen

35. Compare with Dombrowski, *Against Culture*, 117 and 122.

has pointed out, the introduction of western medical care is strongly associated with evangelization and conversion among the Crees.[36]

Similarly, the rapid increase in resource development in the broader region since the 1950s ensured that a growing number of people were exposed to wage labor or environmental damage. These hunters may have perceived their traditional livelihoods to be threatened or perhaps less desirable; such broader awareness of the world may have resulted in dissatisfaction with life in the communities. Some people reportedly left Trout Lake during this period so as not to have to accept relief. Also, the district's first recorded suicide was during the mid-1960s. The beginnings of an industrial economy in the region since the 1950s (including oil exploration, forestry, road building, and a commercial fishery), as well as attendant social changes, likely played a role in promoting insecurity in the region, and thus may have promoted the Evangelical/Pentecostal option at this time. Even so, a full analysis of community life cannot sustain a linkage between Pentecostal commitments and decreased dependence on hunting and other subsistence practices, since everyone in Trout Lake and Peerless Lake (including Pentecostals) survives mainly on bush foods to this day.

The peak of Pentecostalism locally (at least in terms of church membership and attendance) may have occurred very early in its mission: perhaps in the late sixties or early seventies. Another spike in adherence occurred following the poisoning deaths of four Peerless Lake residents from solvent consumption, an event which attracted national media attention, in 1986. During this time local leaders consciously relaxed moral stringency and evangelized both more widely and more sensitively in dealing with drugs, solvents, and alcohol.[37] This short-lived attempt to reach out to people in need, rather than expecting them to give up drinking (to say nothing of smoking) all at once, was successful for a time after 1986, but is no longer so evident. Note that both of these proposed periods of success for Pentecostalism involved socio-economic crises that resulted in the region's appearance on the front pages of major newspapers, suggesting that Pentecostal conversion may be a response to stress for many individuals. Again, the question of how this stress and its epiphenomena (such as religious conversion) are to be differentially measured within small communities is more complicated than simply noting the relatively low social status of Aboriginal people generally.

36. Niezen, "Healing and Conversion."
37. Woodward, "Peerless Lake Church Reaches out to the Community."

The subsequent decline in worshippers (particularly evident since the early 1990s) relates to the common tendency among new adherents of Pentecostalism (as church leader John A. Cardinal alluded to specifically) to backslide or fall away after an initial period of strong involvement.[38] It is unclear whether Trout Lake is currently facing a similar decline, to the same extent as Peerless Lake. Certainly however, church attendance levels in Trout Lake during my fieldwork do not suggest that the majority of the population are regular church attendees. *If* Pentecostalism was a response to a crisis, will it have longevity with or without the crisis' continuance? Could Trout Lake and Peerless Lake be said to be moving *out* of a crisis, with the impending land claim settlement? Will the small number of church attendees gradually be reflected in declining identification with Pentecostalism among the less active group of Census Pentecostals?

Pentecostals act in the local political sphere as electors, testifying commentators, and community leaders. However, there is a practical difficulty in separating the domains of religion and politics. Certainly Pentecostals themselves do not see their movement as primarily political. Issues of concern (i.e., drinking) may be read politically but always have spiritual overtones as well. Land claims, similarly, may be seen either as a potential force for social justice, or as a materialistic distraction. Even so, the characterization of Dominique Legros, that the hope of reaching Jesus's kingdom has depoliticized Aboriginal Pentecostals, and that Pentecostalism has fragmented their communities, seems somewhat limited in comparison with the examples of political activism—both by pastors and lay people—that I document here.[39]

As one example of diversity in the politics of Pentecostalism, I present some perspectives on local land rights. Before the complex and unique BCN claim was accepted for negotiation, promising the flow of compensation and infrastructure to Trout Lake and Peerless Lake, local leaders had undertaken many strategies, including litigation, caveats declaring land ownership, and direct action. One can see the involvement of many Pentecostals in these struggles, including current pastors, in ways that underline the specificity of local meanings attached to the claim and to politics.

As an elder, Pastor Johnny Noskiye has been active in promoting land claims: he is named as a plaintiff in a lawsuit claiming Aboriginal

38. Ibid.

39. Legros, "Communautés Amérindiennes Contemporaines," 55.

title to the region; he was also interviewed as an elder about local land use and history by the Indian Claims Commission, a federal commission of inquiry. Johnny's example shows again that there is no necessary contradiction between Christian leadership and activist politics in support of Aboriginal rights. His older brother, a member of the congregation, has also been active as a political leader in favor of the claim.

Notwithstanding Johnny's example, where Pentecostal leaders have sought, through sermons or electioneering, to comment on public issues, they do not always speak with one voice, particularly about inherently controversial issues such as the land claim.[40] From time to time, individual leaders even appear to contradict themselves. For example, one pastor supported the land claim in his capacity as political leader while, on another occasion, appearing to speak against it as materialistic in his capacity as a church leader. Another Pentecostal and community political leader told me he supported the land claim and wanted new houses for all, but especially for those who would "look after them" (i.e., not drink chronically). Thus, Pentecostals may bifurcate the community through political discourse: they maintain that drinking and "accidents" are mainly personal problems to be addressed spiritually, not mainly social problems to be addressed through political means. Other church leaders feel that increasing justice and prosperity in the region (through the proposed land claim settlement) will have a negative effect on people's spirituality. This dissonance may have a different meaning locally: leaders may feel called upon to improve material standing while remaining concerned about materialism. Apart from Christian theology, this dissonance also reflects a Cree wisdom about what money and power can and cannot do. Many contemporary land claims settlements are strongly contested on a variety of grounds. While Aboriginal Pentecostals may question the utility of land claims and other elements of Aboriginal policy, they are not the only community members to do so, and may not be driven to do so primarily by faith but also by other factors.

The evangelization of the Cree was linked to other aspects of national social and economic development, including expanding transportation networks (Pentecostal and Evangelical missionaries being among the first to bring cars into the region, even before roads were built), but also expanding church mandates and new national organizations dedicated to

40. Ibid., 54.

Aboriginal Evangelical/Pentecostal missions. Both of these trends began in the 1940s. Since the 1970s, the large number of new First Nations-oriented Evangelical and Pentecostal organizations, media outlets, and networks mean native churches are increasingly *interdependent*, with one another, rather than being *dependent* on white denominations and missions.[41] JC Ministries in Alberta provides one such example at the provincial level. Increasingly, such networks are led at the national level by Aboriginal Pentecostals, such as Doug Maracle, who take nuanced stands on lands and rights issues (including the Oka Crisis in Maracle's case),[42] acting to educate Aboriginal and non-Aboriginal Pentecostals alike on political issues.

CONCLUSION

In this chapter, I have been resistant to analyses that see Pentecostal conversion mainly as a predetermined response to economic change. Nevertheless, in studying a marginalized community surrounded by wealth (some of which is generated by despoiling the traditional territory of the marginalized community), one must be attentive to economic, cultural, and social instability, and to the potential role of instability in conditioning or enabling radical social movements, such as Pentecostalism. While my discussion is politically oriented, and while church leaders have always been involved in politics, in my experience Pentecostals do not see their movement as primarily political. Certainly local church leaders have not embraced radical strategies, to the extent of other Cree Pentecostal leaders such as Matthew Coon Come and Billy Diamond, or even (to use the example of a local, traditionalist, politician) Lubicon Chief Bernard Ominayak. However, as I have attempted to show, a more textured consideration of local politics suggests that it is premature to assume that Pentecostals usually oppose land claims and Aboriginal rights.

Religious conversion is partly a response to traumatic social issues. Pastors and lay leaders often become political leaders and activists. As such, Pentecostalism has a political character notwithstanding its other-worldliness. Indeed, scholars often emphasize the political character of Pentecostalism by discussing Pentecostals' positions on land claims, development, and politically oriented cultural revitalization processes. The

41. Guenther, "Ethnicity and Evangelical Christians in Canada," 392.

42. Ibid.

subtleties of political and cultural debates within communities may be lost on outside analysts, many of whom have condemned Pentecostals for rejecting Aboriginal cultural politics or for being on the "wrong" side of disputes over land claims. My research, on Aboriginal Pentecostal networks in northern Alberta as well as nationally, suggests these pronouncements are simplistic. Pentecostalism and politics each have local meanings, and their relationship to one another is not fixed.

To conclude, Pentecostalism among Cree and Métis in Trout Lake and Peerless Lake is not consciously progressive, and certainly not explicitly leftist, in character. In keeping with the Cree emphasis on autonomy, however, there is clearly an element of liberation in the practical consequences of Pentecostal adherence: reduced dependence on drugs, solvents, alcohol, and tobacco among believers, for example. These personal victories also have social consequences, such as improved employment and family stability. Nevertheless, in spite of some efforts to organize politically, Pentecostals have been less successful in addressing the root causes of such widespread despair in their communities. Perhaps one could say that Pentecostals in Trout Lake and Peerless Lake have been partly motivated by progressive social concern, but that this concern has been obviated to some extent by a spiritual or eschatological focus. Progressive tendencies in local politics are further mitigated through the capture of local elites (including religious leaders to some extent) in brokerage politics, a politics ultimately oriented towards conservative political parties supporting resource extraction on Aboriginal lands.

My main concern in this chapter has been to counter arguments that Aboriginal Pentecostals are always or mainly conservative or pro-industry, or just detached from politics altogether; however, in doing so, I am not specifically making the argument that they are always or mainly progressive or radical. Indeed, since the congregations and leadership I studied among do not generally undertake coordinated social action or consistently discuss specific social issues in a given tone (except for alcohol which is deplored as much on a personal as a social level), the data I collected does not resemble the Social Pentecostalism model proposed by scholars such as Miller and Yamamori. In the congregations described by these scholars, progressive elements and practices appear to be more central and explicit in Pentecostal worship and community life, than in the churches I studied.[43] Certainly, Pentecostalism is the religion through

43. Miller and Yamamori, *Global Pentecostalism*.

which the majority of people understand most political struggles in Trout Lake: as such it becomes an important resource or a tool for thinking with, on the part of political activists and leaders within the movement, and also among the community more broadly. Yet it may not be the source or even the main articulation site in believers' engagements with these deeply personal, ethnic, and local political issues. Clearly Pentecostalism is not monolithically conservative or apolitical, yet obviously one must also be cautious in adopting models that suggest Pentecostalism is mainly motivated by a *progressive social politics*, in the sense that this phrase would be understood by most North Americans; this would clearly be an overcorrection.[44] Nevertheless, Cree Pentecostals remain attuned to the needs of fellow believers and family members, who are among the poorest, least healthy, and most marginalized of Canadians. Believers thus carry a burden for their people that is personal and social as well as theological. This burden cannot be easily described or enacted in existing ideological or partisan terms, but it is, potentially, a force for justice and political change in the region.

BIBLIOGRAPHY

Burkinshaw, Robert K. "Native Pentecostalism in British Columbia." In *Canadian Pentecostalism: Transition and Transformation*, edited by Michael Wilkinson, 156–84. Montreal: McGill-Queen's University Press, 2009.

Canada. Census Canada. "Trout Lake/Peerless Lake Aggregated Census Divisions." Ottawa: Census Canada, 2001.

Dombrowski, Kirk. *Against Culture: Development, Politics, and Religion in Indian Alaska*. Lincoln: University of Nebraska Press, 2001.

———. "Subsistence Livelihood, Native Identity and Internal Differentiation in Southeast Alaska." *Anthropologica* 49 (2007) 211–30.

Dorais, Louis-Jacques. *Quaqtaq: Modernity and Identity in an Inuit Community*. Toronto: University of Toronto Press, 1997.

Goddard, John. *The Last Stand of the Lubicon Cree*. Vancouver: Douglas & McIntyre, 1991.

Guenther, Bruce L. "Ethnicity and Evangelical Christians in Canada." In *Christianity and Ethnicity in Canada*, edited by Paul Bramadat and David Seljak, 365–414. Toronto: University of Toronto Press, 2008.

Kan, Sergei. Review of *Against Culture: Development, Politics, and Religion in Indian Alaska*, by Kirk Dombrowski. *American Anthropologist* 105 (2003) 648–49.

44. Smith, *Native Americans and the Christian Right*.

Laugrand, Frédéric, and Jarich Oosten. "Reconnecting People and Healing the Land: Inuit Pentecostal and Evangelical Movements in the Canadian Eastern Arctic." *Numen* 54 (2007) 229–69.

Legros, Dominique. "Communautés Amérindiennes Contemporaines: Structure et Dynamique Autochtones ou Coloniales?" *Recherches Amérindiennes au Québec* 4 (1986–87) 47–68.

MacGregor, Roy. *Chief: The Fearless Vision of Billy Diamond.* Markham, ON: Viking, 1989.

Martin-Hill, Dawn. *The Lubicon Lake Nation: Indigenous Knowledge and Power.* Toronto: University of Toronto Press, 2008.

Miller, Donald E., and Tetsunao Yamamori. *Global Pentecostalism: The New Face of Christian Social Engagement.* Berkeley: University of California Press, 2007.

Nadasdy, Paul. Review of *Against Culture: Development, Politics, and Religion in Indian Alaska,* by Kirk Dombrowski. *American Ethnologist* 29 (2002) 1027–28.

Navarro, Carlos. "Pentecostal Churches and their Relationship to the Mexican State and Political Parties." *Journal of Ritual Studies* 15 (2001) 55–66.

Niezen, Ronald. "Healing and Conversion: Medical Evangelism in James Bay Cree Society." *Ethnohistory* 44 (1997) 463–91.

Noll, Mark A. *A History of Christianity in Canada and the United States.* Grand Rapids: Eerdmans, 1997.

Pelkmans, Mathijs, Virginie Vaté, and Christiane Falge. "Christian Conversion in a Changing World: Confronting Issues of Inequality, Modernity, and Morality." In *Max Planck Institute for Social Anthropology Report 2004–2005,* edited by J. O. Habeck, M. Heintz, J. Knorr, B. Mann, F. Pirie, and L. Yalcin-Heckmann, 23–24. Halle/Salle, Germany: Max Planck Institute for Social Anthropology, 2005.

Polson, Gordon, and Roger Spielmann. "'Once There Were Two Brothers . . .' Religious Tension in One Algonquin Community." In *Papers of the Twenty-First Algonquian Conference,* edited by W. Cowan, 303–12. Ottawa: Carleton University, 1990.

Preston, Richard J. "Belief in the Context of Rapid Change: An Eastern Cree Example," edited by Carole E. Hill, 117–29. Athens, GA: Southern Anthropological Society, 1975.

————. *Cree Narrative: Expressing the Personal Meanings of Events.* Ottawa: National Museums of Canada, 1975.

————. "Transformations Musicales et Culturelles chez les Cris de l'Est." *Recherches Amérindiennes au Québec* XV (1985) 19–28.

————. "Twentieth Century Transformations of East Cree Spirituality and Autonomy." In *Globalization, Autonomy and Indigenous Peoples,* edited by Mario Blaser, Ravi de Costa, Deborah McGregor, and William D. Coleman. Vancouver: UBC Press, forthcoming.

Prince, Raymond. "Psychiatry among the James Bay Cree: A Focus on Pathological Grief Reactions." *Transcultural Psychiatric Research Review* 30 (1993) 3–50.

Robbins, Joel. "The Globalization of Pentecostal and Charismatic Christianity. *Annual Review of Anthropology* 33 (2004) 117–43.

Samson, C. Mathews. "The Martyrdom of Manuel Saquic: Constructing Maya Protestantism in the Face of War in Contemporary Guatemala." *Le Fait Missionnaire* 15 (2003) 1–21.

————. "Maya Evangelical Presence in Guatemala: Contextualization of Religious Practice and Possibilities for Dialogue." *Active Voices: The Online Journal of Cultural Survival* August (1998) 1–10.

Southcott, Chris. "Remarks in a Panel Discussion on Conversion and Community Cohesion." *Heading North, Heading South: Arctic Social-Sciences Research in a*

Global Dialogue. Halle/Salle, Germany: Max Planck Institute for Social Anthropology, 2008.

Smith, Andrea. *Native Americans and the Christian Right: The Gendered Politics of Unlikely Alliances*. Durham: Duke University Press, 2008.

Tanner, Adrian. *Bringing Home Animals: Religious Ideology and Mode of Production of the Mistassini Cree Hunters*. New York: St. Martin's Press, 1979.

———. "The Nature of Quebec Cree Animist Practices and Beliefs." In *La Nature des Esprits/Nature of Spirits*, edited by Fréderic B. Laugrand and Jarich G. Oosten, 133–50. Québec: Les Presses de L'Université Laval, 2007.

Thompson, Edward Palmer. *The Making of the English Working Class*. Harmondsworth, UK: Penguin, 1982.

Thornton, Thomas F. Review of *Against Culture: Development, Politics, and Religion in Indian Alaska*, by Kirk Dombrowski. *Ethnohistory* 52 (2005) 481–83.

Turner-Strong, Pauline. "Recent Ethnographic Research on North American Indigenous Peoples." *Annual Review of Anthropology* 34 (2005) 253–68.

Waugh, Earle H. *Dissonant Worlds: Roger Vandersteene Among the Cree*. Waterloo, ON: Wilfrid Laurier University Press, 1996.

Westman, Clinton N. "Cree Pentecostalism and Its Others." In *Papers of the 40th Algonquian Conference*, edited by Karl Hele et al. London, ON: University of Western Ontario, 2009, forthcoming.

———. "The Making of 'Isolated Communities' in Alberta's Lesser Slave Lake Interior." In *Papers from the 2008 Rupert's Land Colloquium, Rocky Mountain House*, edited by Mallory Richard and M. Anne Lindsay. Winnipeg: Centre for Rupert's Land Studies, The University of Winnipeg, forthcoming.

———. "Faith in God's Temple: Ritual Practice in a Cree Pentecostal Congregation." In *Dynamiques religieuses des autochtones des Amériques (Religious Dynamics of Indigenous People of the Americas)*, edited by Robert Crépeau and Marie-Pierre Bousquet. Paris: Karthala, forthcoming.

———. "A Missionary Tour North from Wabasca, Alberta, 1907." In *Papers of the 39th Algonquian Conference*, edited by Karl Hele and Regna Darnell, 634–51. London: University of Western Ontario, 2009.

———. "Understanding Cree Religious Discourse." PhD thesis, Department of Anthropology, University of Alberta, 2008.

Woodward, Rocky. "Peerless Lake Church Reaches out to the Community." *Windspeaker*, March 30, 1990.

PART TWO

Issues of Class

5

Waxing and Waning of Social Deprivation as a Model for Understanding the Class Composition of Early American Pentecostalism

A Theological Assessment

Peter Althouse

INTRODUCTION

In their recent analysis of global Pentecostalism and social action, Donald Miller and Tetsunao Yamamori note that prevailing stereotypes for explaining the growth of religion along the lines of socio-economic deprivation, psychological angst, or the quest for social order in a chaotic world may help explain some aspects of the growth of Pentecostalism; but they wonder whether this functional approach is adequate.[1] Deprivation theories conveniently bracket the legitimacy of the religious encounter as an experience of the divine and do not address the role of the religious as non-rational motivation for engaging and perhaps changing the

1. Miller and Yamamori, *Global Pentecostalism*, 22.

social structures. Ironically, Miller and Yamamori are willing to accept the evidence that current forms of Pentecostalism consist of the socially affluent and well educated middle class, but they reveal a lingering assumption that its early constituency was predominantly drawn from the lower-class representing the poorly educated and disinherited. "True, Pentecostalism was born among lower-class people," they argue, "and much of its amazing initial growth was due to its connection with impoverished people, including those with animistic religious backgrounds." The rise of Pentecostal socio-economic status is a result of "their embrace of the Pentecostal ethic and lifestyle [which] has resulted in upward social mobility."[2] Miller and Yamamori are not alone in this assumption. There is a growing litany of social theorists who have been unable to support the lower socio-economic class assumptions of religious sects in the case of contemporary Pentecostalism, and conveniently conclude with insufficient evidence that while Pentecostals are predominantly middle class now they must have been lower class in the beginning.[3]

Miller and Yamamori then propose a taxonomy of global Pentecostalism, consisting of 1) legalistic or otherworldly Pentecostalism (of which the Assemblies of God is a prime candidate), 2) prosperity Pentecostalism which emphasizes material prosperity and good health as signs of God's blessing; and 3) progressive Pentecostalism, which "no longer see[s] the world as a place from which to escape—the sectarian view— but instead as a place they want to make better." This last type, the one Miller and Yamamori wish to highlight as a two-thirds world phenomenon, finds Pentecostals involved in social action and social justice as a component of Pentecostal ministry.[4] Progressive Pentecostalism relates to the social sphere as an agent for social transformation in three distinct ways: 1) by alleviating the pain and misery of violations in human rights in a hope for a better world hereafter (Marx's opiate); 2) by creating a "social uplift" in socio-economic status though their prohibitions against "costly" worldly pleasures, thereby producing extra funds for investment in business or education (Weber's ethic of capitalism); and 3) by emphasizing human rights as reflective of the image of God inherent in all life, creating a politically radical ideology of democratic equality, allowing

2. Miller and Yamamori, *Global Pentecostalism*, 21.

3. Gerlach and Hine, *People, Power, Change*, xxi and Hine, "Deprivation and Disorganization Theories," 655.

4. Miller and Yamamori, *Global Pentecostalism*, 29–30.

Pentecostals the right not only to question and perhaps fight against the religious establishments, but also oppressive political regimes. The first two components of social transformation are expressions of deprivation theories. As we shall discover, the latter, according to Miller and Yamamori, is unique to progressive Pentecostals but not readily found in the legalistic Pentecostalism of the West.[5] Miller and Yamamori want to say that within Pentecostalism resides a quality that produces a people who want to change the world and engage the world in an effort to effect that change. However, underneath is still the residing presupposition of social deprivation.

Social theorists tend to argue that early Pentecostalism was a religious sect consisting of poorly educated, immigrant, rural, and lower class workers, who were attracted to its so-called otherworldly spirituality (especially glossolalia) as a way to soothe the socio-economic misery of their life circumstances. Lack of evidence to support socio-economic deprivation has forced social theorists to propose relative deprivation as a way of explaining the rise of religious sects, but with the result that they can no longer justifiably argue that early Pentecostals are from a lower socio-economic class. While willing to admit that Pentecostals today are represented predominantly by the middle class, the prevailing assumption is that early Pentecostals must have been uneducated, lower class, and rural workers. Recent evidence, however, suggests participants in early Pentecostalism consisted of the full spectrum of socio-economic class and education, suggesting, as will become evident, that deprivation theories are inherently flawed. In this chapter I shall explore the development of deprivation theory as a heuristic tool for explaining the rise of sects, and suggest reasons why the theory is ultimately flawed, concluding that early Pentecostalism in the United States reflected the overall socioeconomic class of American society of the time. While engaging sociological sources my assessment will be of a theological nature.

CHURCH AND SECT—A HEURISTIC MODEL FOR SOCIAL DEPRIVATION THEORIES

Early studies of the Pentecostal movement assumed as evident the deprivation theory of social class. Social deprivation emerged from church-sect typologies first developed by Max Weber and Ernst Troeltsch. As a

5. Miller and Yamamori, *Global Pentecostalism*, 32–34.

sociologist, Weber conceptualized sect and church as pure ideal types, rational constructs of social reality for the purpose of "precise conception," but without evaluative content.[6] As a liberal theologian, Troeltsch construed these ideal types to have a value orientation for the purposes of ethical construction.[7] Among the various descriptions of church and sect, Troeltsch writes: "The asceticism of the Church is a method of *acquiring virtue.* . . . The asceticism of the sects, on the other hand, is merely the *simple principle of detachment* from the world (emphasis added)."[8] The implication in Troeltsch's statement is that world denying, counter-cultural activity has little ethical or social value. Notice the value judgment placed on the church and sect. The church is esteemed because it produces a certain set of moral values in its adherents, but because the church allies with the state those moral values are simultaneously the values of the state. The sect is denigrated because it has no capacity to produce moral values instead preferring withdrawal. What if, however, the significance of the sect is resistance to the ungodly powers, giving it a prophetic voice that calls into question the dehumanizing powers of the state?

Nevertheless, while Weber and Troeltsch employed the typology for description and distinction without concern for the origins of new religious groups,[9] H. Richard Niebuhr employs the typology as a means for understanding the relationship between sect and church, specifically the social origins of religious groupings. He states: "the adoption of one or the other type of constitution is itself largely due to the social condition of those who form the sect or compose the church. In Protestant history the sect has ever been a child of an outcast minority, taking its rise in the religious revolts of the poor, of those who were without effective representation in church or state and who form their conventicles of dissent in the only way open to them, on the democratic, antisocial pattern."[10] Not only does he argue that sects are of the lower socio-economic classes, but establishes the sect and church as polar opposites in which over time the sect moves to its opposite in the church. "The sociological character of sectarianism, however, is almost always modified in the course of time by the natural processes of birth and death, and on this change in structure

6. Gerth and Mills, "Introduction," 59.

7. Eister, "Toward a Radical Critique of Church-Sect Typologizing," 87.

8. Troeltsch, *Social Teaching of the Christian Church*, 1:332.

9. Glock, "Role of Deprivation in the Origin and Evolution of Religious Groups," 24.

10. Niebuhr, *Social Sources of Denominationalism*, 19.

changes in doctrine and ethics inevitably follow. By its very nature the sectarian type of organization is valid for one generation."[11] The ethical component in Niebuhr's assessment is telling in *Christ and Culture*, in which "Christ transforming culture" is the ethical model preferred over "Christ against culture," which of course is the worldview of the sect.[12] Craig Carter has argued, however, that Niebuhr's underlying presupposition is a modernist theory of Christendom, which united the religious and the secular authorities in the Christian faith, in order to legitimize Western civilization. "The separated church, [Niebuhr] repeatedly stresses, has no positive effect on the wider society and is therefore selfish in its quest for purity."[13] From the church-sect typology emerges a theory of deprivation associated with the sect, based in ethical-theological considerations rather than in empirical social-scientific evidences. Moreover, in this argument is a value judgment which says that the sects draw their membership from the economically disadvantaged.

Charles Glock, for instance, accepts socioeconomic deprivation as a basis for sect formation, but he is aware of other factors in deprivation relative to socio-economic factors and proposes five kinds of deprivation: economic, social, organismic, ethical, and psychic. Economic deprivation is the limited access of some individuals to resources due to the differential of income. Social deprivation is the difference between groups with more or less prestige, power, status, and opportunity for social participation. Organismic deprivation is the difference between physical and mental health, where some individuals are deprived due to mental disease or physical disability. Ethical deprivation is the disparity between dominant social values and people who seek alternative values because the dominant values no longer offer meaningful social interaction. Psychic deprivation is the denial of psychic rewards even if there are no material advantages.[14] Glock introduces types of deprivation that are not primarily socioeconomic.

Allan Eister's criticism, however, is that the tendency by social scientists to hold church and sect as polar opposites is an assumption that skews

11. Ibid., 19.

12. Niebuhr, *Christ and Culture*.

13. Carter, *Rethinking Christ and Culture*, 18. Carter's commitment to John Yoder's countercultural structure as a model for social formation provides an important critique of Western civilization.

14. Glock, "Role of Deprivation in the Origin and Evolution of Religious Groups," 27–28.

the evidence because the types are too ambiguous to be tested. Moreover, the assumption that the "unidirectional" shift from a sect to a church at which point a schism may occur in the church creating new sects and the assumption of a corresponding shift from lower class to upper class, breaks down under more complex "multidirectional" analyses.[15]

Rodney Stark and William Bainbridge concur with Eister's assessment. They argue that the church and sect "serve as tautological substitutes for real theories and tend to prevent theorizing."[16] Church and sect are "weak correlates" and have "caused frustration" because "empirical cases just would not fit well."[17] Consequently, they conclude: "Clearly, the church-sect typology cannot be applied to religious groups in our society without letting most cases be exceptions to the rule. But what good are categories if we cannot place cases in them with confidence and without ambiguity?"[18] Nevertheless, Stark and Bainbridge still argue that the sect is predominantly lower class and eventually undergoes upward mobility, which eases the tensions between the sect and dominant social norms and values. Yet "no satisfactory mechanism has been suggested to account for this process."[19] Sect transformation is rooted in mobility drift to reduce tensions within the social environment, but the same can also be said for church downward mobility. In other words, transformation from sect to church, from lower socio-economic class to middle and higher socio-economic class, is not deterministic but a function of the degree of tension between religious groups and society-at-large.

The lack of evidence to support the lower socio-economic postulate for sect composition and its subsequent mobility has led some theorists to propose relative deprivation as an explanation for the origins of sects. But even relative deprivation has had a "checkered career, [a]lternatively praised and condemned."[20] The key to relative deprivation is the discrepancy between individual or group expectations and actual life circumstances. David Aberle states: "Relative deprivation is defined as a negative discrepancy between legitimate expectation and actuality. When an in-

---

15. Eister, "Toward a Radical Critique of Church-Sect Typologizing," 88.

16. Stark and Bainbridge, *Future of Religion*, 20.

17. Ibid., 21.

18. Ibid., 22.

19. Ibid., 150.

20. Crosby, Muehrer, and Loewenstein, "Relative Deprivation and Explanation: Models and Concepts," 17.

dividual or a group has a particular expectation and furthermore where the expectation is considered to be a proper state of affairs, and where something less than that expectation is fulfilled, we may speak of relative deprivation. It is important to stress that deprivation is relative and not absolute."[21] Aberle proposes four classifications of deprivation: possessions, status, behavior, and worth, which can be sub-classified as personal, group, or category experience.[22] These classifications revolve around differences between one's past and present circumstances, between one's present and future circumstances, and between one's own and another's circumstances. In other words, if an individual or a group's material, psychic, and spiritual expectations about what should be is different from what is in reality, then the deprivation experienced is relative.

The difficulty is that when members of a sect are from economically or socially advantaged families; "It is argued that what they lack is existential rather than social deprivation, i.e., a lack of meaning in their lives."[23] S. Dein and H. Barlow note a number of problems with deprivation theory. First, while people may feel deprived due to particular life circumstances, they may not experience deprivation. Second, in the numerous historical examples of oppression and deprivation, most do not turn to religion as a consequence. Dein and Barlow thus conclude that deprivation alone cannot explain the formation of new religious movements making it an invalid social theory. Deprivation as a theory can only be used in ad hoc cases to explain why some specific people join specific religious movements.[24]

Studies investigating social deprivation as a model for explaining the rise of new religious groups cannot come to a consensus as to the validity of the theories for explaining the rise and mobility of sects. In her poi-

21. David Aberle, "Note on Relative Deprivation as Applied to Millenarian and Other Cult Movements," 538. Other works include but are not limited to: Baer, "Field Perspective of Religious Conversion," 279–94; Tripathi and Srivastava, "Relative Deprivation and Intergroup Attitudes," 31–18; Kent, "Relative Deprivation and Resource Mobilization," 529–44; Dein and Barlow, "Why Do People Join the Hare Krishna Movement? Deprivation Theory Revisted," 75–84; Runciman, *Relative Deprivation and Social Justice*; Olson, Herman, and Zanna, *Relative Deprivation and Social Composition*; Walker and Smith, *Relative Deprivation: Specification, Development, and Integration*.

22. Aberle, "Note on Relative Deprivation as Applied to Millenarian and Other Cult Movements," 538.

23. Dein and Barlow, "Why Do People Join the Hare Krishna Movement? Deprivation Theory Revisited," 77.

24. Ibid., 77–78.

gnant examination of Caribbean Pentecostals, Judith Soares argues that socioeconomic and relative deprivation theory is "too narrow in its conceptualization and understanding of the religious phenomenon. There is a significant limitation of deprivation theory stating that those of the privileged classes are, in fact, receptive to particular religious messages under adverse social economic and political conditions."[25] Overlooked is the belief in religion that "social change will take place, not as a consequence of the will of the Divine on its own, but through one's association with and participation in its unfolding [h]uman-Divine alliance will, therefore, bring into effect changes in the world and bring healing, protection, and prosperity to all those who are part of the human-Divine alliance."[26] In the Caribbean, the privileged were attracted to neo-Pentecostalism because the millenarian message of hope for a better world here and now, not because they had lost their wealth and status.[27] Although one might assume that Soares is simply speaking about another form of relative deprivation, she is highlighting that the message of hope in Pentecostalism is attractive to a broad range of people and one need not simply assume a form of deprivation. Perhaps it is germane to point out at this juncture that the structure of religious belief is such that expectation of the eschatological kingdom of God as not yet fulfilled in the present is core to Christian belief, but under the relative deprivation model this would be an indication of deprivation not spiritual expectations.

DEPRIVATION AND THE STUDY OF PENTECOSTALISM

When turning to the question of socioeconomic class in American Pentecostalism, we see an influence of social scientific deprivation theories in Pentecostal scholarship. Nils Bloch-Hoell's 1964 study asserted: "When the Pentecostal movement came into being a great deal of the U.S.A. must have been spiritually and socially rootless. Three mutually connected elements converged to bring this about: The mass immigration, the industrial organization and the enormous growth of the cities at the expense of the agrarian districts."[28] The three elements of immigration, industrialization, and urbanization in late-nineteenth-century America,

25. Soares, "Deprivation Theory Deprived," 389.

26. Ibid., 390.

27. Ibid., 391–92.

28. Block-Hoell, *Pentecostal Movement*, 9.

the concomitant rise of class prejudice, and the weakening of traditional forms of authority created a sense of "rootlessness" in the lower classes, spurred a radical and reactionary return to primitive Christianity while simultaneously seeking the democratization of the Christian churches.[29] Bloch-Hoell thus concludes, "The Pentecostal Movement [sic] was, and to a certain extent still is, a class movement, the primitive Christianity of the less educated."[30]

John Nicols complementary study of Pentecostalism likewise assumed that the success and rise of American Pentecostalism was the result of its ability to appeal to the lower classes.[31] The problem, according to Nicol, was that mainline denominations, which had previously directed much of its ministry to the lower classes, had accumulated wealth and prestige to the extent that these denominations started to exclude the lower classes from these newly established middle class denominations.[32] Yet Nicol argues that Pentecostalism was not as radical, sectarian, or cultic as some critics believed, but was well situated within Christian orthodoxy. Despite criticism of so-called "cold and formal orthodoxy" which has replaced a heart-felt Christianity, Pentecostals whole-heartedly subscribed to the ecumenical Creeds of the fourth century and many of the Reformation Confessions. According to Nicol, Pentecostals accept the Reformational doctrine that salvation is a free gift of grace, the view that all Christians constitute a priesthood of believers by virtue of their faith, and the normativity of Scripture for faith and practice, which can be interpreted by each and every Christian.[33] Moreover, Pentecostals adopt many of the beliefs and practices of the Radical Reformation. These include: 1) individual and corporate submission to the ministrations of the Spirit; 2) a return to the primitiveness of apostolic Christianity; 3) separation from the world; 4) believer's baptism as a confession of faith; 5) and the imminent visible return of Jesus Christ to establish his millennial reign.[34]

29. Ibid., 9–13.

30. Ibid., 11.

31. Nicol, *Pentecostalism*, 57 and Aberle, "Note on Relative Deprivation as Applied to Millenarian and Other Cult Movements."

32. Nicol, *Pentecostalism*, 57.

33. Ibid. Nicol's assessment is accurate of the majority of Pentecostalism in the United States, but conveniently glosses over variant streams such as Oneness Pentecostalism. Oneness Pentecostalism's view of the Godhead is not easily reconciled with the Trinitarian position of the Nicene-Chalcedon Creed.

34. Nicol, *Pentecostalism*, 3. I disagree with Nicol that the primitivism tendency

For Nicol, while early Pentecostals were socially deprived, they were still within the broad contours of Christian orthodoxy.

Robert Mapes Anderson's 1979 study of American Pentecostalism is perhaps the culmination of research into Pentecostalism from the perspective of deprivation. Whereas Bloch-Noell and Nicol are limited in their primary resources of Pentecostalism (relying heavily on second generation sources), Anderson's historical-cultural analysis is able to bring together extensive and widespread primary sources of the nascent years. He is fully committed to deprivation theory and argues that the Pentecostal movement is a subspecies of American Fundamentalism, which protests against the dominant culture. He states: "Finally, and very important from my perspective, we can learn from the study of the Pentecostal movement something about the way in which movements of the 'disinherited' that arise out of protest against the social order are transformed into religious forces that serve to perpetuate that order."[35] Pentecostalism is an ecstatic religion, argues Anderson, which represents a protest against urban industrial culture, attempting to return to "the old-time religion."[36] Arguing from a Marxist analysis of cultural and socio-economic history, Anderson proposes:

> Pentecostalism was a movement born of radical social discontent, which however, expended its revolutionary impulses in veiled, ineffectual, displaced attacks that amounted to withdrawal from the social struggle and passive acquiescence to a world they hated and wished to escape. . . . Their social powerlessness was transformed into feelings of religious powerlessness, and its solution was sought through tapping the source of all power in the Baptism of the Holy Spirit. The social consequence of the movement was diametrically opposed to its unconscious intent. Pentecostalism was an instrument forged by a segment of the working class out of protest against a social system that victimized them, but it functioned in a way that perpetuated that very system. A potential challenge to the social system was transformed into a bulwark of it.[37]

---

is an aspect of the radical reformation solely. One can see this tendency in German Pietism, Wesleyanism, and the Anglican context from which Wesley arose.

35. Anderson, *Vision of the Disinherited*, 8.

36. Ibid., 5–9.

37. Anderson, *Vision of the Disinherited*, 222.

In agreement with his predecessors, Anderson saw Pentecostalism as a lower class protest against the modernist process of urbanization, industrialization, immigration, and global expansion, which was sublimated into religious protests against a highly rationalized Christianity with its emphasis on higher biblical criticism, evolutionary theories, and the social role of the church often associated with so-called liberal Christianity.[38] For Anderson, the role of Pentecostalism as a religious movement was to ease the anxiety of social change. "Pentecostalism was a means of acculturation, providing a buffer against the chaotic impact of the urban-industrial milieu upon those migrants. . . . By the repeated ritual renewal of their ties with an older rural-agrarian religious tradition of emotional revivalism, and by the cathartic effects of ecstasy, Pentecostalism made it easier for them to function in their new environment."[39]

Although Grant Wacker agrees that the historical evidence suggests that Pentecostals were of the working class, "A number of studies ranging from 1900 to 1970, indicate that over the years Pentecostals consistently have been found in the upper range of the working class, among artisans and steady wage earners, and occasionally scattered even in the lower middle class." Anderson also assumes the same Pentecostal rhetoric regarding "Anglos Saxon superiority, trade unions, Bolshevism, and so forth, was highly characteristic not of the lower class but of lower-middle-class WASPS."[40] In fact, Wacker points out that Pentecostalism flourishes in prosperous, stable, and traditional societies with strong kinship bonds. Instead, Wacker suggests Pentecostalism is not responding to social strain, but to changes in the symbolic meaning systems within culture.[41] The historian must figure out, retorts Wacker, how Pentecostals who were stratified in a particular social system, lived with significance by giving chaos to an ordered world and order to a chaotic world.[42]

The seeds of an alternative view of socioeconomic class and social status could be seen as early as 1970 with Gerlach and Hine's study of

---

38. Ibid., 223ff. Anderson's rather sweeping statement overlooks the role of the social aspects of Christianity in nineteenth-century evangelicalism, which combined the proclamation of the gospel and the social witness of the gospel. Both the Wesleyan traditions and American revivalism focused on issues such as prison reform, the abolition of slavery, help for the poor and other social issues.

39. Anderson, *Vision of the Disinherited*, 238.

40. Grant Wacker, review of Robert Mapes Anderson, *Vision of the Disinherited*, 57.

41. Wacker, review, 60.

42. Ibid., 62.

social movements—specifically Pentecostalism and Black Power. While they concluded that the rise of early Pentecostalism was linked to socio-economic deprivation, they found that mid-twentieth-century Pentecostals were well situated in the middle class. Gerlach and Hine's focus was on the implications of social movements on changes in society. Their definition of a social movement was "*a group of people who are organized for, ideologically motivated by, and committed to a purpose which implements some form of personal or social change; who are actively engaged in the recruitment of others; and whose influence is spreading in opposition to the established order within which it originated* (authors' emphasis)."[43] They found five key factors that defined and sustained a social movement:

1. A *segmented, usually polycephalous, cellular organization* composed of units reticulated by various personal, structural, and ideological ties.

2. *Face-to-face recruitment* by committed individuals using their own pre-existing, significant social relationships.

3. *Personal commitment* generated by an act or experience which separates a convert in some significant way from the established order (or his previous place in it), identifies him with a new set of values, and commits him to change patterns of behavior.

4. An *ideology* which codifies values and goals, provides a conceptual framework by which all experiences or events relative to these goals may be interpreted, motivates and provides rationale for envisioned changes, defines the opposition, and forms the basis for conceptual unification of a segmented network of groups.

5. *Real or perceived opposition* from the society at large or from that segment of the established order within which the movement has risen.[44]

All five factors are evident in Pentecostalism. Of significance is the polycephalous character of the movement, in which a multiplicity of leaders and organizational structures solidify around various ideological goals, as well as the real or perceived opposition, which forms social identity around various ideologies and leaders, and explains much of the fragmentation in the movement in both its early years and its current multiple manifestations. Perhaps Martyn Percy's analogy best explains

43. Gerlach and Hine, *People, Power, Change*, xvi.

44. Ibid., xvii.

the multidimensional characteristics of Pentecostalism. Percy argues that Pentecostalism and especially its child neo-Pentecostalism are like sand castles on the beach. Each new wave of the Spirit can bring new life, re-shaping existing structures, or completely destroy existing structures. The multifaceted character of Pentecostalism is not easily analyzed or explained because with each new "revival" comes a re-energizing and reorientation of existing forms and structures or even the creation of new orientations, but at the risk of segmentation, erosion, or even disaster.[45]

Returning to Gerlach and Hine, their interest was not to assess the Pentecostal movement in terms of its low class and/or deprived status, but rather to investigate its role in producing social change. While they embarked on their study assuming that Pentecostalism could be classified in one or all of the sociological models of social deprivation, disorgani-zation, or psychological maladjustment, they quickly abandoned these models for lack of evidence. Gerlach and Hine argue, "We spent a good deal of time during the early stages of our research attempting to fit our data into one or another of these three models. We finally abandoned the why-did-it-start for the what-makes-it-tick approach for two reasons. First, too many participants in both movements we studied could not be classified as socially disorganized, even relatively deprived, or psy-chologically maladjusted."[46] Yet they still assumed that the rise of early Pentecostalism could be explained in terms of social deprivation of the lower class, but without supporting evidence. Nevertheless, Gerlach and Hine concluded that as of 1965 (when their study commenced) people within the Pentecostal movement "represent a wide range of socio-economic and educational backgrounds, including the highest."[47] Part of the ambiguity, argue Gerlach and Hine, is the inappropriate definition of Pentecostalism as a sect rather than as a social movement.

Albert Miller's assessment of the deprivation thesis of Pentecostalism is *apropos*, calling into question the sociological and historiographical approaches that maintain deprivation. After an overview of research that supports the Pentecostal deprivation thesis, and especially challenging Anderson's position, Miller notes that recent sociological and psycholog-

45. Percy, "City on a Beach," 207.

46. Gelach and Hine, *People, Power, Change*, xxi; also see Gerlach, "Pentecostalism" 669–99 and "Deprivation and Disorganization Theories of Social Movements," 646–61; Hine, "Pentecostal Glossolalia," 439–61; and Garrison, "Sectarian and Psychological Adjustment," 298–329.

47. Gerlach and Hine, *People, Power, Change*, xxi.

ical research is unable to verify the deprivation thesis. Though perhaps understandable for scholars such as Nicol and Bloch-Hoell, who were contemporaries to Gerlach and Hine, Anderson completely fails to take into account their explanation of tensions, segmentation, and adaptation as dynamic components in the development of social movements. Instead, Anderson chooses to see the early ecclesiastical fragmentation as yet another example of social deprivation for a people disillusioned by their lower class social location in society and struggle to rise in social class.[48] Stated positively, the ecclesial fragmentation in early and present-day Pentecostalism is not a function of social deprivation, where participants feel they need constantly to restructure because their protests are not taken seriously, but a characteristic of social movements in which social groups form identity through real or perceived opposition. Social deprivation theorists simply assumed that participants were drawn into the Pentecostal movement because they felt personal or social deficiencies and hoped somehow to resolve these defects. Completely ignored are the religious claims made by Pentecostals, who were seeking alternative expressions of spirituality. According to Miller, Gerlach and Hine's thesis has not been given due consideration in socio-scientific analyses.[49] Instead of assuming that religious expression and formation is the result of social deprivation and lower class status, Gerlach and Hine insist that social change can be the result of religious motivation. Consequently, they look to one area of Weber's theoretical exposition, nonrational motivation for social change, over against another area, that is social deprivation as a function of the church-sect typology.

RECENT ANALYSES IN PENTECOSTALISM AND SOCIAL CLASS

In the last decade a number of important studies have emerged which seriously challenge the view that early Pentecostals were socioeconomically deprived and therefore of the lower classes. Harvard theologian Harvey Cox's investigation into global Pentecostalism allowed for instances of anomie and relative deprivation within Pentecostalism, but questioned the validity of these explanations to explain the movement. For Cox, the key to unlocking the reasons behind the rise of Pentecostalism was that the movement represented a protest against modernity's myths and val-

48. Miller, "Pentecostalism as a Social Movement," 112.

49. Ibid., 13–14.

ues, which ultimately called into question racial segregation, female subordination, and socioeconomic differences. Pentecostalism was a spiritual groaning for the coming reign of God in this world, tapping into a deep seated, primal spirituality, symbolically represented in primal speech, primal piety, and primal hope. Glossolalia, argues Cox, is not an expression of psychological maladjustment but symbolic enactment tapping into deep-seated human spirituality. Primal piety is a reemergence of deep rooted spirituality, a celebration of vital impulses that an overly rationalistic culture was trying to truncate. Primal hope is a visionary expression of an expectant change. It is a movement that draws deeply on religious symbolic roots in order to make a way for the future. Millenarian hope offers an alternative to what Cox calls modernity's "good life" or what I see as modernity's optimism, to offer hope and thereby transform "chaos, normlessness, and ennui. . . . By embracing ecstatic praise, visions, healing, dreams, and joyous bodily movements, Pentecostal worship lured anarchy into the sacred circle and tamed it."[50] The spiritual groaning of Pentecostals cannot be reduced to a protest against the socioeconomic injustices of this world (though they were in part), but are a declaration that the kingdom of this world must ultimately conform to the biblical vision of God's reign on this earth.[51] Pentecostals themselves resist sociological explanations that define them as victims of deprivation, anomie, or ennui, seeking some sort of psychological compensation for their state.[52] Rather, Pentecostals were "a people who have become what they are because they *wanted* something badly enough to allow themselves to be changed in a fundamental way. And they were willing to embrace the elemental terror that sort of change requires."[53]

Grant Wacker's award winning book *Heaven Below* is a thorough examination of the historical-cultural context in the emergence of Pentecostalism and is the most damaging to the deprivation thesis to date. Wacker claims that the argument that the rise of early Pentecostalism is the result of real or perceived deprivation is too shallow of a reading of the historical sources. Admittedly, early Pentecostals saw themselves as being and operating at the margins of society and were more than willing to thwart accepted social conventions that they believed failed to

50. Cox, *Fire from Heaven*, 120.
51. Ibid., 117.
52. Ibid., 173.
53. Ibid., 182.

conform to the norms and values of Scripture, but one cannot simply assume that operating on the margins of society means that Pentecostals were socioeconomically deprived.[54] Wacker notes, "To hear them tell the story, the wealthy, the well placed, and well educated felt very much at home in their meetings."[55] Scholars who interpret Pentecostals as being socially or psychologically disadvantaged, argues Wacker, are distorting the evidence to fit their preconceived assumptions, looking at a skewed picture of the movement. In reality, the social status of early Pentecostals reflected a cross section of American life. While some Pentecostals were at the lower end of the socioeconomic strata, others were well-to-do. For example, early leaders Carrie Judd Montgomery and Richard Spurling were financially wealthy. Most early Pentecostals, however, were firmly planted in the middle classes.[56]

Backed up by historical evidence, Wacker argues that the average Pentecostal was representative of the average American at that time in American history. Although a slightly higher ratio of women to men, the men who attended Pentecostal meetings were not youthful males seeking their way in life, but mature males. The racial make-up of Pentecostals attending church in the 1930s (the earliest data available) was predominantly white, but with a representation of African-Americans that was twice the percentage of the American population, and two-thirds the population in the South. To suggest that the higher representation of African-Americans in the average Pentecostal church means that Pentecostals were socioeconomically deprived points to a racial bias eschewed by Pentecostals. Instead, the racial mix, while not perfect, suggests that early Pentecostals were concerned for racial equality and integration as depicted in the biblical worldview, that there is neither Greek nor Jew, male nor female, slave nor free (Gal 3:28). Although Pentecostals have been stereotyped as "illiterate yokels," in reality they were functionally literate and typical of the average American of that time in the history of the United States. Early Pentecostals were overall healthy once childhood diseases are factored out, and they were typically American in constituting a stable working class. In sum, early Pentecostals lived comfortably as average middle class Americans, some at the lower end of the social classes, others at the

54. Wacker, *Heaven Below*, 202.

55. Ibid., 198.

56. Ibid., 198–99.

higher end.[57] Early Pentecostals were neither socioeconomically deprived nor materially disadvantaged.

While Pentecostals were on the margins of society, Wacker argues that this was due to their personal autonomy, manifested in their cultural aggressiveness, temperamental independence, and occupational mobility. Pentecostals willingly took risks, moved around, and invested in a vision of God's reign in this world. They were ". . . resourceful, hard working, fired by ideals and, above all, determined to get the job done."[58] In other words, while on the margins of American society, Pentecostals were not marginalized by deprivation but lived on the margins by choice; they were mobile, not because they were forced to follow a job market in the transition from rural to urban and industrial society, but because they chose to follow God's call to the diverse corners of the Unites States and even around the world. Living on the margins was their way of living out their prophetic calling to change the world for the kingdom of God.

THEOLOGICAL ASSESSMENT

My contention is that deprivation theories are unhelpful as social scientific explanations for sect formation and sect to church mobility, or even the terminology of sect itself, because its basis in the church-sect typology is defined by a particular view of Christendom Christianity. Christendom (and its related term Constantinianism) is a view of Western civilization in which the church and civil government(s) represent the religious and secular arms, which work together (albeit with different roles) to establish a unified social reality.[59] Moreover, the church-sect typology is defined within the Protestant liberal tradition, which has a particular interest in aligning Christian faith with modernist notions of universal rationalism and the acquisition of a particular set of moral values that support the ideals of the state. Within the modernist paradigm, the religious is relegated to a private, inward realm of the psyche as a matter of opinion, whereas the values of the state are deemed to be public dealing with verifiable facts. However, as Lesslie Newbigin has so ably argued, the public/

57. Ibid., 205–11.

58. Ibid., 213.

59. Carter, *Rethinking Christ and Culture*, 14.

private, facts/opinions, secular/sacred divide is not coherent to the gospel but is Western Christianity's enculturation of modernist assumptions.[60]

In other words, the church and sect are classified from an elitist position of power, which defines the church according to values that support modernity's national, consumer, and capitalist interests through the unchallenged use of technical rationality. Together they undergird Western civilization. The sect is defined as dysfunctional because it refuses to hold to dominant values and norms, instead withdrawing as a form of resistance, and is dismissed as a prophetic voice "crying in the wilderness." John Yoder's radical Protestant theology is germane on this point. Yoder along with Stanley Hauerwas and other radical Protestant theologians have been dismissed as sectarian, precisely because they refuse to give into the legitimizing forces of modernity.[61] Yoder, for instance, argues that those who are "responsible custodians" of the "majority tradition . . . grant room for criticism," but only by "relegating it to the fringes. The 'saint' and the 'prophet' will find ready recognition from them, but at the price of the concession that their critical vocation is heroic, unique, and not to be taken as normative for others."[62] Yoder claims that the alternative to Christian nationalism, patriotism, the fusion of Christ and culture (Niebuhr), neo-Constantianiam, and "buying into the power game" is not its negation in passive withdrawal but the critical re-conception of values according to the gospel, the beginning of a new game with new rules.[63] In contrast to Troeltsch's church-sect model, Yoder affirms:

> [T]he initial intention of the "sectarian" communities which in the course of Western history have renewed the minority ethic has not been to be as sects. Division was not their purpose. They have called Christians to return to the ethic to which they themselves were called. They did not agree . . . that their position was only for heroes, or that it was only possible for those who would withdraw from the wider society. They did not agree to separate themselves as more righteous from the church at large. They rather called upon the church at large to accept as binding for all Christians the quality of commitment which would in effect lead

60. Newbigin, *Foolishness to the Greeks*, 35–41.

61. Hauerwas has been accused of articulating a sectarian ethic, which he rejects because the terminology has already skewed how that construction of Christian ethics should be approached. Hauerwas, *Christian Existence Today*, 113–14 and throughout.

62. Yoder, "Civil Religion in America," 178–79.

63. Ibid., 179–80.

them all to be separated from the world once again in order to be appropriately in mission to the world.[64]

Sects are branded sects precisely because they refuse to buy into the Christendom worldview, while the church is intrinsically tied to the state and its nationalism.[65] In a turn-about, the church as defined by the church-sect typology is itself a sect with a particular set of values, a particular way of being in the world. By tying itself to the modern nation-state, the church is already parochial and sectarian, just another sect in the broad spectrum of religious bodies.[66]

The prophetic call is critical for evaluating early Pentecostal self understanding. The prophetic call explains why Pentecostals were involved in social ministries. Ron Kydd suggested that "When Pentecostalism was young we did not have an outreach to the poor, we were the poor! We just reached out to ourselves and we were reaching the poor,"[67] but within this claim is a presupposition of socioeconomic deprivation. A more plausible explanation is Steven Land's argument that the prophetic call was rooted in early Pentecostalism's eschatological passion, which instilled a countercultural stance. Being countercultural, Pentecostals were actively involved in rescue missions, schools, orphanages, and medical care, and assumed countercultural positions such as pacifism, racial integration, and the democratization of hierarchical institutions as characteristic of kingdom holiness.[68] Consequently, early American Pentecostalism can be described as progressive in Miller and Yamamori's sense, not because Pentecostals were deprived but because they lived out their prophetic call in alignment with the dawning of the eschatological kingdom, thereby creating a countercultural ethos.

I thus propose that it is unhelpful to define early Pentecostalism as sectarian and therefore consisting of members who are deprived in one form or another. Rather if one defines early Pentecostalism as prophetic in the truest sense of the word, then early Pentecostals called people out of a particular way of thinking about the world as an all encompassing

---

64. Yoder, "Kingdom as Social Ethic," in *The Priestly Kingdom*, 85.

65. Carter, *Politics of the Cross*, 175.

66. Ibid., 176.

67. Kydd, "To See is to Be Called," 11.

68. Land, *Pentecostal Spirituality*, 180.

reality.[69] Though they would not necessarily have articulated it as such, they were calling the churches to reject the Christendom mentality, that there is a rationally universal means of adjudicating the gospel, but that the gospel was calling people to true community and true mission. It was a countercultural resistance to the self-aggrandizing claims of modernity, of nationalism and patriotism and of a form of Christianity that has lost its bearings. In other words, early Pentecostalism was a prophetic call to live the life of true discipleship and mission.

CONCLUSION

What does all this mean for our understanding of the socioeconomic class composition of those who became Pentecostal at the turn of the twentieth century? Early Pentecostals were for the most part from the working class, but what was their stratification? Were they at the bottom of the lower class or in the middle or upper lower class? Were they in the lower middle or middle and upper middle class? Theories of socioeconomic deprivation based in ambiguous assumptions of the relationship between the sect and the church have been used to argue that early American Pentecostals were of the lower class. Social scientific analyses conducted from the 1960s on have revealed that Pentecostals contemporary to the various studies were from the working middle class, but the assumption remained that early Pentecostals must have been lower class because they formed a sect. However, if one sees early Pentecostalism as a movement rather than a sect, then the deprivation model is severely weakened. In response, theorists moved to relative deprivation to explain the rise of early Pentecostalism, but relative deprivation says little regarding socioeconomic considerations. Current investigations suggest that the class composition of early American Pentecostalism was representative of American society of the time, some lower class, some middle class and even a few who were in the upper class. Relative depri-

---

69. Walter Brueggemann for instance argues that the positive role of a sectarian hermeneutic is one in which the alternative practices of the community of faith enter a conversation with the official and monopolizing claims of empire in order to transform the conversation. The prophet is a critical participant in the process. Brueggemann, "Legitimacy of the Sectarian Hermeneutic," 47–48; also see Brueggemann, *Texts under Negotiation*, 18–20 where he argues that the meeting of liturgy and proclamation in a postmodern context offers a "counterimagination of the world" in light of the "failure of the imagination of modernity."

vation and even socioeconomic deprivation may explain some aspects of early Pentecostalism, but certainly not all and therefore distorts our understanding of the relationship between early Pentecostals and social class. More importantly, one cannot claim a causal relationship between social deprivation and sect formation. In the end, Jerry Shepperd's claim is poignant, "Relative deprivation theory, by itself, is unable to explain why there is a discrepancy between the reality and the stereotype of Pentecostal social involvement."[70]

However, from the perspective of a postliberal and postmodern context, we start to see that the church-sect distinction is merely another strategy for supporting modern liberal legitimization. Early Pentecostals resisted identification with the sect and saw it as a violation of the gospel. Instead they preferred to see themselves as prophetic communities, calling people out of the monolithic and overarching values of modernity, in order to live as Spirit indwelt people under the gospel of Jesus Christ.

BIBLIOGRAPHY

Aberle, David. "Note on Relative Deprivation as Applied to Millenarian and Other Cult Movements." In *Reader in Comparative Religion: An Anthropological Approach*, 2nd ed., edited by William A. Lessa and Evon Z. Vogt, 537–41. New York: Harper & Row, 1979.

Anderson, Robert Mapes. *Vision of the Disinherited: The Making of American Pentecostalism*. 1979. Reprinted, Peabody, MA: Hendrickson, 1992.

Baer, Hans A. "A Field Perspective of Religious Conversion: The Levites of Utah." *Review of Religious Research* 19 (1978) 279–94.

Block-Hoell, Nils. *The Pentecostal Movement: Its Origins, Development, and Distinctive Character*. London: Allen & Unwin, 1964.

Brueggemann, Walter. "The Legitimacy of the Sectarian Hermeneutic." In *Interpretation and Obedience: From Faithful Reading to Faithful Living*, 41–69. Minneapolis: Fortress, 1991.

———. *Texts under Negotiation: The Bible and Postmodern Imagination*. Minneapolis: Fortress, 1991.

Carter, Craig A. *The Politics of the Cross: The Theology and the Social Ethics of John Howard Yoder*. Grand Rapids: Brazos, 2001.

———. *Rethinking Christ and Culture: A Post-Christendom Perspective*. Grand Rapids: Brazos, 2006.

Cox, Harvey. *Fire from Heaven: The Rise of Pentecostal Spirituality and the Reshaping of Religion in the Twenty-First Century*. Reading, MA: Addison-Wesley, 1995.

70. Shepperd, "Sociology of World Pentecostalism," 1085.

Crosby, Faye, Peter Muehrer, and George Loewenstein. "Relative Deprivation and Explanation: Models and Concepts." In *Relative Deprivation and Social Comparison: The Ontario Symposium*, vol. 4, edited by James M. Olson, C. Peter Herman, and Mark P. Zanna, 17–32. London: Erlbaum, 1986.

Dein, S., and H. Barlow, "Why Do People Join the Hare Krishna Movement? Deprivation Theory Revisted." *Mental Health, Religion and Culture* 2 (1999) 75–84.

Eister, Allan W. "Toward a Radical Critique of Church-Sect Typologizing: Comment on 'Some Critical Observations on the Church-Sect Dimension.'" *Journal for the Scientific Study of Religion* 5 (1967) 85–90.

Garrison, Vivian. "Sectarian and Psychological Adjustment: A Controlled Comparison of Puerto Rican Pentecostals and Catholics." In *Religious Movements in Contemporary America*, edited by Irving I. Zaretsky and Mark P. Malone, 298–329. Princeton: Princeton University Press, 1974.

Gerlach, Luther P. "Pentecostalism: Revolution or Counter Revolution?" In *Religious Movements in Contemporary America*, edited by Irving I. Zaretsky and Mark P. Malone, 669–99. Princeton, NJ: Princeton University Press, 1974.

Gerlach, Luther P., and Virginia H. Hine. *People, Power, Change: Movements of Social Transformation*. New York: Bobbs-Merrill, 1970.

Gerth, H. H., and C. Wright Mills. "Introduction." In *From Max Weber: Essays in Sociology*, edited by H. H. Gerth and C. Wright Mills, 3–74. New York: Oxford University Press, 1946.

Glock, Charles Y. "The Role of Deprivation in the Origin and Evolution of Religious Groups." In *Religion and Social Conflict*, edited by Robert Lee and Martin E. Marty, 24–36. New York: Oxford University Press, 1994.

Hine, Virginia H. "Deprivation and Disorganization Theories." In *Religious Movements in Contemporary America*, edited by Irving I. Zaretsky and Mark P. Maloney, 646–64. Princeton: Princeton University Press, 1974.

———. "Pentecostal Glossolalia: Toward a Functional Interpretation." In *Speaking in Tongues: A Guide to Research on Glossolalia*, edited by Watson E. Mills, 439–61. Grand Rapids: Eerdmans, 1986.

Kent, Stephen A. "Relative Deprivation and Resource Mobilization: A Study of Early Quakerism." *British Journal of Sociology* 33 (1982) 529–44.

Kydd, Ron[ald] "To See is to Be Called." *Pentecostal Testimony* (January, 1996) 9–12.

Land, Steven J. *Pentecostal Spirituality: A Passion for the Kingdom*. Journal of Pentecostal Theology Supplement Series 1. Sheffield, UK: Sheffield Academic, 1993.

Miller, Albert G. "Pentecostalism as a Social Movement: Beyond the Theory of Deprivation." *Journal of Pentecostal Theology* 9 (1996) 97–114.

Miller, Donald E., and Tetsunao Yamamori. *Global Pentecostalism: The New Face of Christian Social Engagement*. Berkeley: University of California Press, 2007.

Nicol, John Thomas. *Pentecostalism*. New York: Harper & Row, 1966.

Niebuhr, H. Richard. *Christ and Culture*. New York: Harper & Row, 1951.

———. *The Social Sources of Denominationalism*. New York: World, 1929.

Olson, James M., C. Peter Herman, and Mark P. Zanna. *Relative Deprivation and Social Composition: The Ontario Symposium*, vol. 4. London: Erlbaum, 1986.

Percy, Martyn. "The City on a Beach: Future Prospects for Charismatic Movements at the End of the Twentieth Century." In *Charismatic Christianity: Sociological Perspectives*, edited by Stephen Hunt, Malcolm Hamilton, and Tony Walter, 205–28. London: McMillian, 1997.

Runciman, W. G. *Relative Deprivation and Social Justice: A Study of Attitudes to Social Inequality in Twentieth-Century England*. Berkeley: University of California Press, 1966.

Shepperd, J. W. "Sociology of World Pentecostalism." In *The New International Dictionary of Pentecostal and Charismatic Movements*, rev. ed., edited by Stanley M. Burgess and Eduard M. Van Der Maas, 1083–90. Grand Rapids: Zondervan, 2002.

Soares, Judith. "Deprivation Theory Deprived." *Peace Review: A Journal of Social Justice* 18 (2006) 389–93.

Stark, Rodney, and William Sims Bainbridge. *The Future of Religion: Secularization, Revival and Cult Formation.* Berkeley: University of California Press, 1985.

Tripathi, Rama Charan, and Rashmi Srivastava. "Relative Deprivation and Intergroup Attitudes." *European Journal of Social Psychology* 11 (1981) 31–18.

Troeltsch, Ernst. *The Social Teaching of the Christian Church.* Vol. 1 of 2. Translated by Olive Wyon. Louisville: Westminster John Knox, 1992.

Wacker, Grant. *Heaven Below: Early Pentecostals and American Culture.* Cambridge: Harvard University Press, 2001.

———. Review of *Vision of the Disinherited: The Making of American Pentecostalism*, by Robert Mapes Anderson. *Pneuma* (Fall 1982) 53–62.

Walker, Iain, and Heather J. Smith, editors. *Relative Deprivation: Specification, Development, and Integration.* Cambridge: Cambridge University Press, 2002.

Yoder, John Howard. "The Kingdom as Social Ethic." In *The Priestly Kingdom: Social Ethics as Gospel*, 80–101. Notre Dame, IN: University of Notre Dame Press, 1984.

6

Re-Visioning the Disinherited

Pentecostals and Social Class in North America

Adam Stewart

INTRODUCTION

For much of the last one-hundred years, when the nomenclature "Pentecostal" has been uttered by both the media and within the regnant academic discourse, it was usually done so with reference to either its substantial growth in the developing world, or its preponderance among members of the lower class in North America. While these references describe Pentecostalism in two very different contexts, they often reveal the same prevailing assumption: Pentecostalism is largely a religion of the socially, culturally, or economically deprived, consisting of either the dislocated members of the massive rural-to-urban migration in the developing world, or the desire for status among the indigent dregs of the rural backwater boondocks or urban industrial cities of North America. Scholars have commonly assumed that individuals primarily sought affiliation with the Pentecostal movement in order to gain compensation for the social, cultural, or economic status that they otherwise lacked in their broader social settings.

The idea that Pentecostalism is the desperate response of the disinherited to the anxieties created by modernity fails to account for Pentecostal affiliation in at least two important ways; the first empirical and the second theoretical. First, the assumption that individuals join the Pentecostal movement due to deprivation fails to explain why many members of the middle, upper-middle, and even upper-classes, have been drawn to the Pentecostal tradition, not just in recent years, but since the very inception of the movement. Second, the assumption that objective structures, such as class, wholly determine subjective behavior including religious affiliation, fails to take into consideration the very real influence that individual subjectivity exerts on the determination of religious belief, practice, and affiliation.

In this chapter I provide a reconceptualization of the relationship between Pentecostalism and social class that accounts for the socioeconomically diverse membership of Pentecostalism, as well as the influence of subjective intentionality on the part of Pentecostal adherents. I aim to achieve this, however, without ignoring the important influence that objective structures such as social class do indeed exert on the determination of religious affiliation. In other words, while I intend to provide a corrective to the idea that social class wholly determines Pentecostal affiliation, at the same time I do not want to swing so far to the side of subjectivity, as has been common in recent decades, so as to perpetuate the myth that people are the sole authors of their own histories.[1] Instead, I argue that while deprivation is indeed both an empirically and theoretically problematic way to conceptualize Pentecostal affiliation because it tends to overemphasize the influence that objective structures exert on subjective behavior, I also claim that it is as equally empirically and theoretically problematic to ignore the very real influence that objective structures such as social class do exert on human behavior. In order to make this argument, I will do three things. First, I will briefly outline the ways that scholars have historically attempted to explain Pentecostal affiliation as the result of social, cultural, and economic deprivation.

1. For a discussion of the development of this idea in one of its earliest and most entrenched forms in the discipline of anthropology, see Asad, *Genealogies of Religion*, 1–24.

Second, using both contemporary and historical examples, I will demonstrate the deficiency of deprivation theory to explain Pentecostal affiliation. Finally, building on the work of social theorist, Pierre Bourdieu, I will suggest a more nuanced way of envisioning the relationship between Pentecostalism and social class that does not view Pentecostals as either completely passive objects or entirely free agents in the construction of their own religious identities.

PENTECOSTALISM AND DEPRIVATION

On first appraisal, deprivation theory appears to be an improvement over earlier scientific explanations of religious affiliation, which argued that individuals were drawn to certain religious traditions due to inherent biological tendencies. From the late nineteenth through to the middle of the twentieth century, a whole plethora of scientific explanations for religious affiliation predicated on the eugenics thesis, originating in such fields as biology, evolutionary anthropology, psychology, and sociology, argued that biologically degenerate, morally depraved, and socially deviant individuals either created or joined questionable social and religious movements. The deviants were usually identified as under-evolved, lower class, rural whites, or urban minorities. It naturally followed, then, that the religions of these rural whites and urban minorities, including sectarian and emotive forms of conservative Protestantism such as Pentecostalism, as well as African Spirituality, and Roman Catholicism, and not to mention Judaism and new religious movements, were largely categorized as the primitive and irrational pathologies of those existing on the outermost periphery of society.[2] After the logical conclusion of the eugenics thesis was witnessed in the barbarities of the Holocaust, biological explanations of religious affiliation began to give way to social-scientific explanations, and the cause of religious affiliation shifted from biological to social-scientific determinism.

It is important to briefly note, however, that these kinds of social-scientific explanations of religious affiliation were already being made well before the conclusion of the Second World War, particularly in the writings of Karl Marx, Émile Durkheim, Max Weber, Ernst Troeltsch, and H.

---

2. For a discussion of the modern American eugenics movement, see Haslan, *Rhetoric of Eugenics in Anglo-American Thought*; Kelves, *In the Name of Eugenics*; and Rosen, *Preaching Eugenics*.

Richard Niebuhr. Marx, for instance, wrote in *The German Ideology*: "The phantoms formed in the human brain are also, necessarily, sublimates of their material life-process, which is empirically verifiable and bound to material premises. Morality, religion, metaphysics, all the rest of ideology and their corresponding forms of consciousness, thus no longer retain the semblance of independence."[3] Marx was convinced that material conditions and, more specifically, underlying economic structures, directly determined human experience, including, of course, religion. Marx also wrote that, "Religious suffering is at the same time an expression of real suffering and a protest against real suffering. Religion is the sigh of the oppressed creature, the feeling of a heartless world, and the soul of soulless circumstances. It is the opium of the people."[4] This passage makes apparent the fact that for Marx, religious suffering, or alienation from God, is simply an emulation of real or economic suffering, and so religion is ultimately an illusion that serves to distract people from focusing their attention on ameliorating the true source of humanity's discontent, which is, according to Marx, capitalism.

Marx's conviction that religion is strongly influenced by material conditions was also advanced, although less deterministically, by the sociologist Max Weber, as well as Ernst Troeltsch, and H. Richard Niebuhr. These thinkers were responsible for the initial development of the church-sect typology, which suggested a correlation between social class and religion. While it is true that Weber, Troeltsch, and Niebuhr each modified and discarded elements of Marx's theory, they all ultimately saw a connection between social class and religious subjectivity.[5] Weber, for instance, somewhat echoing Marx, wrote that, "not ideas, but material and ideal interests, directly govern men's conduct," revealing his firm belief in the power of objective social structures such as class to influence human behavior such as religion.[6]

Despite the early thinkers who paid careful attention to the social sources of religious affiliation, these kinds of social-scientific explanations did not achieve academic ascendancy until the near dissolution of the eugenics movement following World War II, and in particular in the

---

3. Marx, "German Ideology," 180–81.

4. Marx, "Towards a Critique of Hegel's Philosophy of Right," 72.

5. Niebuhr, *Social Sources of Denominationalism*; Troeltsch, *Social Teaching of the Christian Churches*; and Weber, *Sociology of Religion*.

6. Weber, "Social Psychology of the World Religions," 280.

1960s. One of the most important of these emerging social explanations that developed in the second half of the twentieth century, and the most relevant for any discussion concerning Pentecostalism, was deprivation theory. Attesting to the popularity of deprivation theory to explain the existence of sectarian and new religious movements, sociologist Virginia Hine wrote in 1974, "The view that movements of all types arise out of deprivation, however it is defined, is almost universal."[7]

In contrast to eugenics theory, deprivation theory, in its most basic form, holds that people establish or join new religious movements, not because they are biologically inferior, but, rather, because they are economically deprived, and seek the usually soteriological rewards that these supposedly subversive religious groups provide their members.[8] This early form of deprivation theory, however, failed to account for the many upwardly mobile members of sectarian or marginal religious groups, not to mention the variety of new religious movements that emerged in the 1960s and 1970s, which drew their membership disproportionately from the upper-middle class.[9] In order to account for the rising socioeconomic status of both individual sect members, and entire religious organizations, sociologists began to distinguish between "absolute" and "relative" deprivation.[10] Charles Y. Glock, the most important progenitor of the relative deprivation thesis, argued that individuals do not need to experience absolute or objective deprivation in order to form or join a new religious movement, but only relative, or subjective deprivation. In other words, people need only imagine that they are in some way deprived, which they subsequently attempt to ameliorate by seeking out the compensations offered by a new or sectarian religious movement. Glock wrote: "a necessary precondition for the rise of any organized social movement, whether it be religious or secular, is a situation of felt deprivation."[11]

By broadening the definition of deprivation to include subjective as well as objective forms of deprivation, Glock was able to greatly expand

---

7. Hine, "Deprivation and Disorganization Theories of Social Movements," 651.

8. Dawson, *Comprehending Cults*, 72 and 73.

9. Machalek and Snow, "Conversion to New Religious Movements," 53–74; Stark and Bainbridge, *Future of Religion*, 395; and Wilson, *Sects and Society*.

10. Aberle, "Millennial Dreams in Action," 209–14; Glock, "Role of Deprivation in the Origin and Evolution of Religious Groups," 24–36; Gurr, *Why Men Rebel*; and Merton, *Social Theory and Social Structure*, 4.

11. Glock, "Role of Deprivation in the Origin and Evolution of Religious Groups," 29.

the ways in which people could be conceived to experience deprivation
that far exceeded the realm of material conditions. Glock developed a
five-fold taxonomy of deprivation that could be both objective or subjective, which included: (1) economic deprivation, (2) social deprivation,
(3) organismic deprivation (deficiencies in physical or mental health),
(4) psychic deprivation (a lack of psychic rewards such as love and affec-
tion), and (5) ethical deprivation (being deprived of a sense that society
provides a meaningful order to one's life).[12] Through the differentiation
of real from felt deprivation, Glock and others were then able to account
for the presence of members from the upper socioeconomic classes who
joined new religious movements. The disproportionately young, white,
highly educated, and middle-to-upper class members who joined new
religious movements, could now be explained as responding not to real
socioeconomic distress, but, rather, their either real or imagined economic, social, organismic, psychic, or ethical deprivation.

The type of relative deprivation theory developed by Glock and others
was extremely influential in shaping the way that subsequent sociologists
came to explain affiliation in new and sectarian religious movements, with
possibly no religious group receiving more attention from scholars eager
to prove the merits of deprivation theory than Pentecostalism. Writing
in the early 1980s, when deprivation theory was still the most widely
used schema to explain affiliation within new religious movements, the
historian Grant Wacker remarked, "the presumption that Pentecostalism
arose as a more or less functional adaptation to social and cultural dis-
equilibrium has acquired the status of an orthodoxy."[13] Similarly, religious
studies scholar, Sean McCloud, observes: "It is no exaggeration to suggest
that one could trace the twentieth-century history of theories of religious
affiliation by singularly focusing on Pentecostalism."[14] It was no accident
that deprivation theorists were drawn to Pentecostalism. Pentecostalism's
emphasis on an apocalyptic eschatology marking a sharp distinction between the material and supernatural, as well as strict group boundaries,
its emphasis on ecstatic and emotive religious practices such as speaking in tongues, prophesying, faith healing, dancing, and being slain in

---

12. Glock, "Role of Deprivation in the Origin and Evolution of Religious Groups,"
27–29.

13. Wacker, "Taking Another Look at the *Vision of the Disinherited*," 19.

14. McCloud, *Divine Hierarchies*, 90.

the spirit, and its assumed preponderance among members of the lower classes, seemed to fit the deprivation paradigm perfectly.

Among the most notable and widely cited studies of Pentecostal affiliation utilizing some aspect of deprivation theory are those conducted by John Holt, Liston Pope, Elmer Clark, and Gary Schwartz.[15] While the work of Holt and Pope well predates the post-World War II predominance of deprivation theory, they anticipated the work of later scholars such as Clark and Schwartz who similarly argued that Pentecostalism drew its membership disproportionately from those who were seeking some kind of compensation for their various forms of deprivation. In no other work, however, was the application of deprivation theory to Pentecostalism more carefully developed and meticulously demonstrated than in Robert Mapes Anderson's highly influential work, *Vision of the Disinherited: The Making of American Pentecostalism*.[16]

Anderson chronicles how during the late nineteenth and early twentieth centuries, large numbers of African Americans from the Southern states, whites, largely from Appalachia and the Ozarks, and immigrants from Southern and Eastern Europe and Latin America, relocated to the burgeoning northeastern centers of industry (many relocated to California as well) in order to fill the increasing demand for labor.[17] He argues that the severe socioeconomic deprivation that these largely lower class migrants and immigrants experienced in their attempts to adapt from their previous rural-agrarian, or to borrow Ferdinand Toennies's term, *gemeinschaft*, forms of community, to the new urban industrial, or *gesellschaft*, social order, resulted in their being drawn to Pentecostalism.[18] The Pentecostal movement, Anderson writes, "may be viewed as one small part of a widespread, long-term protest against the whole thrust of modern urban-industrial society."[19] Of these mainly dispossessed members of the lower-class, Anderson explains that, "rejecting all secular solutions to their problems, they found in Pentecostalism a religious resolution that was almost wholly other-worldly, symbolic, and psychotherapeutic."[20]

15. Clark, *Small Sects of America*; Holt, "Holiness Religion," 740–47; Pope, *Millhands and Preachers*; and Schwartz, *Sect Ideologies and Social Status*.

16. Anderson, *Vision of the Disinherited*.

17. Ibid., 225 and 226.

18. Anderson, *Vision of the Disinherited*, 113; and Toennies, *Community and Society*, 65.

19. Anderson, *Vision of the Disinherited*, 80, 96, 113 and 223.

20. Ibid., 229.

Symptomatic of the compensatory language developed by Glock and the other early deprivation theorists, Anderson asserted that Pentecostalism's apocalyptic eschatology and ecstatic religious practices provided both order to, and escape from, life in modern industrial society. "For the Pentecostals," he wrote, "ecstasy was a mode of adjustment to highly unstable circumstances over which they had little or no control."[21] The most interesting aspect of Anderson's analysis of the origins of early American Pentecostalism is his assertion that the early Pentecostal's construction of an essentially religious critique of modern society was largely unpropitious. He viewed the Pentecostal response to their socioeconomic situation as unfortunate and ineffectual because it "deflected social protest from effective expression, and channeled it into the harmless backwaters of religious ideology."[22] "[T]he radical social impulse inherent in the vision of the disinherited," he argued, "was transformed into social passivity, ecstatic escape, and finally, a most conservative conformity."[23]

Anderson, however, did not limit his explanation of Pentecostal affiliation to the historical era with which his study so carefully chronicled. In an entirely unsubstantiated claim, he writes, "I would hazard the hypothesis that status deprivation and an anti-rationalist, anti-bureaucratic—i.e., anti-modern-temper has combined to predispose most of the recruits of the neo-Pentecostal movement."[24] Here Anderson asserts that his proposed explanation of Pentecostal origins and affiliation within the earliest decades of the movement apply equally to the Pentecostal movement in the late twentieth century, as well as the neo-Pentecostal or Charismatic movements, which had emerged within Roman Catholicism and most other mainline Protestant denominations during the 1960s and 1970s. Grant Wacker was indeed correct to claim that Anderson's *Vision of the Disinherited* is "the standard that subsequent interpreters simply shall have to come to terms with, one way or another," and that it "still constitutes the most compelling example of the genre."[25] The reduction of Pentecostal origins and affiliation to deprivation, however, as Wacker was among the first to point out, fails as a comprehensive explanation for the appeal of either the early or contemporary Pentecostal movement. In the following

21. Ibid., 231.
22. Ibid., 239.
23. Ibid., 240.
24. Ibid., 229.
25. Wacker, "Taking Another Look," 16; and *Heaven Below*, 199 and 200.

two sections I will briefly examine some of the more salient empirical, as well as theoretical problems with the use of deprivation theory to explain Pentecostal affiliation.

EMPIRICAL PROBLEMS WITH DEPRIVATION THEORY

Some of the earliest critiques of deprivation theory came from sociologists whose primary interests were the formation and development of social movements, such as the early work of Luther P. Gerlach, Virginia H. Hine, and Clark McPhail.[26] While these sociological critiques were multifaceted, they focused on two major logical inconsistencies in the deprivation paradigm.

First, most deprivation theorists did not provide empirical evidence of the correlation between real or felt deprivation and religious affiliation, or, as Joan Neff Gurney and Kathleen J. Tierney wrote, they failed to "link convincingly psychological states with antecedent societal conditions on the one hand and with subsequent movement participation on the other."[27] Many deprivation theorists simply assumed the relationship between deprivation and affiliation in certain religious groups such as Pentecostalism, resulting in a kind of circular logic where it was assumed that an individual was deprived because they established or joined a particular religious group, and that they established or joined a particular religious group because they were deprived. Luther P. Gerlach, for instance, argued that the only evidence that deprivation theorists had that deprived individuals established or joined a sectarian or new religious movement was the very existence of these religious groups; such individuals must be deprived because they joined religious groups that deprivation theorists classified as being composed of the deprived.[28] Both Gerlach and his colleague, Virginia H. Hine, argued that deprivation theory fails to completely or adequately explain Pentecostal affiliation because its singular focus on deprivation as the source of participation ignores the influence that other factors exert on the determination of religious affiliation, as well as the possibility of "positive motivation."[29]

26. Gerlach and Hine, *People, Power, Change* and McPhail, "Civil Disorder Participation," 1058–73.

27. Gurney and Tierney, "Relative Deprivation and Social Movements," 40.

28. Gerlach, "Pentecostalism: Revolution or Counter-Revolution?" 669–99.

29. Hine, "Deprivation and Disorganization Theories of Social Movements," 654.

Second, and probably deprivation theory's most serious sociological weakness, is the inability of deprivation theorists to account for the large amounts of individuals who experience some sort of deprivation, but who choose not to join the so called religions of the deprived. It is entirely possible that there are more deprived individuals who either choose to join another religious movement or none at all, than those who choose to join the particular religious movements that the deprivation theorists identify as common to the deprived. Bryan Wilson aptly summarizes this critique when he writes "Why . . . do some people not feel deprived when by all objective criteria, they are deprived, and why, even of those who feel deprived do only a proportion become absorbed by religious groups?"[30] The fact is that there are millions of people around the world who would fit the deprivation theorist's criteria of deprived individuals, who either affiliate with established or elite religious traditions, or do not practice religion at all. The very existence of these individuals seriously calls into question explanations of religious affiliation predicated on deprivation.

Sociological critiques played an important role in calling the deprivation paradigm into question, causing it to fall into serious disfavor from the 1980s onward. The most devastating critiques of deprivation theory, however, can be found in the careful ethnographic and historical studies of both the contemporary and early Pentecostal movement, which seriously challenge any homogeneous understanding of Pentecostalism as a collection of the economically deprived or culturally dispossessed. Chief among these analyses is Mary Jo Neitz's, *Charisma and Community*, a close study of a Roman Catholic Charismatic prayer group in the United States.[31] Here she describes a group that is comprised of mainly white, middle-to-upper-middle class, well educated members, which seriously challenges the explanation of Pentecostal-Charismatic affiliation as a result of deprivation, social, economic, cultural, or otherwise.

Neitz's study confirms the earlier work of Michael Harrison, Joseph Fichter, and Max Heinrich who argued that (1) the best predictor of involvement in the Charismatic movement is prior religious commitment, (2) the acceptance of religious beliefs plays the most important role in an individual's decisions to affiliate with the movement, and (3) socioeconomic stresses do not account for conversion.[32] Responding directly

---

30. Wilson, *Social Dimension of Sectarianism*, 195.

31. Neitz, *Charisma and Community*.

32. Harrison, "Preparation for the Life in the Spirit," 387–414; Harrison, "Sources of

to Robert Mapes Anderson's assertion that Pentecostal affiliation is the result of a "hunger for God,"[33] which he conflates with deprivation, Neitz comments:

> One wonders what deprivation means, in this sense. Theologians might define the religious as deprivation, as Anderson seems to be using it here, and consider it a part of the human condition. . . . Those more psychologically inclined might say that such feelings of deprivation stem from the early experience of being separated from the mother, and also consider it a part of the human condition. "Deprivation" loses its explanatory power as a sociological concept if the only place it is not experienced is in the womb.[34]

Instead of attempting to uncover the underlying social, economic, cultural, or psychological reasons why people join the Charismatic movement, Neitz suggests that scholars should reorient their attention to questions of meaning: "We must look at what people believe and how beliefs are interpreted and used by participants in religious organizations."[35] Neitz argues that as a result of the destabilizing tendencies of modernity, and, more significantly, after what many conservative Roman Catholics view as the largely negative affects of the liberalization of the Catholic church in the wake of Vatican II, many Catholics were drawn to the Charismatic Renewal because its religious contents provided adherents with a new social reality whose sources of legitimation and plausibility structures have remained intact in spite of the modern, pluralistic situation.[36]

Again, highlighting the lack of emphasis placed on the possibility of positive motivation for Pentecostal affiliation among the deprivation theorists, Neitz writes: "These were people who had other options. Becoming a Charismatic represented a positive choice—for them it was the preferred alternative. This is in marked contrast to the way that those committed to orthodox religious beliefs are often described by sociologists who tend to see them as those on the periphery whom modern

---

Recruitment to Catholic Pentecostalism," 49–64; Fichter, *Catholic Cult of the Paraclete*; and Heinrich, "Change of Heart," 653–80.

33. Anderson, *Vision of the Disinherited*, 229.

34. Neitz, *Charisma and Community*, 18. On this issue also, see Miller, "Pentecostalism as a Social Movement," 97–114.

35. Neitz, *Charisma and Community*, 5.

36. Ibid., 83, 128, 188, 221, 246, and 249–60.

society has by-passed."[37] In short, Neitz's study provides one of the most compelling refutations of the various attempts to explain Pentecostal affiliation as a result of deprivation, and did much to call attention to the fact that most individuals are drawn to Pentecostalism due to the merits that they see in the tradition's religious content, making conversion of reaffiliation to Pentecostalism, as Neitz writes, a "positive choice."

Another important source pointing to the socioeconomic diversity of the Pentecostal movement is Grant Wacker's unsurpassed study of early American Pentecostalism, *Heaven Below*.[38] Wacker does agree with the research of Robert Mapes Anderson and others, which carefully catalogs the socioeconomic deprivation of many of the early American Pentecostals: "There is much to be said for Anderson's portrait. Without question, poverty, hunger, homelessness, minimal education, and ill health defined the lives of thousands."[39] Wacker continues, however, by asking the question, "Where did the rank-and-file believers fit in the social system?" to which he replies, "Contrary to stereotype, the typical convert paralleled the demographic and biographical profile of the typical American in most though not quite all respects."[40] With careful attention to statistical and historical evidence, Wacker explains that in terms of gender, health, marital status, rural and urban residence, formal education, occupation, employment, wealth, and population distribution, Pentecostals were no different than the average American.

In only three important ways did Pentecostals differ significantly from the general American population.[41] First, the average Pentecostal was significantly older than the average American, which is not uncommon for a new religious movement drawing a largely voluntaristic, adult membership. Wacker notes that in 1910 the average American was in their mid-twenties, while the average Pentecostal was in their late thirties or forties, making them, Wacker writes, "a mature adult, not an emotionally mercurial adolescent, as commonly supposed."[42] Second, Wacker observes that in 1930 African Americans made up 10 percent of the general population, but represented 20 percent of Pentecostal adherents,

---

37. Ibid., 258.

38. Wacker, *Heaven Below*.

39. Ibid., 201.

40. Ibid., 205.

41. Ibid., 205–16.

42. Ibid., 206.

meaning that there was twice the proportion of African Americans in the early Pentecostal movement than in the general American population.[43] Finally, Wacker explains that early American Pentecostals exhibited a significantly higher degree of personal autonomy, one of the most highly appreciated American values, than did the average American. He explains that early American Pentecostals exhibited a standard of self-sufficient individualism that exceeded that of the common American, which translated into the missional activity that the movement is known for, and may have resulted in greater financial prosperity.[44] In short, Wacker very convincingly demonstrates that the average early American Pentecostal was female, middle-aged, in good health, white, married, an urban dweller, with a middle-school education, most likely a skilled laborer with a steady job and average earnings, who could be from just about anywhere in the country, and exhibited a high degree of personal autonomy. In other words, early American Pentecostals were virtually identical to other American Protestants: "In the early twentieth century it would have been hard to find any definable religious tradition, except Methodists, that presented its face more broadly and in more diverse geographic and social settings. Normal Americans they were in almost every respect."[45]

My own research into early Canadian Pentecostalism mirrors many of Wacker's observations concerning the socioeconomic diversity of early American Pentecostalism. Much of the evidence available from the first site of the Pentecostal movement in Canada located at 651 Queen Street East in Toronto, Ontario, known as the East End Mission, or, more commonly, as the Hebden Mission, indicates that these earliest Canadian Pentecostals were not identical to the average working class Canadian of the time, but, to the contrary, were most likely from the upper-middle class echelons of Torontonian society. The Hebden Mission was led by recent immigrants from England, James and Ellen Hebden. James was a successful contractor who purchased a large building almost immediately upon arriving in Toronto that he subsequently had renovated and transformed into a mission, which was attended by converts from established Protestant churches in the area. The Hebdens also owned a large home at 191 George Street in Toronto, and the five extant editions of the Hebden's own journal, *The Promise*, indicate that several of the mission's

43. Ibid., 206 and 207.

44. Ibid., 212–16.

45. Ibid., 212.

early adherents were college graduates, professionals, and doctors, who when traveling abroad as missionaries, took the time to learn the languages of the locals, a practice not common within the early American Pentecostalism of the working class.[46]

What the sociological analyses of Gerlach, Hine, Gurney, and Tierney, the close ethnographic observations of Neitz, and the historical evidence from Wacker and early Canadian Pentecostalism all clearly demonstrate is that deprivation theory is an inadequate explanation of Pentecostal affiliation. The assertion that people are drawn to the Pentecostal movement because of either real socioeconomic deprivation arising from their place on the class hierarchy, or felt deprivation as a result of other cultural or psychological deficiencies is simply not supported by empirical and historical evidence.

THEORETICAL PROBLEMS WITH DEPRIVATION THEORY

The second major problem with the assertion that socioeconomic deprivation is the cause of Pentecostal affiliation is that it fails to account for the role that individuals play in the construction of their own religious realities.[47] In other words, objective structures, such as social class, or external forces exerting pressure on individuals and communities, such as the massive relocation of many Americans during the rural-to-urban shift of the late nineteenth and early twentieth centuries, are not alone capable of adequately explaining Pentecostal affiliation. Rather, religious affiliation is better understood as a complex interplay between both objective and subjective influences. Pierre Bourdieu, the French social theorist, attempted to reconcile the relationship between structure and human agency through the revitalization of the concept of the "habitus" previously discussed by theorists such as Marcel Mauss and Norbert Elias.[48] Contrary to historical materialism, Bourdieu wrote in *Outline of a Theory of Practice*: "it is necessary to abandon all theories which explicitly or implicitly treat practice as a mechanical reaction, directly determined

46. *The Promise* 1 (May, 1907) 1–4; *The Promise* 2 (June, 1907) 1–4; *The Promise* 12 (February, 1909) 1–8; *The Promise* 14 (October, 1909) 1, 2, 7, and 8; and *The Promise* 15 (March, 1910) 1–8.

47. For a particularly salient discussion of this shortcoming, see Best, *Passionately Human, No Less Divine*, 33.

48. Elias, *Civilizing Process* and Mauss, *Gift*.

by the antecedent conditions and entirely reducible to the mechanical functioning of pre-established assemblies, 'models,' or 'rôles.'"[49] This is where many critiques of deprivation theory stop. They point to the obvious problem with a strictly deterministic understanding of the relationship between objective structures such as class and religious affiliation, which easily crumbles under the weight of any evidence that people often choose different affiliations than their social conditions would normally suggest. This type of a critique, however, opens itself up to an entirely new problem, which is the need to explain the very real correlation, either historical or contemporary, between the lower socioeconomic classes and affiliation with many forms of conservative Protestantism including Pentecostalism.[50] This is where Bourdieu's theories of practice and the habitus are particularly helpful.

In addition to denying any kind of strict determinism, Bourdieu also insisted on a very comprehensive understanding of the role that structure has in the determination of human behavior:

> But rejection of mechanistic theories in no way implies that, in accordance with another obligatory option, we should bestow on some creative free will the free and willful power to constitute, on the instant, the meaning of the situation by projecting the ends aiming at its transformation, and that we should reduce the objective intentions and constituted significations of actions and works to the conscious and deliberate intentions of their authors.[51]

In other words, Bourdieu argued that human behavior should not be viewed as the sole result of either objective structure, as the structuralists following Émile Durkheim and Talcott Parsons advocate, or subjective intentionality, as the interactionists following George Herbert Mead

---

49. Bourdieu, *Outline of a Theory of Practice*, 73.

50. For recent evidence of this correlation, see Beyerlein, "Specifying the Impact of Conservative Protestantism on Educational Attainment," 505–18; Glass and Jacobs, "Childhood Religious Conservatism and Adult Attainment Among Black and White Women," 555–79; Keister, "Religion and Wealth," 175–207; Massengill, "Educational Attainment and Cohort Change Among Conservative Protestants, 1972–2004," 545–62; McCloud, *Divine Hierarchies*; McCloud, "Putting Some Class into Religious Studies," 840–62; Pyle, "Trends in Religious Stratification," 61–79; Reimer, "Class and Congregations," 583–94; Smith and Faris, "Socioeconomic Inequality in the American Religious System," 95–104; and Stewart, "Praying with the Hand You Are Dealt," 35–53.

51. Bourdieu, *Outline of a Theory of Practice*, 73.

and Herbert Blumer, as well as a whole host of postcolonialist theorists propose. Instead, Bourdieu suggested that behavior should be viewed as a "dialectical relationship between the objective structures and the cognitive and motivating structures which they produce and which tend to reproduce them."[52] He insisted that it is crucial to recognize that "objective structures are themselves products of historical practices and are constantly reproduced and transformed by historical practices whose productive principle is itself the product of the structures which it consequently tends to reproduce."[53] In terms of our discussion, this means that it is important to recognize that while the determination of religious affiliation is not simply determined by one's social location, that it is not always an entirely free choice either, but is decided through a complex negotiation between both objective structures and subjective intentionalities.

Bourdieu's understanding of the dialectic between objectivity and subjectivity is not all that different from what many social theorists have argued before him: individuals and groups tend to externalize their own ideas about the meaning of the world that are then transposed as objective reality, and internalized as a set of dispositions exerting an immense degree of pressure on the determination of human behavior.[54] Bourdieu called this set of dispositions a habitus, which he defined as "a system of lasting, transposable dispositions, which, integrating past experiences, functions at every moment as a *matrix of perceptions, appreciations, and actions.*"[55] Understood in this way, human behavior is not an entirely deterministic process because the habitus, first, is only partially constructed by truly objective structures such as class in addition to the individual's own subjective projection of what constitutes objective reality, and, second, does not determine what types of behavior are possible, but, rather, those types of behavior appear more or less reasonable, depending on a particular behavior's coherence with the habitus. Bourdieu explains:

> Practical evaluation of the likelihood of the success of a given action in a given situation brings into play a whole body of wisdom, sayings, commonplaces, ethical precepts ("that's not for the likes of us") and, at a deeper level, the unconscious principles of the

52. Ibid., 83.
53. Ibid.
54. See for instance, Berger and Luckmann, *Social Construction of Reality*, 61.
55. Bourdieu, *Outline of a Theory of Practice*, 82 and 83 (emphasis in original).

ethos which, being the product of a learning process dominated by a determinate type of objective regularities, determines "reasonable" and "unreasonable" conduct for every agent subjected to those regularities.[56]

In short, then, Bourdieu proposed that an individual's or group's habitus, which is the result of the complex dialectic between both objective and subjective realities, makes certain life choices either more or less likely in as far as those choices align with one's habitus, or, rather, the whole matrix of objective and subjective influences. The habitus of working class children, for instance, does not necessarily determine that all working class children will find themselves in working class occupations and neighborhoods, as many working class children do indeed decide to go on to college, find professional employment, and move to the suburbs. Rather, the habitus only makes these contingencies much more likely, often to the degree that they appear determined to the statistician or demographer, and even oftentimes to the individuals themselves. It is very difficult for children to become socialized into a mode of behavior and assume roles with which they have not been exposed, or which have not been demonstrated to them as desirable or even possible.

In the context of our present discussion, this means that the decision to affiliate with a particular religious tradition results from the combination of objective realities and the subjective response to these realities that make certain religious options either physically possible, or appear desirable in as far as they relate to or support the habitus. Bourdieu explains:

> Because the dispositions durably inculcated by objective conditions . . . engender aspirations and practices objectively compatible with those objective requirements, the most improbable practices are excluded, either totally without examination, as *unthinkable*, or at the cost of *double negation* which inclines agents to make a virtue of necessity, that is, to refuse what is anyway refused and to love the inevitable.[57]

Bourdieu similarly commented in his analysis of class in France, *Distinction: A Social Critique of the Judgment of Taste*: "Taste is *amor fati* [love of fate], the choice of destiny, but a forced choice, produced by conditions of existence which rule out all alternatives as mere daydreams and leave

56. Ibid., 77 (emphasis in original).

57. Bourdieu, *Outline of a Theory of Practice*, 77 (emphasis in original).

no choice but the taste for the necessary."[58] It is easy to see why Bourdieu is commonly viewed as little different from the same structuralists who he himself critiqued. It is important to recognize, however, that Bourdieu always reserves the possibility that individuals may break away from what their habitus deems reasonable, but that these decisions are simply less likely. It is much more likely, for instance, that two people sharing a similar habitus would choose to wear similar clothing, consume similar media, purchase similar products, drive similar vehicles, reside in similar neighborhoods, work in similar occupations, and, where it becomes relevant for our discussion, choose similar religions, because they also share a relatively similar life experience that makes certain choices either more or less available, or seem more or less reasonable.[59] As Sean McCloud similarly observes, "the material conditions produced by social class and status differentiation make individuals and groups more or less available and constrained when exploring certain religious groups."[60]

So, what does Bourdieu have to do with understanding the relationship between Pentecostalism and social class? Bourdieu is important because he provides a framework through which we can at once acknowledge the very real pressure that objective structures such as class exert on the determination of religious affiliation, and, at the same time, assert that individuals and groups are not the completely passive victims of these structures as the deprivation theorists assumed. Instead of viewing the preponderance of individuals from the lower socioeconomic classes in some segments of the Pentecostal movement, say in the Ozarks and Appalachia of the early twentieth century, the urban centers of North America, or throughout much of the developing world, as resulting from the need of these individuals to compensate for some form of deprivation, we can alternatively understand it as the very natural process of the primary socialization of the children, and the reaffiliation or conversion of individuals within the same social networks and inhabiting the same or similar habitus as the individuals who make up these communities. In other words, members of the working class do not affiliate with a working class Pentecostal church because their social conditions determine it, but, rather, because they share the same or similar social networks and inhabit the same or similar habitus as the members who already comprise

58. Bourdieu, *Distinction*, 474.

59. Bourdieu, *Outline of a Theory of Practice*, 85.

60. McCloud, *Divine Hierarchies*, 15–16.

this congregation, which simply makes their decision to affiliate in this church appear to them as much more "reasonable," and, as a result, makes it much more likely, but not inevitable, than another religious option.

Likewise, it would seem much less reasonable, and be much less likely for members of the middle or upper middle class who do not share the same or similar social networks and habitus, to join the same working class Pentecostal church. While members of these classes do sometimes affiliate with these types of churches, their habitus, which includes an entirely different set of experiences, social networks, aspirations, and possibilities makes it more likely that they will choose to affiliate with another type of congregation, which may still be Pentecostal, but not likely with a predominantly working class membership. This means that some segments of the Pentecostal tradition that have either historically been or are structurally more likely to be comprised of members from the lower class are much more likely to continue to attract these types of members, leaving the deprivation theorists to mistake this correlation with the cause for affiliation. An application of Bourdieu's theory to an understanding of the relationship between social class and Pentecostalism makes it possible, then, to understand the existence of lower class Pentecostal congregations and denominations, and, indeed, even middle and upper middle class Pentecostal congregations and denominations, as a result of the "positive choices" made in an attempt to select a religious option that explains, reinforces, or sometimes even challenges, the individual's entire objective and subjective experience of reality.

CONCLUSION

I have demonstrated that both absolute and relative deprivation theory fails as an empirically convincing explanation of Pentecostal affiliation because it cannot account for those individuals who are somehow deprived who do not join the Pentecostal movement or a similar religion of the deprived, and also because it does not explain the presence of members of the middle and upper-middle classes within both the early and contemporary Pentecostal movement. I have also shown how deprivation theory fails as a theoretically convincing explanation of Pentecostal affiliation because it does not take into account the very real influence that subjective intentionality exerts on the determination of objective social reality, which in turn creates the range of religious possibilities available to the individual. At the same time, however, I have argued that it is important not to ignore the role that objective structures such as class do play in the determination of religious affiliation, as has been common in the recent anti-Marxist, postcolonial, and postmodern scholarly milieu. Borrowing ideas from Pierre Bourdieu, I propose that the determination of religious affiliation is the result of the complex dialectic between both objective structures and the subjective intentionalities that create these structures, and which in turn are only made possible through the very objective structures that they themselves create. I propose that this dialectic makes it possible to recognize both the very real pressure that objective structures such as class exert on the determination of religious affiliation, and, at the same time, the fact that religious affiliation is not determined, but, rather, simply made either more or less likely depending on one's social location. Understood in this way, the preponderance of members from the lower class in any particular Pentecostal congregation, or even locality or region, can simply be explained as the natural outplay of social network relations and the similar range of decisions commonly made by individuals inhabiting a similar form of habitus.

BIBLIOGRAPHY

Aberle, David. "Millennial Dreams in Action." In *Comparative Studies in Society and History, Supplement II*, edited by S. L. Thrupp, 209–14. The Hague: Mouton, 1962.

Anderson, Robert Mapes. *Vision of the Disinherited: The Making of American Pentecostalism*. New York: Oxford University Press, 1979.

Asad, Talal. *Genealogies of Religion: Discipline and Reasons of Power in Christianity and Islam*. Baltimore: Johns Hopkins University Press, 1993.

Berger, Peter, and Thomas Luckmann. *The Social Construction of Reality: A Treatise in the Sociology of Knowledge*. Garden City, NY: Doubleday, 1966.

Best, Wallace D. *Passionately Human, No Less Divine: Religion and Culture in Black Chicago, 1915–1952*. Princeton: Princeton University Press, 2005.

Beyerlein, Kraig. "Specifying the Impact of Conservative Protestantism on Educational Attainment." *Journal for the Scientific Study of Religion* 43 (2004) 505–18.

Bourdieu, Pierre. *Distinction: A Social Critique of the Judgment of Taste*. Translated by Richard Nice. Cambridge: Harvard University Press, [1979] 1984.

———. *Outline of a Theory of Practice*. Translated by Richard Nice. New York: Cambridge University Press, 1977.

Clark, Elmer T. *The Small Sects of America*. Rev. ed. Nashville: Abingdon, 1965.

Dawson, Lorne L. *Comprehending Cults: The Sociology of New Religious Movements*. 2nd ed. Toronto: Oxford University Press, 2006.

Elias, Norbert. *The Civilizing Process: The History of Manners*. 2 vols. Translated by Edmund Jephcott. New York: Urizen, [1939] 1978–1982.

Fichter, Joseph. *The Catholic Cult of the Paraclete*. New York: Sheed & Ward, 1975.

Gerlach, Luther P. "Pentecostalism: Revolution or Counter-Revolution?" In *Religious Movements in Contemporary America*, edited by Irving I. Zaretsky and Mark P. Leone, 669–99. Princeton: Princeton University Press, 1974.

Gerlach, Luther P., and Virginia H. Hine. *People, Power, Change: Movements of Social Transformation*. Indianapolis: Bobbs-Merril, 1970.

Glass, Jennifer, and Jerry Jacobs. "Childhood Religious Conservatism and Adult Attainment among Black and White Women." *Social Forces* 84 (2005) 555–79.

Glock, Charles Y. "The Role of Deprivation in the Origin and Evolution of Religious Groups." In *Religion and Social Conflict*, edited by Robert Lee and Martin Marty, 24–36. New York: Oxford University Press, 1964.

Gurney, Joan Neff, and Kathleen J. Tierney. "Relative Deprivation and Social Movements: A Critical Look at Twenty Years of Theory and Research." *The Sociological Quarterly* 23.4 (1982) 33–47.

Gurr, Ted. *Why Men Rebel*. Princeton: Princeton University Press, 1970.

Harrison, Michael. "Preparation for the Life in the Spirit." *Urban Life and Culture* 2 (1974) 387–414.

———. "Sources of Recruitment to Catholic Pentecostalism." *Journal for the Scientific Study of Religion* 13 (1974) 49–64.

Haslan, Marouf Arif, Jr. *The Rhetoric of Eugenics in Anglo-American Thought*. Athens: University of Georgia Press, 1996.

Heinrich, Max. "A Change of Heart." *American Journal of Sociology* 83 (1977) 653–80.

Hine, Virginia. "The Deprivation and Disorganization Theories of Social Movements." In *Religious Movements in Contemporary America*, edited by Irving I. Zaretsky and Mark P. Leone, 646–61. Princeton: Princeton University Press, 1974.

Holt, John. "Holiness Religion: Cultural Shock and Social Reorganization." *American Sociological Review* 5 (1940) 740–47.

Keister, Lisa. "Religion and Wealth: The Role of Religious Affiliation and Participation in Early Adult Asset Accumulation." *Social Forces* 82 (2003) 175–207.

Kelves, Daniel J. *In the Name of Eugenics: Genetics and the Uses of Human Heredity*. Berkeley: University of California Press, 1985.

Machalek, Richard, and David A. Snow. "Conversion to New Religious Movements." In *Religion and the Social Order*, vol. 3, *The Handbook on Cults and Sects in America*, Part B, edited by David Bromley and Jeffrey Hadden, 53–74. Greenwich, CT: JAI, 1993.

Marx, Karl. "The German Ideology." In *Karl Marx: Selected Writings*, edited by David McLellan, 175–208. New York: Oxford University Press, 2000.

———. "Towards a Critique of Hegel's Philosophy of Right: Introduction." In *Karl Marx: Selected Writings*, edited by David McLellan, 71–82. New York: Oxford University Press, 2000.

Massengill, Rebekah Peeples. "Educational Attainment and Cohort Change among Conservative Protestants, 1972–2004." *Journal for the Scientific Study of Religion* 47 (2008) 545–62.

Mauss, Marcel. *The Gift: The Form and Reason for Exchange in Archaic Societies*. Translated by W. D. Halls. London: Routledge, [1923–1924] 1990.

McCloud, Sean. "Putting Some Class into Religious Studies: Resurrecting an Important Concept." *Journal of the American Academy of Religion* 75 (2007) 840–62.

————. *Divine Hierarchies: Class in American Religion and Religious Studies.* Chapel Hill: University of North Carolina Press, 2007.

McPhail, Clark. "Civil Disorder Participation: A Critical Examination of Recent Research." *American Sociological Review* 36 (1971) 1058–73.

Merton, Robert K. *Social Theory and Social Structure.* New York: Free Press, 1968.

Miller, Albert G. "Pentecostalism as a Social Movement: Beyond the Theory of Deprivation." *Journal of Pentecostal Theology* 4 (1996) 97–114.

Neitz, Mary Jo. *Charisma and Community: A Study of Religious Commitment within the Charismatic Renewal.* New Brunswick, NJ: Transaction, 1987.

Niebuhr, H. Richard. *The Social Sources of Denominationalism.* New York: Meridian, 1957.

Pope, Liston. *Millhands and Preachers: A Study of Gastonia.* New Haven: Yale University Press, 1942.

Pyle, Ralph E. "Trends in Religious Stratification: Have Religious Group Socioeconomic Distinctions Declined in Recent Decades?" *Sociology of Religion* 67 (2006) 61–79.

Reimer, Sam. "Class and Congregations: Class and Religious Affiliation at the Congregational Level of Analysis." *Journal for the Scientific Study of Religion* 46 (2007) 583–94.

Rosen, Christine. *Preaching Eugenics: Religious Leaders and the American Eugenics Movement.* New York: Oxford University Press, 2004.

Schwartz, Gary. *Sect Ideologies and Social Status.* Chicago: University of Chicago Press, 1970.

Smith, Christian, and Robert Faris. "Socioeconomic Inequality in the American Religious System: An Update and Assessment." *Journal for the Scientific Study of Religion* 44 (2005) 95–104.

Stark, Rodney, and William Sims Bainbridge. *The Future of Religion: Secularization, Revival and Cult Formation.* Berkeley: University of California Press, 1985.

Stewart, Adam. "Praying with the Hand You Are Dealt: Revisiting Social Class in the Study of Religion." *Illumine* 7 (2008) 35–53.

Toennies, Ferdinand. *Community and Society.* Translated by C. P. Loomis. New York: Harper & Row, 1963.

Troeltsch, Ernst. *The Social Teaching of the Christian Churches.* 2 vols. New York: Harper, 1960.

Wacker, Grant. *Heaven Below: Early Pentecostals and American Culture.* Cambridge: Harvard University Press, 2001.

————. "Taking Another Look at the *Vision of the Disinherited.*" *Religious Studies Review* 8 (1982) 15–22.

Wilson, Bryan R. *Sects and Society: A Sociological Study of the Elim Tabernacle, Christian Science, and Christadelphians.* Berkeley: University of California Press, 1961.

————. *The Social Dimension of Sectarianism: Sects and New Religious Movements in Contemporary Society.* Oxford: Clarendon, 1990.

Weber, Max. "The Social Psychology of the World Religions." In *From Max Weber: Essays in Sociology,* edited by H. H. Gerth and C. Wright Mills, 267–301. New York: Oxford University Press, 1946.

————. *The Sociology of Religion.* Translated by Ephraim Fischoff. Boston: Beacon, 1963.

PART THREE

Issues of Gender

7

Your Daughters Shall Prophesy (As Long as They Submit)

Pentecostalism and Gender in Global Perspective

Andrea Hollingsworth and Melissa D. Browning

"The prevalence of women preachers is a fair measure of the spirituality of a church, a country, or an age. As the church grows more apostolic and more deeply spiritual, women preachers and workers abound in that church; as it grows more worldly and cold, the ministry of women is despised and gradually ceases altogether. It is of the nature of paganism to hate foreign people and to despise women, but the spirit of the gospel is exactly opposite."

—Church of God in Christ minister Charles E. Brown, 1939[1]

"A woman can most certainly function prophetically; she can be anointed by God to serve in delegated authority as a prophetess. But when she insists

---

1. "Women Preachers," *The Gospel Trumpet* (May 27, 1939) 5, quoted in Sanders, *Empowerment Ethics for a Liberated People*, 63–64.

161

upon recognition, when she manipulates or entirely disregards the male leadership in the church, when she calls herself a prophetess, beware."

—Neopentecostal author and pastor Francis Frangipane, 1989[2]

INTRODUCTION

In their book *Global Pentecostalism*, Donald E. Miller and Tetsunao Yamamori argue that in non-Western areas of the globe, Pentecostal Christians are increasingly involved in social engagement and that the message of the Holy Spirit's equal availability to all persons is a distinctive and "subversive" element of this trend.[3] Yet regarding women's leadership and authority, they note a stark contradiction: even though Pentecostalism preaches equal access to the gifts of the Spirit and has historically been "one of the more egalitarian movements within Christianity," in their four years of travels—which included visits to hundreds of Pentecostal congregations all over the world—the authors encountered only one church headed by a woman.[4]

This gender-based power disparity in the face of Pentecostalism's egalitarian roots and doctrines begs critical inquiry. What are the sources of the marked contrast between Pentecostalism's emancipatory rhetoric and its real-life restriction of women? How do racial and cultural factors shape Pentecostal women's experiences? How do the lived experiences of Pentecostal women in the global north compare with those of women in the global south?

This chapter takes up these and related questions by discussing ways in which Pentecostalism is paradoxically both limiting and liberating for women in their ongoing struggles for agency and equality in contexts of faith. We suggest that where Pentecostalism is *limiting*, the influences of European cultural, theological, and ecclesiastical traditions are largely at work. Most Pentecostal congregations in North America and the world over are deeply shaped by the European patriarchal standard of women's subordination to male headship.[5] But where Pentecostalism is *liberating*,

2. Frangipane, *Three Battlegrounds*, 128.

3. Miller and Yamamori, *Global Pentecostalism*, 4–5 and 177.

4. Ibid., 208.

5. Feminist theologians and theorists have argued that patriarchal presuppositions implicitly shape European theologies and ideologies. See, for example, Ruether, *Sexism*

the ingenuity and courage of Spirit-filled women and men is largely at work. In spite of structural hindrances, many Pentecostal beliefs and practices hold powerful resources which, when mined, enable Pentecostal women to transcend the limitations they face.

In keeping with the concentration of the present volume, our main focus in this chapter is on North American Pentecostalism. The two main sections that comprise the body of the essay treat limiting and liberating aspects of Pentecostalism for women. In each section we discuss two major groupings of Pentecostalism in the United States: first, the Neopentecostal (or Neocharismatic) movement, which contains mostly White, middle-to-upper-class adherents, and second, the Sanctified Church—which is comprised of primarily African American Christians of Holiness, Pentecostal, and apostolic traditions.[6] Since Pentecostalism in the United States can only be amply understood in global context, we also consider the experiences of Pentecostal women in the global south.[7] We close each section by spelling out theological correlates to Pentecostalism's limiting and liberating aspects in relation to women's agency and flourishing. To conclude, we offer the metaphor of "discerning the voice of the Spirit" as a hermeneutical framework for analyzing what constitutes women's flourishing within Pentecostalism.

---

and God-Talk and Lerner, *Creation of Patriarchy*. Global feminist/womanist theologies have critiqued and extended this argument by pointing out that not only patriarchy, but the sexism, racism, and imperialism present in European colonialism and missionary movements have lessened the safeguards present for women in pre-colonial societies. See, for example, Oduyoye, *Daughters of Anowa* and Dube, *Postcolonial Feminist Interpretation of the Bible*.

6. Pentecostalism in North America is vast, diverse, and continually changing, and space does not permit us to examine women's experiences in each group and subgroup. Choosing to err on the side of incisiveness of analysis rather than breadth of coverage, we limit our primary analysis to Neopentecostalism and the Sanctified Church. These represent two populous and prominent Pentecostal groups in North America which, while holding much in common, diverge from each other in significant ways on account of race-ethnicity factors and thus provide a helpful framework in which to analyze the multiple contextual dynamics that shape North American Pentecostal women's experiences.

7. In this essay we employ multiple geographical terms in order to speak as precisely as possible about Pentecostalism in global perspective. By "global north" and "global south" we refer to the (ever-shifting) socio-economic and political division that exists between countries that are wealthier and more developed (many of which are in North America and Europe) and poorer, developing countries (many of which are in Asia, Africa, Central America, and South America). By "North America" we mean the United States and Canada.

Pentecostal women in the global north and global south are united by several broad structural and theological trends that inform their experiences to greater or lesser degrees. However, these overall trends are always shaped by and expressed within the concrete particularities of each woman's sociocultural context. Therefore, while the chapter is organized along the lines of two broad generalities (limitation and liberation), in each section we attend to the diversity of Pentecostal beliefs and practices by illustrating our points with context-specific data.

PENTECOSTALISM AND THE LIMITATION OF WOMEN

The Pentecostal movement's beginnings at Azusa Street (1906–1909) and the years immediately following were marked to a large degree by egalitarianism.[8] However, Pentecostal women gradually lost their leadership platforms as the twentieth century progressed.[9] This gradual suppression of women was due largely to the ways in which European theological and ecclesial traditions shaped later Pentecostal communities. As they sought increased structure, organization, and respectability in the years following the movement's inception, Pentecostal churches looked to traditional, mostly-White Protestant denominations that upheld the patriarchal standard of women's subordination to male headship.[10] Institutionalization based on European-derived theologies and models of church organization made sexism such a constitutive part of Pentecostal church polity that today, most Pentecostal women seeking ordination and full clergy rights encounter insurmountable obstacles based on gender biases.

Although it began as an interracial movement, Pentecostalism in North America has also become increasingly racially segregated over the years. Therefore, as we examine the limitations contemporary North American Pentecostal women face, we distinguish between traditions that have evolved separately from each other along racial lines, and note ways in which inequalities related to gender and race are linked within traditions.

8. For an illuminating look at the stories of four early Pentecostal women preachers and denominational founders, see Alexander, *Limited Liberty*. For a discussion on reasons for the gradual decline of opportunities for women's leadership in Pentecostal churches over the course of the twentieth century, see Alexander, "Introduction," in *Philip's Daughters*, 1–15.

9. Sanders, *Empowerment Ethics*, 63.

10. Cf. Keller, Ruether, and Cantlon, *Encyclopedia of Women and Religion in North America*, 397–405.

Neopentecostalism

North American Neopentecostalism is a mostly-Caucasian, middle-class subculture within North American Pentecostalism that emerged out of Evangelicalism in the 1980s and is sometimes referred to as the "Neo-charismatic" or "Third Wave" movement.[11] Persons and revivals generally considered to be under the Neopentecostal umbrella include C. Peter Wagner, John Wimber, Joyce Meyer, Rick Joyner, the "Toronto Blessing," the "Brownsville Revival," and the "International House of Prayer" (IHOP) in Kansas City. Neopentecostals, who are at the "cutting edge" of the Pentecostal movement,[12] "generally have no clear connection to traditional Pentecostal and Charismatic Renewal churches, but nevertheless embrace charismatic forms of spiritual experience and worship."[13] Often Neopentecostal churches designate themselves as "nondenominational."

Within this movement there exist several influential leaders who warn of the dangers of women who do not remain underneath the "spiritual covering" of husbands and male pastors.[14] Francis Frangipane—pastor of a large church in Cedar Rapids, Iowa[15] and founder of his own parachurch organization and publishing company[16]—is known among Neopentecostals for his teachings on "the Jezebel spirit." Drawing on the narrative of King Ahab, Queen Jezebel, and the prophet Elijah as found in 1 and 2 Kings, Frangipane presents Jezebel as an evil spirit that manifests in our society as "obsessive sensuality," "unbridled witchcraft," and "hatred for male authority."[17] While Jezebel can defile anyone, this spirit "seeks the disposition of the feminine nature."[18] If a woman is under the

---

11. According to Miller and Yamamori, modern Neopentecostal churches and parachurch ministries are generally founded by independent, theologically unschooled, market-savvy individuals who "embrace the reality of the Holy Spirit but package the religion in a way that makes sense to culturally attuned teens and young adults, as well as upwardly mobile people who did not grow up in the Pentecostal tradition" (Miller and Yamamori, *Global Pentecostalism*, 27). For another description of Neopentecostal/Neocharismatic Christianity, see Studebaker, "Introduction," 1–10.

12. Miller and Yamamori, *Global Pentecostalism*, 27.

13. Studebaker, "Introduction," 3.

14. Bevere, *Under Cover.*

15. River of Life Ministries, www.riveroflife.org.

16. Ministries of Francis Frangipane, www.frangipane.org; Arrow Publications, arrowbookstore.frangipane.org.

17. Frangipane, *Three Battlegrounds*, 124.

18. Ibid., 128.

influence of Jezebel, she seeks recognition, challenges God-instituted male authority figures,[19] and becomes strong-willed at home, rendering her husband unable to serve as the "head of the household."[20]

For Frangipane, Jezebels must be violently opposed in the church; for, if left unchecked, they will destroy God's prophets. This warlike opposition to female power can also be observed in the writings of Steve Sampson, a Neopentecostal "prophet" and leader of his own parachurch organization based in Birmingham, Alabama. Commenting on King Jehu's slaughter of Jezebel (2 Kgs 9:33), Sampson writes: "He immediately commanded those eunuchs to throw her down. . . . Those who have been victims of this treacherous spirit must rise up in the power of God and be ruthless against it. Let God use you to be an instrument in throwing her down."[21] Sampson's violent interpretation of the slaughtering of Jezebel is meant to be allegorical; men (and women) are to wage "spiritual warfare" against Jezebel to "throw her down." However, in both Frangipane's and Sampson's writings, the line between the Jezebel of the Bible, the Jezebel of the spirit world, and the Jezebel in everyday homes and churches is fuzzy; a vague "she" is often employed as the object of the authors' vehement rhetoric. Moreover, in speaking of the kind of submission that is antithetical to the haughty Jezebel spirit, Sampson points out that at Calvary Jesus was in an "abusive situation" and "chose to entrust His life to the Father's hands, not taking things into His own hands."[22] Put in context, the implicit message here is that women are to follow Jesus's example by submitting to male authority, even in situations of abuse.

In some Neopentecostal communities, a woman who dares exercise agency by challenging male authority in home or church risks being labeled a "Jezebel," ostracized from the community, and possibly subjected to some form of abuse. Frangipane and Sampson's teachings on "the Jezebel spirit" send women a clear message: you are only Spirit-filled when you refuse to challenge or even question male authority. Despite the message of the Holy Spirit's freedom and empowerment so foundational to Pentecostal spirituality, the feminization of sin and evil through images such as the Jezebel serve to drastically restrict women's freedom. Since Neopentecostalism emerged out of conservative strands of mostly-white

19. Ibid., 127.

20. Ibid., 146.

21. Sampson, *Confronting Jezebel*, 20. Citations are to the Chosen Books edition.

22. Ibid., 60.

North American Evangelicalism (which in turn emerged out of Calvinist and Wesleyan strands) the limitation of women's agency that the Jezebel image represents may be interpreted as a vestige of patriarchal European religious ideologies.[23]

The Sanctified Church

In the United States the Jezebel motif has long functioned as a symbol of ways in which both sexism and racism collide in life-denying ways, and is therefore an apt entrée into our discussion of the experiences of African American Pentecostal women in the Sanctified tradition. It was in the antebellum Christian South that the biblical image of the Jezebel morphed into a dehumanizing stereotype applied to black women. In pre-abolition America, Jezebel gradually came to be equated with the "loose black woman" functioning as a justification of White men's sexual exploitation of female slaves.[24] According to Kelly Brown Douglas, today the Jezebel image "has come to symbolize an evil, scheming, and seductive woman" in popular thought, and has developed into the oppressive stereotype of Black woman as "welfare mother/queen."[25]

The Jezebel image is only one manner in which racism and sexism shape African American women's experiences of God, self, church, and family. Cheryl Townsend Gilkes argues that European forms of church organization that presume the subordination, marginalization, and "silence" of women have profoundly influenced African American religion in the United States, including Pentecostal traditions.[26]

To understand the import of Gilkes's thesis for our discussion, it is necessary to first consider specific ways in which Black Pentecostal women are "silenced" in their churches. The Church of God in Christ (COGIC) is

23. For a discussion on ways in which Reformed Theology's patriarchal ideologies influenced Pentecostalism through the charismatic movement, see Hyatt, "Your Sons and Your Daughters," 57–65.

24. Gilkes, "Liberated to Work Like Dogs!," 161–80. Originally published in *The Experience and Meaning of Work for Women*, ed. Nia Lane Chester and Hildy Grossman (Hillsdale, NJ: Erlbaum, 1990) 165–88.

25. Douglas, *Sexuality and the Black Church*, 36.

26. Gilkes, "Politics of 'Silence,' Dual-Sex Political Systems and Women's Traditions of Conflict," 92–117. Originally published as "'The Politics of 'Silence'" Dual-Sex Political Systems and Women's Traditions of Conflict in African American Religion," in *African American Christianity: Essays in History*, ed. Paul E. Johnson (Los Angeles: University of California Press, 1994) 80–110.

an African American Pentecostal denomination in the Sanctified Church tradition that has its origins in both the nineteenth-century Holiness movement and the twentieth-century Pentecostal movement. COGIC—currently the largest Pentecostal ecclesial body in North America[27]—has long endorsed the view that women are not called to "preach," though they may "teach." In addition, COGIC women are not allowed to serve the Lord's communion, though they may set the communion table, nor may they become ordained ministers in the denomination, though they may be "missionaries" and "evangelists."

As we will see in the next section, many Sanctified Church women have challenged and worked around these formal hindrances and have become indispensable leaders in their churches and communities. Regardless of such accomplishments, however, structural limitations barring Sanctified Church women from executive church leadership positions remain firmly in place.

Gilkes sets forth a persuasive argument that sexism in the Black church is largely due to the influence of Euro-American patriarchy, and that it is inextricably bound up with the dynamics of White racism in America. She shows that both West African religion and slave religion in the American South were rooted in an egalitarian "dual-sex politics" wherein men and women maintained equally valuable roles in the community. However, during Reconstruction and on into the twentieth century, sexist ecclesial politics gradually infiltrated Black religious communities, many of which were facing pressure from White church leaders to conform to European organizational standards. "In order for the free black church to conform to its counterpart in the dominant culture, it was necessary to suppress the freedom with which black church women had exercised their roles in the churches of the antebellum South."[28]

Despite this repression, Gilkes maintains that the egalitarian ethos so deeply woven into the fabric of Black religion has enabled African American women to make great strides in overcoming male domination in their churches. Furthermore, she suggests that this latent sense of gender equality has meant that "Black women have a sense of their own importance in their churches and communities that is perhaps unmatched in the sense of self-importance felt by women in other racial-ethnic com-

27. Butler, *Women in the Church of God in Christ*, 1–2.
28. Gilkes, "Politics of 'Silence,'" 102.

munities in the United States."[29] Gilkes's nuanced and compelling historical reading therefore carries with it an important implication for our present investigation; namely, that mostly-White Neopentecostal women, on account of their direct immersion in an ethnic and religious tradition more immediately shaped by patriarchal European theologies and ideologies, may have developed fewer resources to subvert gender oppression as compared to Pentecostal women within the Sanctified Church tradition.

Limitation and Pentecostalism in Global Perspective

Not only in North American contexts but also in the global south, Pentecostal women struggle for equality in their homes, churches, and communities. During the twentieth century as Pentecostal missionaries spread the Pentecostal gospel from North America to various parts of the globe, they frequently formed congregations modeled after the White Euro-American patriarchal standard. Often, previous European (and North American) Christian missionaries to these areas had already laid the groundwork for male-dominated church structures.[30]

Eurocentric patriarchy transmitted through missionary efforts has had a profound influence on African Pentecostal Christianity. Writing from a South African Pentecostal context, Sarojini Nadar points out that while it is technically possible for women to be ordained in her denomination (the Full Gospel Church of God in Southern Africa), in reality there are deep-seated structural hindrances that prevent women from occupying top ministerial positions.[31] Women's seminary education is restricted in ways that make it nearly impossible to graduate, and women are consistently relegated to tasks "such as helping with women's meetings, organizing the nursery, and making tea."[32]

Patriarchy also is deeply ingrained in Latin American Pentecostal belief systems. According to Lesley Gill, who has researched Pentecostals in Peru, "belief in the innate inferiority of women is so firmly entrenched

---

29. Gilkes, "Introduction: Community, Churchwork, Culture, and Crisis: Toward a Sociology of Indispensable Black Women," 1–12; quote p. 7; Cf. "Politics of 'Silence,'" 115.

30. Ghanaian theologian Mercy Oduyoye notes the tendency of African missionaries to neglect the integral roles women played in religion and religious ritual throughout the continent. See Oduyoye, *Beads and Strands*, 78–89.

31. Nadar, "On Being the Pentecostal Church," 354–67.

32. Ibid., 358.

in Pentecostal ideology that many believers view the subordination of women as part of the natural order."[33] In other parts of Latin America the situation is much the same.[34] Thus not only in North America but also in Africa, Central America, and South America, Pentecostal women find themselves up against rigid structural hindrances that inhibit the full expression of their gifts and abilities for leadership in their religious communities.

Theological Correlates: Dualism and Literalism

To better understand the limitations Pentecostal women face, we must examine theological correlates to patriarchal attitudes that serve to further the continuance of gender-based power imbalances in Pentecostal communities. One such correlate is the harsh dichotomization between "spiritual" and "worldly" realms, and the concurrent overvaluation of the former in relation to the latter. Here the prioritization of the experience of the otherworldly Spirit results in a clouding and underestimation of concrete everyday realities, including those related to gender-based prejudices.

In North America and elsewhere, the split between "the spiritual" and "the worldly" deeply affects Pentecostal women's experiences—often in disempowering ways.[35] For example, Neopentecostal author Lisa Bevere confesses that she has often thought to herself, "If only I were a man, things would be so much easier. If I were a man, I would not be judged so harshly. If I were a man, my voice would be heard."[36] While a holistic, integrated worldview might regard the challenging of gender-based discrimination as a holy endeavor, Bevere's response to being silenced by men is to retreat into more prayerful and spiritual realms in which she is assured that because "God is enough," she can gladly and peacefully self-

33. Gill, "Like a Veil to Cover Them," 708–21; quote p. 716.

34. Berryman, *Religion in the Megacity*, 89.

35. Several scholars have noted ways in which dualistic worldviews prove limiting for Pentecostal women in the global south. Cf. Attanasi, "Getting in Step with the Spirit," 193–208; Nadar, "On Being the Pentecostal Church;" Katy Tagenberg, "Culture, Social Relationships, and Self-Perceptions of Pentecostal Women," 229–42.

36. Bevere, *Fight Like a Girl*, 47. Lisa's husband John Bevere is author of the book *Under Cover* which argues (among other things) that if wives are not submitted to their husbands unconditionally, they forfeit God's spiritual protection. Cf. John Bevere, *Under Cover*, 201–4.

silence in humble submission to divinely ordained male authority.[37] Here spiritual dualism and deeply entrenched patriarchy combine to close off avenues that might lead to gender justice.

Another important theological correlate to Pentecostal bias against women is the tendency to shun critical, hermeneutically-nuanced approaches to Scripture. Some Pentecostals in North America and the world over read the Bible in a simplistic or literalistic fashion due to the belief that, if one is Spirit-filled and believes that the Bible is the Word of God, one cannot interpret the Bible incorrectly. While not necessarily and ubiquitously detrimental, this approach to Scripture becomes problematic in Pentecostal interpretations of Paul's admonitions regarding women (e.g., Eph 5:24; 1 Pet 2:18–19; 1 Tim 2:11). Nadar argues that in the Full Gospel Church of God in Southern Africa, the "most limiting notion of spirituality" for women is the pervasive ahistorical view of Scripture: "Since the Bible is perceived to be beyond history and therefore read in a literal way, inequality in the areas of ordination, divorce, dress codes, and issues of salary ensue."[38] The belief that the Holy Spirit is the interpreter of Scripture and one need not engage in exegetical research prevents readers from acknowledging the shaping role of context (literary and historical), and thus keeps them from embracing more critical and emancipatory interpretations that might emerge from such acknowledgement.[39] As seen above in Steve Sampson's interpretation of the Jezebel narrative in the Hebrew Bible, this singular reliance upon supposedly Spirit-led interpretive methods can serve to conceal and perpetuate deeply misogynistic and even abusive postures toward women. The limitations faced by Pentecostal women in North America and across the globe are real and serious. But there is another, more hopeful side to the story.

PENTECOSTALISM AND THE LIBERATION OF WOMEN

One suspects that something interesting is going on when the first few results gathered from an internet search using the terms, "Pentecostalism" and "Women" are Christian fundamentalist websites that condemn Pentecostalism as "the only religion founded by women who usurp their

---

37. Bevere, *Fight Like a Girl*, 47; cf. 60–61.

38. Nadar, "On Being the Pentecostal Church," 359.

39. Ibid., 360.

place"[40] and chide Pentecostal Christian men for "failing God" because "they didn't shut up a woman!"[41]

For all its limitations, Pentecostalism has earned a reputation for being one of the more freeing Christian traditions with respect to women's opportunities. Gilkes notes that in its early days COGIC grew as a result of women from Baptist and Methodist churches moving to the Sanctified Church to break free from restrictive environments in their own mainline traditions.[42] From its earliest days, Pentecostalism has been a Spirit-space where women could find voice. As Pentecostalism spread throughout the globe over the course of the twentieth and early twenty-first centuries, Spirit-filled women and men have creatively and courageously challenged gender-based oppression by tapping into the liberative undercurrents of their cultural traditions and Pentecostal faith itself.

Neopentecostalism

Above we showed that, like the conservative, mostly-White Evangelical traditions from which it emerged, North American Neopentecostalism has been deeply influenced by the belief that women are to be silent and submissive to male headship in homes and churches. But occasionally in contemporary Neopentecostal circles there are persons who directly challenge sexist ideals and practices precisely by drawing on Pentecostal values such as cultural critique, freedom in the Spirit, and deliverance from bondage.

Sheri and Danny Silk—Family Life Pastors at Bethel Church in Redding, California[43]—preach a message of women's authority and freedom that calls into question the supposition that women are inherently inferior or not fit to lead. In a sermon preached on June 3, 2007 at Bethel Church entitled "Powerful and Free: Women in the Church,"[44] Danny Silk begins by stating that women have been "banging their head on a glass

---

40. Sometimes Truth Makes Love Hurt. Online: www.bible.ca/tongues-women-usurp.htm.

41. Men Who Failed God: They Didn't Shut Up a Woman! Online: www.touchet1611.org/PentecostalWomen.html (accessed December 8, 2008).

42. Gilkes, "Role of Women in the Sanctified Church," 76–91. Originally published in *Journal of Religious Thought* 43 (1986) 24–41.

43. Bethel Church. Online: www.ibethel.com.

44. Danny and Sheri Silk, "Powerful and Free: Women in the Church," MP3 recording of sermon preached at Bethel Church, June 2007 (Redding, CA: ibethel.org).

ceiling in the church for centuries." While women occupy top leadership positions in economic, political, business, educational, scientific, technological, and artistic domains, the church consistently restricts their freedom and refuses to place them in executive leadership roles. Silk openly denounces this state of affairs even as he proclaims the approach of a new day of emancipation: "The closer a woman gets to the church, the more confined her existence in life becomes. The closer a woman gets to the church, the less free she is to happen." After a pause, "I believe that is about to change!"

In view of the fact that Christian arguments for women's inferiority normally hinge on appeals to Scripture, in his sermon, Silk aims to expose ways in which cultural biases can influence biblical interpretation in horrific ways. Drawing on the lessons of American history, he leads his audience through the biblical argument in favor of slavery. Congregants become increasingly quiet as he sets forth a perfectly well argued and scripturally grounded thesis that supports the dehumanization, commodification, and subjugation of human beings. "The scriptures are interpreted *through church culture!*" Silk insists. "What are you looking for? You will find what you're looking for in this book!"[45]

Having raised a measure of hermeneutical awareness, Silk declares that it is incumbent upon Christians to intentionally "look for" freedom in the Scriptures by prioritizing Jesus's message of good news to the poor, release for the captives, recovery of sight for the blind, and freedom for the oppressed (Luke 4:18). The message of the gospel is freedom and equality for all people, he proclaims (Gal 3:28). "Ladies, go out there and be powerful! Go out and occupy the highest positions available in the land! It is embarrassing that the church is bringing up the rear in the effort for [your] freedom!"

Pastor Sheri Silk (Danny's wife) closes the message by praying for those in the audience. She specifically addresses the Neopentecostal Jezebel doctrine, framing it in terms of spiritual release from evil and bondage: "The Lord showed me . . . some of you women have been spoken over, and . . . the word 'Jezebel' is always used to describe women when they have some power and they're trying to walk in it, and they're not 'under covering' or whatever . . . this 'Jezebel' thing is always on it, and I just want to break it off of you right now in Jesus's name! No more of that! No more residue!" By naming and "breaking" the destructive power of

45. Danny and Sheri Silk, "Powerful and Free: Women in the Church."

the Jezebel teaching, Silk communicates to women that God wants them to be free from the disempowering and damaging label of "Jezebel."

The Silks are contemporary North American Neopentecostals who employ a creative use of resources within their faith tradition to expose and denounce the oppressive sexist ideologies and simplistic hermeneutics that underlie many Pentecostal belief systems. While it appears that this mining of and capitalizing upon liberative traces in culture and faith for the sake of women's flourishing is a relatively new trend in Neopentecostal circles, it has been going on for a long time in the Sanctified Church. As Cheryl Sanders argues, when it comes to issues that matter to women, the Holiness tradition has a "usable past" that many mainline denominations lack.[46]

The Sanctified Church

We have observed ways in which Black North American religious traditions have been impacted by the European legacy of women's subordination and silencing. However, as Gilkes shows, the egalitarian undercurrents of West African religion have influenced and continue to shape the Black Pentecostal church today.[47] Furthermore, when compared to White religious traditions in America, the African American Sanctified Church has generally afforded greater degrees of freedom, power, and leadership opportunities for women.[48]

In her various essays on women in the Sanctified Church, Gilkes details ways in which Black Pentecostal women have, from the earliest days of the movement, functioned as the founders and backbones of Sanctified Churches across the United States. When it was time to plant a church, it was the women who came first "to preach a revival in order to organize a church, dig out the church (build the physical plant), and then send back to the headquarters for a pastor."[49] When a charismatic leader passed away, it was the women who provided the leadership, organization, and authority needed to enable churches to survive.[50] When they were barred

---

46. Here Sanders quotes Susie Cunningham Stanley to speak of a "usable past" within the Holiness tradition. See Sanders, "History of Women in the Pentecostal Movement." For original quote see, Morgan, "Stained-Glass Ceiling," 52.

47. Gilkes, "Politics of 'Silence,'" 108.

48. Gilkes, "Role of Women," 81–82.

49. Ibid., 84.

50. Ibid., 82.

from ordination, it was the women who "never let the matter [of gender discrimination] rest,"[51] and "managed to impose themselves on the political process of their churches through collective strategies."[52] When they were told they could not preach, it was the women who became influential evangelists, revivalists, educators, economic supporters, and agents of church order in their communities.[53] When the Civil Rights movement erupted, it was the women whose activism helped shape the "ethical and political culture of the black experience."[54] In sum, Gilkes argues, "If one looks beyond the pulpit, it is possible to view the Sanctified Church as a women's movement."[55]

Anthea Butler sheds further light on the nature of the liberative undercurrents in the Sanctified Church. In her book *Women in the Church of God in Christ*, Butler argues that the major reason behind COGIC women's remarkable level of empowerment—both now and throughout the denomination's history—has been the continual quest for spiritual empowerment through pursuit of the "sanctified life." The emphasis on personal holiness, realized through spiritual disciplines such as fasting, prayer, Scripture study, and other practices have "enabled COGIC women to attain status within the confines of the denomination without being ordained. Their pursuit of sanctification was not simply a quest for personal meaning; it was also a pursuit to be shared with the world."[56] According to Butler, COGIC women have made the most of their tradition's emphasis on personal sanctity. The pursuit and acquisition of deeper levels of holiness have gone along with the negotiation and attainment of greater levels of power, both in the church and in broader society.

A number of men in the Sanctified Church have also spoken out on behalf of women's equality. In 1939, COGIC pastor Charles E. Brown wrote, "As the church grows more apostolic and more deeply spiritual, women preachers and workers abound in that church; as it grows more worldly and cold, the ministry of women is despised and gradually ceases

---

51. Gilkes, "Together and in a Harness," 43–60; quote p. 48. Originally published in *Signs: Journal of Women in Culture and Society* 10 (1985) 678–99.

52. Gilkes, "Politics of 'Silence,'" 116.

53. Gilkes, "Role of Women," 83.

54. Ibid., 88.

55. Ibid., 84.

56. Butler, *Women in the Church of God in Christ*, 3.

altogether."[57] More recently, in a 1996 article pastor H. Carlyle Church Jr. denounces ways in which COGIC women "have had to accommodate to the church rules and the male leadership of the church"[58] and have for too long been "the marginalized people of the church."[59] Thus even amid the confines of an ecclesial framework formed along the lines of patriarchal Euro-American church organization, inspirited men and women in the Sanctified Church have attuned to and sounded forth the voice of the Spirit who calls persons into communities of freedom and equality.

Liberation and Pentecostalism in Global Perspective

With few exceptions the highest positions of church leadership in traditional or "mainline" churches remain inaccessible to Pentecostal women in the global south. However, as in North America, Spirit-filled individuals and communities creatively subvert patriarchal entrenchments by mining and appropriating emancipatory resources within their cultures and faith traditions.

Today on the African continent, it could be argued that the strongest form of Pentecostalism is not found in "mainline" missionary Pentecostal movements but in African Instituted Churches (AIC),[60] many of which were founded by or are led by women.[61] In these churches, the Spirit is seen to empower both men and women and is manifest through prayer, healing, and connecting the faithful with the person of Jesus Christ. Mercy Oduyoye notes that in charismatic AIC churches, women have au-

---

57. Brown, "Women Preachers," 5, quoted in Sanders, *Empowerment Ethics for a Liberated People*, 63–64.

58. Church, "Accommodation and Liberation of Women in the Church of God in Christ," 77.

59. Ibid., 88.

60. African Instituted Churches (also known as African Independent or Indigenous Churches) began as a reaction to "mainline" missionary movements, which were not inculturated within African cultures. There are two broad categories for AIC churches, Ethiopian-type and Spirit-type. Within the Spirit-type churches, which would be considered Pentecostal-charismatic in their worship style and understandings of the Holy Spirit, are the Zionist and Apostolic movements. For more on AIC churches and their relation to Pentecostalism, see Anderson, "Newer Pentecostal and Charismatic Churches," 167–84.

61. For examples of AIC churches founded by women, see Damaris Seleina Parsitau, "'Arise Oh Ye Daughters of Faith': Women, Pentecostalism and Public Culture in Kenya," Paper presented at the annual meeting of the *American Academy of Religion*, Religion and Politics Section, Chicago, IL, November 2, 2008.

thority and are "on a par with men in the matter of singing and praying."[62] And praying and singing are not inconsequential things;[63] rather than existing as ministries of support (as is common in some North American Pentecostal Churches), in charismatic AIC churches prayer and song are directly connected with ritual and healing. This connection resonates with African culture, as women have always been connected with religious and communal rituals of healing and reconciliation.[64]

In addition, the Pentecostal emphasis on spiritual transformation is an important resource for African Pentecostal women in their ongoing struggles for gender equality. Kenyan Theologian Damaris Seleina Parsitau argues that within Kenyan Pentecostal movements, "the conversion experience [leads to] a valuing of the self in relation to God and others that increases women's autonomy and undermines traditional patriarchy."[65] Parsitau goes on to argue that this sense of worth engendered by a powerful conversion experience "set[s] Pentecostals apart from much of the rest of the Evangelicals in Kenya."[66]

Evidence also suggests that Latin American Pentecostal women benefit from the liberative undertones in Pentecostal faith, regardless of formal restrictions on female executive leadership. In Colombia, Pentecostal conversion appears to provide women with a powerful moral voice in certain domestic situations in which they might otherwise be voiceless (such as a husband's infidelity or drunkenness).[67] In Chile, Pentecostal Spirit-ecstasy is a means by which Pentecostal women find the agency and energy to transform themselves and their communities.[68] And in Brazil, as Pentecostal women testify before the congregation, they are better able to cope with domestic conflict and to celebrate "the power of transforma-

---

62. Oduyoye, "Empowering Spirit of Religion," 254.

63. In her work on Pentecostal women in Ghana, Adelaide Boadi emphasizes the importance of prayer ministries and the ways in which they empower Pentecostal women. See Adelaide Boadi, "Pentecostal Theologies of the Global South and their Reshaping of Global Pentecostalism/Christianity: Some Insights from (West) Africa." Paper presented at the American Academy of Religion, History of Christianity Section and Pentecostal-Charismatic Movements Consultation, Chicago, IL, November 2, 2008.

64. Oduyoye, *Beads and Strands*, 84.

65. Parsitau, "Arise Oh Ye Daughters of Faith," 31.

66. Ibid., 31.

67. Brusco, "Reformation of Machismo," 143–58.

68. Sjorup, "Pentecostals: The Power of the Powerless," 16–25.

tion" in their lives. [69] Thus even in contexts of gender inequality, as Spirit-filled Latin American Pentecostal women utilize their voices in powerful and public ways through *glossolalia*, preaching, prophesying, singing, and testifying, they are increasingly empowered to express themselves freely, teach and lead others, develop a sense of personal agency, and effectively cope with suffering in their lives.[70]

Theological Correlates: Text and Voice

Within Christianity and more specifically within Pentecostalism, theological and spiritual resources exist for women to both subvert gender oppression and find empowerment. These resources, which offer enormous potential for women's freedom, must be continually retrieved and appropriately contextualized by Pentecostal communities around the globe. Text and voice (or, interpretation and proclamation) are two theological motifs that, when analyzed in light of Pentecostal beliefs and practices, can reveal ways in which key Pentecostal theological and spiritual resources have accompanied Pentecostal women's movement toward greater levels of freedom.

The book of Joel is the source of the crucial Pentecostal conviction that God's Spirit is poured out on "all flesh," and so offers an apt starting point for considering Pentecostal approaches to biblical texts. Joel the prophet of Israel declares, "Your sons and your daughters shall prophesy, your old men shall dream dreams, and your young men shall see visions. Even on the male and female slaves, in those days, I will pour out my spirit."[71] This text and its counterpart in the second chapter of Acts are central to Pentecostalism's core claim that the Spirit-baptism of Pentecost, which empowers people to bear witness to Jesus Christ, is available today for everyone without discrimination or restriction.

Yet, as we have seen, sexism has encroached upon the egalitarian Spirit-space that first emerged from original Pentecostal interpretations of these texts.[72] When texts that silence women are overemphasized and

---

69. Burdick, *Looking for God in Brazil*, 108.

70. Cf. Hollingsworth, "Spirit and Voice," 189–213.

71. Joel 2:28–29, NRSV.

72. As Janet Everts Powers has pointed out, many seem to have forgotten that Pentecostalism's doctrine of Spirit-baptism for all believers was first developed by nineteenth century Holiness teacher Phoebe Palmer as part of her argument for the ministry of women. Cf. Powers, "Pentecostalism 101," 133–51.

texts that give women voice are neglected or de-gendered, a hermeneutic of suspicion is necessary to restore balance. Pentecostalism, which tends to value transformation, cultural critique, and equality, is well equipped to reinterpret these texts with such a hermeneutic, and to thereby begin to clear away the stifling constraints of gender bias. A Pentecostal hermeneutic of suspicion is then followed by a Pentecostal hermeneutic of liberation, which prioritizes the gospel message of good news to the poor and freedom to the oppressed, and affirms the ubiquitousness and indiscrimination of the Spirit's outpouring upon and infilling of *all flesh*.

As Pentecostals draw on resources in their faith tradition to reinterpret texts in liberating ways, a new sense of vocality and spontaneity is found in worship. The sermon is no longer a place to disparage women as "Jezebel" but a place of liberative proclamation wherein women are set free from the "residue" of oppressive stereotypes.[73] Inspired voices from diverse members of the body of Christ prophetically announce that all are invited to participate in the work of the liberating Spirit.

The Pentecostal emphasis on vocality is manifested in different ways according to diverse cultural contexts. For example, in Nairobi, Kenya there is a charismatic church that is organized according to a typical patriarchal gender-hierarchy. When a man gets up to "testify," if he speaks for too long, the women will begin to sing—softly at first, but with gradually increasing volume. Usually the man will continue to speak over their singing, but eventually the voices of the women will drown him out and he will rejoin the congregation as the service continues with song. This is an example of inspirited voice-finding that creatively works within patriarchal structures to clear the way for greater levels of equality and mutuality in the church.[74]

Pentecostals believe that it is the liberating Spirit who must be present in each textual interpretation and every vocal utterance. But we will remain forever deaf to the infinitely complex harmonies (and dissonances) of the Spirit's voice if the daughters are denied space in which to attune to the text with their own ears, and to sound forth its intuitions with their own voices.

73. In using the word "residue" we quote Sheri Silk's prayer wherein she calls on women to get ride of the "residue" of the Jezebel stereotype. Cf. Danny and Sheri Silk, "Powerful and Free: Women in the Church."

74. One of the authors (Melissa Browning) learned this from a colleague while doing fieldwork at the Maryknoll Institute of African Studies in Nairobi, Kenya (April 2004).

CONCLUSION: DISCERNING THE VOICE OF THE SPIRIT

We began by noting the paradox that Pentecostalism can be both limiting and liberating for women. We continued by suggesting that where Pentecostalism is limiting, the influences of European cultural, theological, and ecclesiastical traditions are largely at work, but where it is liberating, the ingenuity and courage of Spirit-filled women and men is at play. We looked at the Neopentecostal tradition and the Sanctified Church tradition as two primary examples, and nuanced these with examples from global Pentecostalism, showing the ways women subvert yet still struggle with the oppressions present within their faith traditions. We ended by offering an interpretation of two important resources within the tradition—text and voice—and showed how these can be mined in ways that allow the liberative Spirit to breathe new life into Pentecostal communities.

In conclusion, we offer a metaphor that we hope can function as a theo-ethical, hermeneutical tool for analyzing what constitutes women's flourishing within the Pentecostal tradition. That metaphor is "discerning the voice of the Spirit." In relation to the issue of Pentecostalism and gender, discerning the voice of the Spirit involves asking in what ways particular Pentecostal beliefs or practices cultivate (or impede) women's flourishing. This question, by its very nature, belongs to a communal hermeneutic; discernment is an ongoing interpersonal interpretive event that asks women and men in Pentecostal churches around the world to learn together to recognize the sound of the Spirit's voice.

But how do communities come to recognize the Spirit's vocatives? How may we speak of the pitch, resonance, timbre, tone, or ring of the voice of the Spirit as it is experienced by and mediated through communities of Pentecostal disciples? We suggest that the sound of the Spirit's voice can be metaphorically described as both evocative and provocative. These adjectives, both derived from the root word "vocative," are generally used to describe persons, places, or things that call forth or rouse. They are inherently dynamic terms. As Pentecostal women and men experience the evocations and provocations of the voice of the liberating Spirit, they are increasingly brought into their vocation—that is, their call to embody God's love, truth, and justice in the world.

The evocative voice of the Spirit can be described as the calling-forth of hope in the midst of a world filled with degradation and oppression. It is the voice of comfort and consolation in deep suffering and subjugation. It is the voice of advocacy and instruction that reminds us of the truth of God's saving love in and for creation, and that speaks peace to our hearts (John 14:16, 26; 16:6–8). It is the promising sound of future resurrected life (2 Cor 1:21–22; 2 Cor 5:5) that empowers us to work responsibly and creatively for women's freedom and justice in the world. In Spirit-filled communities, the Spirit's evocations draw forth expressions of encouragement and solidarity. In communal Pentecostal worship, the evoking Spirit is experienced in and mediated through words of prophesy and tongues, songs of praise, expressions of wonder, testimonies of healing, and words of instruction. In sum, we can say that the evocative voice of the Spirit, which calls us toward renewed life, has a certain ring to it as it is discerned by the church. That ring—whether it is described as compassionate, comforting, healing, friendly, instructive, empowering, connecting, thankful, promising, delightful, or peaceful—is the ring of the summons toward hope.

The provocative voice of the Spirit can be described as the disturbing prophetic denunciation of injustice and domination. This voice convicts the world of sin (John 16:8) by interrupting systems of oppression (including gender oppression), and confronts those who are complicit in wrongdoing with a call toward repentance and conversion. It resounds in the cries of the poor, despised, and forgotten sufferers of the world—many of whom are Pentecostal women and their dependent children in the global south. The Spirit's provocative voice is experienced as Pentecostals critically consider the damaging implications of Jezebel doctrines and dualistic ontologies, and embrace a dual hermeneutic of suspicion and liberation that can uproot entrenched patriarchal interpretive norms. Although disquieting and disrupting, the Spirit's provocations rouse believers to take action—to be transformed into persons whose words and deeds overflow with divine justice. In sum, we can say that the provocative voice of the Spirit, which calls us toward converted life, has a certain resonance as discerned by the church. That resonance—whether it is described as disturbing, interrupting, confronting, crying, groaning, subverting, lamenting, demanding, upsetting, disquieting, or reproaching—is the resonance of the call toward transformation.

The evocative and provocative voice of the liberating Spirit must be discerned within inspired Pentecostal communities as they seek modes of belief and practice that promote fullness of life for women. In these inspirited spaces of mutual discovery and transformation, Pentecostal churches can listen again for the voice of the Spirit, declaring, "Your daughters shall prophesy."

BIBLIOGRAPHY

Alexander, Estrelda Y. "Introduction." In *Philip's Daughters: Women in Pentecostal-Charismatic Leadership*, edited by Estrelda Alexander and Amos Yong, 1–15. Princeton Theological Monograph Series 104. Eugene, OR: Pickwick Publications, 2009.

———. *Limited Liberty: The Legacy of Four Pentecostal Women Pioneers.* Cleveland: Pilgrim, 2008.

Anderson, Allan H. "The Newer Pentecostal and Charismatic Churches: The Shape of Future Christianity in Africa?" *Pneuma: The Journal of the Society for Pentecostal Studies* 24 (2002) 167–84.

Attanasi, Katy. "Getting in Step with the Spirit: Applying Pentecostal Commitments to HIV/AIDS in South Africa." *Political Theology* 9 (2008) 193–208.

Berryman, Phillip. *Religion in the Megacity: Catholic and Protestant Portraits from Latin America.* 1996. Reprinted, Eugene, OR: Wipf & Stock, 2006.

Bevere, John. *Under Cover.* Nashville: Nelson, 2001.

Bevere, Lisa. *Fight Like a Girl: The Power of Being a Woman.* New York: Faith Words, 2006.

Boadi, Adelaide. "Pentecostal Theologies of the Global South and their Reshaping of Global Pentecostalism/Christianity: Some Insights from (West) Africa." Paper presented at the American Academy of Religion 2008 Annual Conference, Chicago, IL, History of Christianity Section and Pentecostal-Charismatic Movements Consultation. November 2, 2008.

Brown, Charles E. "Women Preachers." *Gospel Trumpet*, May 27, 1939.

Brusco, Elizabeth. "The Reformation of Machismo: Asceticism and Masculinity among Colombian Evangelicals." In *Rethinking Protestantism in Latin America*, edited by Virginia Garrard-Burnett and David Stoll, 143–58. Philadelphia: Temple University Press, 1993.

Burdick, John. *Looking for God in Brazil: The Progressive Catholic Church in Urban Brazil's Religious Arena.* Berkeley: University of California Press, 1993.

Butler, Anthea D. *Women in the Church of God in Christ: Making a Sanctified World.* Chapel Hill: University of North Carolina Press, 2007.

Church, H. Carlyle, Jr. "The Accommodation and Liberation of Women in the Church of God in Christ." *Journal of Religious Thought* 52–53:2–1 (1996) 77–90.

Douglas, Kelly Brown. *Sexuality and the Black Church.* Maryknoll, NY: Orbis, 1999.

Dube, Musa W. *Postcolonial Feminist Interpretation of the Bible.* St. Louis: Chalice, 2000.

Frangipane, Francis. *The Three Battlegrounds.* Cedar Rapids, IA: Arrow, 2006.

Gilkes, Cheryl Townsend. "Introduction: Community, Churchwork, Culture, and Crisis: Toward a Sociology of Indispensable Black Women." In Cheryl Townsend Gilkes, *'If It Wasn't for the Women . . .': Black Women's Experience and Womanist Culture in Church and Community*, 1–12. Maryknoll, NY: Orbis, 2001.

———. "Liberated to Work Like Dogs! Labeling Black Women and Their Work." In Cheryl Townsend Gilkes, 'If It Wasn't for the Women . . .': Black Women's experience and Womanist Culture in Church and Community, 161–80. Maryknoll, NY: Orbis, 2001.

———. "The Politics of 'Silence,' Dual-Sex Political Systems and Women's Traditions of Conflict." In Cheryl Townsend Gilkes, 'If It Wasn't for the Women . . .': Black Women's experience and Womanist Culture in Church and Community, 92–117. Maryknoll, NY: Orbis, 2001.

———. "The Role of Women in the Sanctified Church." In Cheryl Townsend Gilkes, 'If It Wasn't for the Women . . .': Black Women's experience and Womanist Culture in Church and Community, 76–91. Maryknoll, NY: Orbis, 2001.

———. "Together and in a Harness: Women's Traditions in the Sanctified Church." In Cheryl Townsend Gilkes, 'If It Wasn't for the Women . . .': Black Women's Experience and Womanist Culture in Church and Community, 43–60. Maryknoll, NY: Orbis, 2001.

Gill, Lesley. "'Like a Veil to Cover Them': Women and the Pentecostal Movement in La Pas.'" American Ethnologist 17 (1990) 708–21.

Hollingsworth, Andrea. "Spirit and Voice: Toward a Feminist Pentecostal Pneumatology." Pneuma: The Journal of the Society of Pentecostal Studies 29 (2007) 189–213.

Hyatt, Susan. "Your Sons and Your Daughters: A Case for Pentecostal-Charismatic Egalitarianism with Special Emphasis on Kephale in the Pauline Literature." MA thesis, Oral Roberts University, 1993.

Keller, Rosemary Skinner, Rosemary Radford Ruether, and Marie Cantlon, editors. The Encyclopedia of Women and Religion in North America, vol. 1. Bloomington: Indiana University Press, 2006.

Lerner, Gerda. The Creation of Patriarchy. Oxford: Oxford University Press, 1986.

Miller, Donald E., and Tetsunao Yamamori. Global Pentecostalism: The New Face of Christian Social Engagement. Berkeley: University of California Press, 2007.

Morgan, Timothy C. "The Stained-Glass Ceiling." Christianity Today (May 16, 1994) 52.

Nadar, Sarojini. "On Being the Pentecostal Church: Pentecostal Women's Voices and Visions." The Ecumenical Review 56 (2004) 354–67.

Oduyoye, Mercy. Beads and Strands: Reflections of an African Woman on Christianity in Africa. Maryknoll, NY: Orbis, 2004.

———. Daughters Of Anowa: African Women and Patriarchy. Maryknoll, NY: Orbis, 1995.

———. "The Empowering Spirit of Religion." In Lift Every Voice: Constructing Christian Theologies from the Underside, edited by Susan Brooks Thistlethwaite and Mary Potter Engel, 251–64. Maryknoll, NY: Orbis, 1998.

Parsitau, Damaris Seleina. "'Arise Oh Ye Daughters of Faith': Women, Pentecostalism and Public Culture in Kenya." Paper presented at the annual meeting of the American Academy of Religion, Religion and Politics Section, Chicago, IL, November 2, 2008.

Powers, Janet Everts. "Pentecostalism 101: Your Daughters Shall Prophesy." In Philip's Daughters: Women in Pentecostal-Charismatic Leadership, edited by Estrelda Y. Alexander and Amos Yong, 133–51. Eugene, OR: Pickwick Publications, 2008.

Ruether, Rosemary Radford. Sexism and God-Talk. Boston: Beacon, 1983.

Sampson, Steve. Confronting Jezebel: Discerning and Defeating the Spirit of Control. Grand Rapids: Chosen, 2003.

Sanders, Cheryl J. Empowerment Ethics for a Liberated People: A Path to African American Social Transformation. Minneapolis: Fortress, 1995.

————. "History of Women in the Pentecostal Movement." 1996 PCCNA National Conference, Memphis, Tennessee. October 1, 1996. Reprinted online at: *Cyberjournal for Pentecostal-Charasmatic Research* 2 (1997). Online: www.pctii.org/cyberj.

Silk, Danny and Sheri. "Powerful and Free: Women in the Church." Sermon preached at Bethel Church in Redding, CA, 2007.

Sjorup, Lene. "Pentecostals: The Power of the Powerless." *Dialog: A Journal of Theology* 41 (2002) 16–25.

Studebaker, Steven M. "Introduction: The Dynamism of Pentecostal Theology." In *Defining Issues in Pentecostalism: Classical and Emergent*, edited by Steven M. Studebaker, 1–10. McMaster Theological Studies Series 1. Eugene, OR: Pickwick Publications, 2008.

Tagenberg, Katy. "Culture, Social Relationships and Self-Perceptions of Pentecostal Women," *International Social Work* 50 (2007) 229–42.

8

Acts 29 and Authority

*Towards a Pentecostal Feminist
Hermeneutic of Liberation*

Pamela M. S. Holmes

INTRODUCTION

I am an ordained Pentecostal pastor who has spent all of her life worshipping and ministering within a Canadian Pentecostal context.[1] I am also a feminist and systematic theologian currently employed by a theological college housed within a major Canadian university that explicitly emphasizes liberation and justice for all.[2] When Canadian Pentecostalism

1. As I have worshipped and ministered within Canadian Pentecostalism and have studied and interacted with American Pentecostalism, this project will only reference these two countries within the North American context. This is not to disparage a Mexican perspective. Rather, it is intended to acknowledge my limitations.

2. Ordained with the Canadian Fellowship of Christian Assemblies. Ministered in Edmonton, AB, Ottawa and Trenton, ON. Currently employed by Queen's Theological College, Queen's University to direct field Education and to teach in the areas of spirituality and theology.

emerged in the early years of the twentieth century, hermeneutical discussions were not an issue. Interpretation of Scripture was assumed to be one of the functions of the Spirit. Anyone, lay or clergy, male or female, young or old, white, brown or black, who had the "anointing"[3] could understand and preach or teach the Scriptures effectively. Academic or theological training was deemed unnecessary. Human efforts to understand the Bible were typically scorned as a second rate approach for those not Spirit filled.[4] As the movement grew and institutionalized, professional clergy became the norm. Pentecostal Bible Colleges were established for their training. However, the professors who staffed these colleges were often educated in various evangelical institutions. As a result they brought into the Pentecostal colleges an evangelical approach to the interpretation of Scripture with its more rational and academic basis.[5] In addition, within Canada, as the movement institutionalized and evangelicalized, men placed women in positions of submission to ordained male leaders within organized structures, following the accepted interpretation of Scripture within evangelicalism.[6]

In recent years, the question has been raised concerning a Pentecostal hermeneutic. Is there such a thing? If so, what would it look like? Although some Pentecostal scholars are content to adopt miscellaneous evangelical methodologies,[7] many Pentecostal scholars desire a hermeneutic that

3. "Anointing" refers to the idea of being Spirit anointed. Such an anointing is a drenching not just a sprinkle similar to the way the kings of Israel were anointed with oil in the Hebrew Scriptures by having oil poured over their heads indicating that they were the chosen ones. Oil is understood to symbolize the Spirit. Pentecostal people often anoint people with oil (small amounts, not a drenching) as a ritual symbolizing the Spirit's presence. However, God also anoints people with the Spirit indicating that they have some special gifts.

4. For a fuller discussion of this material, see Archer, *Pentecostal Hermeneutic for the Twenty-First Century*, 35ff.

5. For an example of a Pentecostal trained in and using evangelical methodology see Spittler, "Scripture and the Theological Enterprise," 85ff. and R. Johnston, "Pentecostalism and Theological Hermeneutics," 51–66.

6. See my "Ministering Women in the Pentecostal Assemblies of Canada," and "'Place' of Women in Pentecostal/Charismatic Ministry Since the Azusa Street Revival," 171–96.

7. Many Pentecostals, particularly in Europe and North America, utilize an evangelical hermeneutic as part of their assimilation into the broader evangelical movement. Such assimilation is considered positive in that evangelicalism is thought to provide a stabilizing factor for the diversity of interpretations possible within a Pentecostal hermeneutical approach while at the same time Pentecostalism revives and restores the emphasis on the Spirit within evangelicalism. Menzies, "Methodology of Pentecostal Theology," 1.

represents the ethos and traditions of Pentecostalism.[8] For the latter, the rationalistic approaches adopted by various evangelical groups are insufficient. Rather, a truly Pentecostal hermeneutic must specifically ask questions regarding both the Spirit's role and the community's role in the interpretative task. As John Christopher Thomas points out, "It is, indeed, one of the oddities of modern theological scholarship that both liberal and conservative approaches to Scripture have little or no appreciation for the work of the Holy Spirit in interpretation."[9] Issues have been raised and debated, but, at this point, no consensus has been raised as to what a Pentecostal hermeneutic should look like.

Except for a few yet significant efforts, within these discussions feminist insights are minimal or absent.[10] This is due to the fact that many Pentecostals tend to be indifferent to feminist thought (scholarship) or even anti feminist. Within Pentecostalism, feminism is viewed as a Western, middle class, academic, humanistic pursuit that neglects or dismisses movements of the Spirit. Therefore, when feminism is mentioned at all, it is typically in a derogatory fashion.[11] Rare are the suggestions that feminists have something positive to say.[12]

8. Not all Pentecostals consider the assimilation of Pentecostalism into evangelicalism positive. Therefore, they are engaged in developing a hermeneutic that takes seriously the distinctiveness of the Pentecostal movement particularly in the early years of its emergence before it became enmeshed in evangelicalism. See McLean, "Towards a Pentecostal Hermeneutic," 35–56.

9. Thomas, "Women, Pentecostals and the Bible," 42.

10. The work of Amos Yong in *Spirit-Word-Community: Theological Hermeneutics in Trinitarian Perspective* is a refreshing exception to this rule in that he at least attempts to engage some feminist material. Additionally, Estrelda Alexander brings a welcome biblical womanist perspective to her scholarly endeavours. And, finally, Hollingsworth's article in *Pneuma*, "Spirit and Voice: Towards a Feminist Pentecostal Pneumatology," 189–213, is an important first for that periodical.

11. For example, speaking of "*sensus plenior*, or fuller meaning" of Scripture Gordon Anderson states that the "obvious and dangerous circularity of this approach can [be] seen by considering the hermeneutics and theology of a radically biased methodology, a radical feminist or homosexual interpretation, for example. The proper criticism of such a method is to assert that the interpreter never got a sound theology in place to begin with, resulting in a constant rereading of theological biases back on to the text." Anderson, "Pentecostal Hermeneutics," 8. Claiming that the concern to develop a Pentecostal hermeneutic is "misguided," Richard Israel explains that such a hermeneutic would be "motivated either by an ideology (as some Marxist and Feminist hermeneutics are) or an epistemology of the Spirit." Israel, Albrecht, and McNally, "Pentecostals and Hermeneutics," A8–9.

12. I did find one brave soul, Timothy B. Cargal, who dared suggest that feminists might be illumined by the Spirit. Cargal, "Beyond the Fundamentalist-Modernist Controversy," 22.

It is my intention to insert feminist thinking into these fledgling discussions regarding a Pentecostal hermeneutic before the discussion solidifies. I shall begin by first briefly examining the hermeneutical approaches of two feminists—Elisabeth Schüssler Fiorenza and Phyllis Trible —and then compare their thinking with ongoing Pentecostal discussions. As this has not been attempted before, I shall have to draw on my own insights and experience as an ordained Pentecostal clergyperson who was raised within the Canadian Pentecostal branch of the Christian church and continues to worship and minister in that context.

SCHÜSSLER FIORENZA, TRIBLE, AND PENTECOSTALISM COMPARED

Positioning her work within the context of the liberation movement, feminist studies, and theological academia, Elisabeth Schüssler Fiorenza has formulated a hermeneutical approach that uses a variety of insights and methods.[13] It is her intention to recast biblical studies in rhetorical terms in the hopes of displacing supposed objective and non-political approaches presently gaining ground in biblical women's studies.[14]

13. These other methods include the "revisionist" strategy, an apologetic approach often used by evangelical women that claims that the Bible authorizes the equal rights and liberation of women and others; the "text and translation" approach which focuses on the androcentric character of biblical texts and explores a proper translation; an "imaginative identification" approach which highlights personal identification and biblical imagination focusing on women characters in biblical stories whether explicitly mentioned or not; the "women as authors and biblical interpreters" approach which attempts to recover women's writings; the "historical interpretation" strategy which focuses on the historical studies of biblical, Jewish, Greek, or Roman women; the "sociocultural reconstruction" strategy developed in Schüssler Fiorenza's *In Memory of Her* that attempts to reconceptualize the task of early Christian historiography as consciously constructive narrative reflecting power relationships and struggles rather than as history in a positivist sense as what really happened; the "ideological inscription" approach, whether formalist, reader-response oriented, structuralist, or narratological, which demonstrate how androcentric texts construct the politics of gender and feminine representation; the "women as subjects of interpretation" approach that highlights women as reading and thinking subjects within an androcentric symbol-system encouraging them to identify with what is culturally normative, that is "male;" and the "sociopolitical location" strategy whose advocates often speak from the social location of double or triple marginalization and insist on articulating the sociopolitical, global-cultural, and pluralistic religious locations and contexts of biblical readings in order to establish that an "interested" reading of biblical texts is not less scholarly or less historically adequate than a so-called value neutral one. Schüssler Fiorenza, *But She Said*, 24–38.

14. Schüssler Fiorenza, *But She Said*, 24–38.

Schüssler Fiorenza's "critical feminist interpretation for liberation," as she calls it, utilizes a rhetorical reading approach. First, in this strategy any grammatically masculine language of the Bible is assumed to be conventional generic language unless examination indicates that it is functioning in a gender-specific fashion. Second, explicitly gendered language and images are translated as conventional language that must be understood both in its traditional and present-day contexts. Third, the interlocking systems of domination that Schüssler Fiorenza labels kyriarchy, including racism, sexism, classism, and colonialism, are recognized.[15] Schüssler Fiorenza's approach attempts "to exploit the contradictions and silences inscribed in the text" not only to reconstruct the worldview of the biblical text but also the social and historical situations behind that worldview.[16]

Phyllis Trible also uses a rhetorical approach to biblical interpretation. For Trible the voice of God can be found within the biblical text through the use of metaphor and literary criticism.[17] In order to find out the intention of God the biblical exegete must listen to and interpret the text as accurately as possible. Therefore, Trible chooses as her interpretative method rhetorical criticism that she claims concentrates on the movement of the text rather than on extrinsic historical factors. Classical rhetoric, literary critical theory, literary study of the Bible and form criticism all form the background for rhetorical criticism.[18] Trible also adds psychoanalytic thought, existentialism, philosophical hermeneutics and Zen Buddhism to her rhetorical and literary criticism.[19]

Rhetorical criticism is a text centered literary method that insists upon the organic unity of form and content. A "proper articulation of form-content yields proper articulation of meaning" according to Trible.[20] Trible insists on recognizing the texts' own concern for language and speech. Therefore, she pays particular attention to two hermeneutical issues. First, insisting that the "hermeneutical clue is the clue within the

15. Kyriarchy she defines as the "rule of the emperor/master/lord/father/husband over his subordinates" indicating that "not all men dominate and exploit all women without difference." Schüssler Fiorenza, *Jesus: Miriam's Child, Sophia's Prophet*, 14 and *But She Said*, 43.

16. Schüssler Fiorenza, *But She Said*, 39–40.

17. Trible, "Eve and Miriam," 6.

18. Trible, *Rhetorical Criticism*, 5.

19. Trible, *God and the Rhetoric of Sexuality*, xvii.

20. Trible, "Editor's Preface," in *Rhetorical Criticism: Context, Method, and the Book of Jonah*, vii–viii.

text," she attempts to demonstrate how stylistic and rhetorical features of the Hebrew language illuminate the text's interpretations.[21] As far as Trible is concerned, this "inner hermeneutic of Scripture" is the clue to understanding.[22] Second, Trible is concerned about the use of inclusive language in translation.[23]

Using an explicitly feminist hermeneutic which defines feminism not as a narrow focus on women but rather as a critique of culture in light of misogyny, Trible sets about to redeem the Bible from "bondage to patriarchy" convinced that "redemption is already at work in the text."[24] As she explains, "to bring together the self-critique that operates in the Bible with the concerns of feminism is to shape an interpretation that makes a difference for all of us—an interpretation that begins with suspicion and becomes subversion, but subversion for the sake of redemption, for the sake of healing, wholeness and well-being."[25]

In her approach, Trible personifies the text using the metaphor of a "pilgrim." She notes that, "the bible is a pilgrim wandering through history to merge past and present . . . engaging in new settings, and ever-refusing to be locked in the box of the past. Every generation or group that engages the text comes to it from certain perspectives not adopted by others, with certain questions not asked by others, and with certain issues not raised by others."[26] Exegetes then become "pilgrims" themselves, partners in the pilgrimage of the text through the centuries. By appealing to the intrinsic meaning of the text itself, imagery that, on its own, may appear either straightforwardly neutral or sexist is defined by its placement and working in a text. As a result, Trible's literary analysis not only focuses feminists' attention on the inseparability of form and content in terms of the work of the text itself but also offers a corrective to the his-

---

21. Trible, *God and the Rhetoric of Sexuality*, 1–5.

22. Ibid.

23. Ibid., xvii.

24. As a critique of culture and Christianity, Trible considers feminism to be a prophetic movement that examines the status quo, pronounces judgement, and calls for repentance. As such, it involves Scripture in various ways. It may bring to light misogynist texts that promote the assumed inferiority, subordination, and abuse of women in ancient Israel and the early church. It may discern within the Bible itself critiques of patriarchy. Or, it may combine the two as Trible's own work does. Trible, *Texts of Terror*, 3.

25. Trible, *Feminist Approaches to the Bible*, 8.

26. Ibid., 9.

torical searches for meaning that often attempt thematic unification of biblical books or of scripture as a whole.[27]

Classical Pentecostals are convinced that the whole Bible, as the inspired word of God, is a reliable revelation of God stating the truths the Spirit intends to convey.[28] While being both the Word of God and the words of men and women in history it holds an authoritative position as the basic rule of faith and practice that supplies the "corrective and interpretative authority for all religious experience," maintains Scott Ellington. As he explains, "What the Bible says" is considered identical with "what God says." He then follows up with the point that stemming from this conviction, the central question in biblical interpretation is, "How do we live a Christian life according to the Scriptures?"[29]

Pentecostals insist that the Spirit's involvement is a major factor in understanding the Bible as the Word of God; there is an importance to the biblical text that goes beyond its function as a work of literature that can only be perceived with the aid of the Spirit. The assumption is that the Bible can be read by a non-Christian without anything of spiritual value being gained. Non-believers are thought to be blind to the reality of God's revelation in Scripture unless the Spirit opens their eyes. It is only when the Spirit illumines the Bible that it becomes spiritually meaningful for readers. In this sense, the language and grammatical aspects of the text are not what makes the writings the Word of God but God's use of them. As the Word of God, the Spirit illumined Scriptures are understood to possess transformative power and authority.[30] This strong emphasis on

27. Such a corrective could be extended to a similar practice of feminist theologians, which separates form and content in the historical recovery and appropriation of past meanings. For example, the retrieval of an early Christian egalitarian discipleship (Schüssler Fiorenza) or of the liberating prophet (Rosemary Radford Ruether) are ideas that may have become separated from their original literary context. The conclusion that male imagery for God automatically means the deification of man (Mary Daly) results from the assumption that certain ideas are always patriarchal or sexist. In contrast, the conclusion that female imagery for God (Elizabeth Johnson) is always affirming and liberating results from similar assumptions. Examining these imageries within their literary context could prove otherwise. Trible's approach highlights these assumptions.

28. Arrington, "Use of the Bible by Pentecostals," 101.

29. "Pentecostals approach the Bible with very practical questions, expecting to encounter in the Scripture the very words of God speaking directly to their needs and guiding them in the transformation that the Holy Spirit is actively carrying on in their lives." Ellington, "Pentecostalism and the Authority of Scripture," 21–22.

30. Many Pentecostals in the Canadian churches within which I have ministered and worshipped, following the lead of conservative Fundamentalists, would strongly

the Holy Spirit in interpreting the Bible is derived by Pentecostals from the Scriptures themselves that emphasize the role of the Spirit in revealing God and God's will.[31]

Pentecostals also stress the role of the Spirit in inspiring both the original writers and current readers. While a distinction is made between the original Spirit *inspired* authors—resulting in the text being granted ultimate authority—and the current Spirit *illuminated* interpreter—resulting in a less binding appropriation—"within a Pentecostal setting these 'illuminated' meanings exercise far more power over Pentecostal believers since they are perceived as carrying divine sanction and authority."[32] As it is the same Spirit guiding and assisting both the original authors and the modern interpreters, the gap between past and present is assumed to be bridged.[33]

Expressions such as "the Spirit showed me" or "the Holy Spirit revealed to me" are commonly heard from both the pulpit and the pew regarding the interpretation and possible application of Scripture. As a result, multiple meanings of the biblical text are understood to apply to various situations as they arise—situations that never occurred to the original author(s).

Trible's approach reinterprets texts in such a way that biblical texts are open to multiple interpretations that may be "teased out." [34] Such an approach acknowledges the diversity of Scripture filled with various voices and points of view. A single text can appear "in different versions with different functions in different contexts. Through application, it confesses,

---

react to what I have just stated and insist that the words of the Bible are God's words. However, if pressed to think about their own practice and position, they would admit that what I have outlined is correct. The understanding is that there is meaning in the Bible that is not tied up with its status as a work of literature and, in distinction from conservative Fundamentalist, not even historical facts. Not everything that is meaningful is historically true.

31. For examples, such passages as John 14:26 and 16:13; 1 Cor 2:10ff.

32. Cargal, "Beyond the Fundamentalist-Modernist Controversy," 10–12.

33. Stronstad, "Pentecostalism, Experiential Presuppositions and Hermeneutics."

34. As Trible explains, "the Bible itself comes to us full of struggles, battles, contradictions and problems. It refuses to be the captive of any one group or perspective. . . . Even the winners who prevail in Scripture—those whose points of view tried to stamp out other points of view—bear witness to the stories of the losers. And in the very process of trying to discredit these stories, the winners gave them canonical status." Trible, *Feminist Approaches to the Bible*, 89.

challenges, comforts, and condemns. What it says on one occasion, it denies on another. Thus scripture in itself yields multiple interpretations of itself." [35] Obviously, the potential for abuse exists in such practices. However, acknowledging that there are several interpretations of a text is not the same as saying that all interpretations are correct. A text can be misinterpreted.[36]

Regardless, within Pentecostalism restricting the text's meaning to what the original authors thought is considered too restrictive. As one Pentecostal article explains, "*understanding* involves the creative capacity of the interpreter to open up new insights which transcend the time-bound situation of the original author and the original audience. It is at this juncture where creative transcendence is needed, where the Spirit may indeed teach us and lead us into all truth."[37] Interpretation is thought to be both an art and a technique that involves the Word and the Spirit. Both faithfulness to the text, which provides a relatively objective control, and inspired creativity, which allows God's Spirit to move, are important in the interpretative process.

Along with the Spirit, Pentecostals also place a great deal of emphasis on experience in the interpretation of Scripture. However, the emphasis is on the human experience of God as Spirit and not specifically on women's experience. Pentecostalism is an experientially expressed spirituality.[38] Pentecostals believe that they experience the same Spirit who is at work in this world since creation and empowering them to live out the ramifications of that encounter.[39] Pentecostals are constantly seeking to discern and experience the Spirit's presence.

35. Trible, *God and the Rhetoric of Sexuality*, 1–5.

36. Israel, Albrecht, and McNally, "Pentecostals and Hermeneutics," 145.

37. Ibid.

38. Pentecostals emphasize experience as a way of interacting with God as Spirit rather than the rational, liturgical or sacramental expressions of human/divine interaction emphasized in many other branches of the Christian Church. Although "experience" in this sense is difficult to define, one suggestion has been to view it as "one's interpretation of the reality and value of a phenomenological encounter based on one's pattern of beliefs about the world." Cargal, "Beyond the Fundamentalist-Modernist Controversy," 15 n. 43.

39. As the Spirit is understood to be God, wherever the Spirit is to be found, there is God. The Spirit is assumed to reveal Christ, the Self-revelation of God. As the immediate Person of God experienced by creation, the Spirit serves as a primary lens through which all life experiences are interpreted. As Ellington explains, "A faith which in no way attempts to express a personal encounter with a living God is deeply suspect for many Pentecostals, simply because it is a foreign concept. God is intensely interested in

When it comes to their relationship with Scripture, Pentecostals tend to move from their experience of God to the Bible.[40] If their experiences are not supported by the Pentecostal community's interpretation of Scripture (which, in distinction to much of the rest of Christianity until recently, takes seriously the narratives of the Bible such as Luke–Acts) they are suspect.[41] Such an approach has advantages in that the authority of Scripture is not founded on a "bedrock of doctrine," but rather doctrine rests on the experience of encountering God as Spirit. Doctrines are *descriptive* of lived experience rather than generative. Therefore these doctrinal positions, various practices, and even unexamined assumptions about how things should be, such as the patriarchy evident in Canadian Pentecostalism, can be challenged and corrected without doing damage to the core of Pentecostal faith—i.e., an encounter with God as Spirit and the outworking of that encounter. Pentecostals are not likely to enter into a "fight to the death" in defence of rational doctrinal statements and the potential is there to think critically about their practices and positions in light of lived experience even as these experiences are informed by their descriptive doctrines.[42]

Elisabeth Schüssler Fiorenza explicitly dismisses the idea of the authority of Scripture insisting that "biblical texts and interpretations must be seen as rhetorical discourses . . . perspectival, historically and socially conditioned, 'embodied' discourses."[43] Therefore, in her opinion,

---

relationship with his creation and Pentecostals understand God's invitation to relationship in very literal and concrete terms and have testimonies of encounters with God which form the basis of their faith and theology" (Ellington, "Pentecostalism and the Authority of Scripture," 20).

40. Hermeneutically, a common criticism of Pentecostals, particularly by evangelicals, is that they "eisegete their experience into the text." However, many Pentecostals feel no need to defend this approach. See for example Stronstad, "Pentecostal Experience and Hermeneutics," 16–26.

41. Archer, "Pentecostal Hermeneutics," 77–78 quoting McLean, "Toward a Pentecostal Hermeneutic," 38.

42. The exception, of course, is those Pentecostal groups that have aligned themselves with the more fundamentalistic evangelicals. As well, this is not to suggest that doctrines are unimportant to Pentecostals. Doctrines are very important. However "Pentecostals base their faith *first* on the God that they have met and know in relationship, and only then do they attempt, with greater or lesser success, to articulate their experiences in normative, doctrinal ways . . . the basic fodder of the doctrinal process within Pentecostalism is the experience of the community of faith." Ellington, "Pentecostalism and the Authority of Scripture," 17–18.

43. Schüssler Fiorenza, *But She Said*, 11.

the biblical texts are making relative rather than absolute truth claims. Her hermeneutic involves the idea of "inspiration as the divine breath of life invigorating all and everyone" rather than that of a divine reality or truth revealed in canonical texts. Authority is not located in the Bible but rather derives from the "experience of God's liberating presence in today's struggles to end patriarchal domination."[44] She cautions that because both oppressed and oppressors are "manifestations of dehumanization," the methodological starting point for hermeneutics cannot be a "commonsense" type of experience alone. Rather experience must be critically reflected upon and analyzed.[45]

She suggests viewing the Bible as a "historical prototype" rather than a "mythic archetype." As a "historical prototype" the Bible can be reclaimed as an "experiential enabling authority" for the new community she calls "women church" rather than as a normative document for patriarchal repression.[46] Women church she defines as "the congress of full decision-making citizens" and "the movement of self-identified women and women-identified men in biblical religion."[47] Viewing the Bible as a historical prototype assists in the process of redirecting the locus of revelation from the Bible or the patriarchal church to women church thereby authorizing those who have been viewed as "other."[48]

As all are believed to be "enlivened and empowered by the life-giving breath of Sophia-Spirit," the authority involved in inspiration is not restricted to a select few but given to the whole women church.[49] Therefore, biblical texts do not have to be accepted and obeyed. Instead "discerning the spirits," a critical process that she claims occurs in the midst of women church as a deliberative rhetorical practice, is required.

44. Ibid., 156.

45. Schüssler Fiorenza, *Sharing Her Word*, 82.

46. Schüssler Fiorenza, "Will to Choose or to Reject," 136.

47. Schüssler Fiorenza, *Sharing Her Word*, 112 and *Bread Not Stone*, xiv.

48. As she describes it, her concept of women church is not a "site of competing confession discourses," but a "rhetorical space from where to assert women's theological authority to determine the interpretation of Christian scripture, tradition, theology, and community" that neither neglects "biblical interpretation as the site of competing discursive practices" nor ignores that "the Bible is a cacophony of interested historical voices and a field of rhetorical struggles in which questions of truth and meaning are being negotiated." Schüssler Fiorenza, *But She Said*, 150–52.

49. Schüssler Fiorenza, *But She Said*, 156.

The central theological question then becomes "what kind of G-d[50] Christians believe in and proclaim" rather than "whether G-d exists."[51]

According to Schüssler Fiorenza, within women church, feminist discourses seek "to persuade the democratic assembly and to adjudicate arguments in order to make decisions for the sake of everyone's welfare."[52] These feminist rhetorical discourses include, first of all, the "rhetorics of liberation" and make "visible the oppressive structures and power relations within biblical texts" while questioning "the 'common-sense' assumptions in biblical interpretation that naturalize, theologize, and mystify kyriarchal relations of subordination, exploitation, and oppression." Second, the "rhetorics of differences (not just of difference)" examines the "biblical texts from different subject-locations, amplifying and valorising not only 'feminine' identity strategies but also those elaborated on the basis of race, culture, class, and religion." Third, the "rhetorics of equality does not understand biblical truth and revelation as given but rather as constituted in and through the practices of the 'democratic' vision of the *basileia* which spells well-being for all." Fourth, the "rhetorics of vision" carefully studies the biblical texts looking for "religious visions that foster equality, justice, and the logic of the *ekklesia* rather than that of patriarchal domination."[53]

Within Canadian and American Pentecostalism, the community also plays an important role in the interpretation of biblical texts. It is within the Pentecostal worshipping community that experiences are evaluated as various individuals tell their stories of life transforming encounters with God.[54] Whether in their testimony times, preaching, teaching, or

---

50 In recognition that language is "not capable of adequately expressing the Divine," Schüssler Fiorenza first used this manner of spelling God and later G*d. Schüssler Fiorenza, "Cartography of Struggle," 10 n. 13. In her book, *Jesus: Miriam's Child, Sophia's Prophet: Critical Issues in Feminist Christology*, Schüssler Fiorenza "switched from the orthodox Jewish writing of G-d which she had adopted in *But She Said* and *Discipleship of Equals* in order to indicate the brokenness and inadequacy of human language to name the Divine to this spelling of G*d, which seeks to avoid the conservative malestream association which the writing of G-d has for Jewish feminists." Schüssler Fiorenza, "Introduction: Feminist Liberation Theology as Critical Sophialogy," xxxv n. 4.

51. Schüssler Fiorenza, *But She Said*, 156.

52. Ibid., 131.

53. Ibid., 131–32.

54. As Thomas remarks, "Given the community orientation of Pentecostalism on the one hand and the excesses of a somewhat rampant individualism among interpreters generally (both liberal and conservative) on the other hand, reflection on the place

chorus singing, Pentecostals are constantly telling and retelling the stories about "what God is doing in their lives." If those stories do not line up with what is understood to be scriptural teaching on the matter, correction can be made. Because the practice is decidedly oral and experiential, all can participate. No special knowledge is required. Each member of the community is invited and encouraged to share testimonies of his or her experiences of God and to offer interpretations of what those experiences mean in light of Scripture so that the others may add an "amen" to the accounts. Speaking and interpreting Scripture is not the sole privilege of the preacher or some presiding ordained person. The opportunity and the responsibility to participate are expected from all during different parts of a service. If a problem arises with a seriously questionable testimony, the person presiding (lay or ordained) is expected to intervene. There is authority granted to the presiding person in this sense. However this rarely ever occurs and, in my experience, when it does occur it is only for serious error.[55] The tendency is to allow various opinions to prevail. The result of this approach is that "authority is not imposed from 'above' by church leadership, but the Bible is experienced as authoritative as the Holy Spirit is found to be at work in and through Scripture in the lives

of the community in the hermeneutical process would appear to be a natural next step in the development of a Pentecostal hermeneutics" (Thomas, "Women, Pentecostals, and the Bible," 42).

55. It is commonly understood that "grace" is exercised in situations where people's interpretation of their experiences and Scripture are questionable. Any questioning or correcting is often done informally and privately by both members of the congregation and the leaders so as not to discourage people from participating. However, there are rare occasions when public rebukes are mounted. I have only witnessed a presiding person intervene on two occasions during my lifetime. In one case, an older, lay leader with a "holiness" background was insisting that if you were a Spirit-filled Christian you could not sin. As everyone in the room seemed to indicate that they were Spirit-filled Christians, but still did things that they knew were wrong, this lay leader then went on to insist that they were not Spirit-filled Christians. The presiding person gently pointed out that that although that may be the opinion of "holiness" people, many other Spirit-filled Christians "agreed to disagree" with the opinion. A second instance was much more serious. An ordained person sitting with the congregation stood up and gave a scathing condemnation of the whole group due to their lack of faith in believing in God to perform the miracles necessary to gain material prosperity (commonly known as "Word of Faith" or "Name it and Claim it" or "Prosperity" teaching). The presiding person, at first gently, and then forcefully, told the person speaking to be quiet and sit down. The presiding person then read from Romans 8, "There is now, therefore, no condemnation." The ordained person who had been so condemning, to his credit, accepted the rebuke and humbly apologized to the congregation.

of each member of the church community."[56] Biblical authority therefore involves the participation of the community.[57]

This communal aspect of Pentecostalism at first appears to be similar to what Schüssler Fiorenza is advocating when she places her hermeneutical approach within the context of women church. I would certainly agree with her that we need creative communities. That is, communities that celebrate the participation of all in envisioning new ways of being, contexts that allow everyone to dream dreams and have visions, congregations that enact and demonstrate the "now but not yet" reality of what we are meant to be and empower each other to live in that reality. Institutionalized denominations may call this confusion and chaos; Pentecostals, and perhaps also some feminists, call it "having church." However, while in principle this communal aspect should be a strength of the Pentecostal movement, in practice not all voices are being equally heard or heeded. A problem exists.

Canadian and American Pentecostal interpretative practices, after the first couple of decades of the emergence of the movement, have generally borrowed from American conservative evangelicals. Within conservative evangelicalism, the Bible is considered the final authority in matters of faith and practice and in fundamentalist groups it is considered inerrant. This often stood in stark contrast to the earlier emphasis within the Pentecostal movement on the Spirit's authority to inspire, empower, and guide. This conflict is strikingly noticeable as it has played out within the lives of women within the movement. Whereas in the early years women were actively involved in all areas of ministry following the Spirit's leading, as the movement institutionalized and evangelicalized women were placed in positions of submission to male leaders within organized structures following the accepted interpretation of Scripture within evangelicalism. Now when women are mentioned in hermeneutical discussions it is typically related to the ongoing debate regarding their right to ordination and leadership positions. I, and others, have

---

56. Ellington, "Pentecostalism and the Authority of Scripture," 29–31.

57. While the Bible is authoritative for the community, such authority "arises from personal and communal experiences of the transformative power of the Holy Spirit in the lives of individuals, in the community of faith and in the world. The Spirit utilizes and works in harmony with and through Scripture to transform the lives of individuals and to empower them supernaturally to become instruments of God's transformation and restoration of fallen creation . . . Scripture acts as a corrective for experience and the biblical text has the last word." Ellington, "Pentecostalism and the Authority of Scripture," 31.

recently been challenging this "evangelicalization of Pentecostalism." One area where this challenge must be mounted is in regards to the use of Scripture. As it pertains to women, I am curious as to whether or not feminist thinking can be of assistance.

In the early years of the movement when a high premium was placed on the Spirit's authority and power to equip, women were actively involved in all areas of ministry following the Spirit's gifting and leading.[58] Women, as well as men, were understood to have an obligation as well as a right to respond to the call to spread the good news based on passages of Scripture such as Acts 2 and Joel 2.[59] However, a hierarchy was soon established whereby men were institutionally awarded senior positions of leadership over women following the teachings of such passages as Ephesians 5, 1 Timothy 2, and Titus.[60] As a result, a transition occurred in the movement from that of a Spirit filled people seeking to reach others with the good news of the gospel to an institutionalized organization with men in charge. And many of the women were, and still are, supportive of the male hierarchy![61] An egalitarian model of mutual ministry based on the Spirit's authority and ability to empower has been effectively suppressed within Pentecostalism. Women's experience and contribution has systematically been downplayed and ignored by a movement rife with patriarchal practices. Significantly for this discussion, the interpretations

58. Blumhofer, *Assemblies of God*, 137 and Holm, "Organizational Blues," 2.

59. Based on Acts 2, Spirit baptism was understood to equip and empower anybody, including women, to minister in fulfilment of the prophesy found in Joel 2. If a woman was empowered and called by the Spirit to be a particular type of minister, it was not her choice but the Spirit's. Her obligation was to be obedient. This attitude can be seen in the words of Appleby and Beatrice Simms in the December 1922 issue of the *Canadian Pentecostal Testimony* 2.12 (December 1922) 1–4.

60. Within the United States where the movement began, women's activities in establishing the new movement is well documented. See Brumback, *Sound From Heaven*, 62–81 and Blumhofer, *Assemblies of God*, 116. Within Canada the recovery of women's early involvement has not yet occurred. However, from my own research it is obvious that women also were actively involved in the Pentecostal Assemblies of Canada, the largest Canadian Pentecostal group, from its beginning. The *Canadian Pentecostal Testimony*, the "Official Organ of the Pentecostal Assembles," edited and published by R. E. McAlister, regularly reported on the ministry of women within its ranks in its early days.

61. In 1988, Margaret Gibb, who is described as pastoring Greenfield Park Pentecostal Church, near Montreal, along with her husband Robert, writes in the July 1988 issue of the *Pentecostal Testimony* (10–11), "Pentecostal women in our nation hold firmly to the Biblical principle of male leadership and headship." She places this position in contrast to the "feminist message of women's rights for power and authority" that "has fallen on deaf ears, as far as our women are concerned."

of various passages of Scripture have played prominent roles in defending both the egalitarian and patriarchal approaches.

While many Pentecostals assume that the current patriarchal practice within Pentecostalism is the natural order of things, if not divinely ordered, Elisabeth Schüssler Fiorenza would argue that "meaning is always politically constructed insofar as interpretation is located in social networks of power/knowledge relations that shape society."[62] Therefore, scholarly discourses regarding biblical interpretation are not disinterested, but have a political context and content. Within the Canadian and American Pentecostal context, the power/knowledge relations that have been affirmed are those that benefit particular men in charge of the institution. The challenge is to develop an approach to the interpretation of Scripture that does not reinforce patriarchy but rather is liberative for all. I would suggest that this process cannot even begin within Pentecostalism until women themselves become aware of what has and still is occurring within their movement. Whether deliberate or not, men and women have agreed together to select and emphasize those passages of Scripture which seem to teach a male headship/female submission model of church and family life while downplaying or ignoring those passages which insist on the involvement of all based on the Spirit's authority to blow where she will.[63] At present, men and women with patriarchal assumptions and a commitment to the authority of Scripture are highlighting particular passages of Scripture that affirm those patriarchal assumptions. It would seem that a feminist critique is needed in order to expose and to correct such a vicious circle.

In insisting that feminist theological hermeneutics must derive its authority from within the emancipatory struggles of women church, Schüssler Fiorenza mentions that "the prophetic traditions and the struggles of the 'sisters of the Spirit' provide such a different contextualization for a feminist theological rhetoric."[64] As a discipleship of equals, women church includes women who have equal status, dignity, and rights as people made in the divine image and "equal access to the multifarious gifts of the Spirit."[65] Schüssler Fiorenza further explains, using the metaphor

---

62. Schüssler Fiorenza, *But She Said*, 3.

63. Pentecostals prefer to use the pronoun "he" rather than "it" for the Spirit. "She," which I prefer, is rare.

64. Schüssler Fiorenza, *But She Said*, 11.

65. Schüssler Fiorenza, *Sharing Her Word*, 114.

of a "messianic community" that such "equality in the Spirit does not mean that all are the same." Instead, the gifts vary while their individual functions are necessary. Therefore, no one gift or the person gifted, in Schüssler Fiorenza's opinion, can be viewed as superior because all are necessary for the building up of the community. Thus "solidarity and collaboration are the 'civic' virtues in the political order (*politeuma* of Christ), which is best characterized as a 'pneumatic' or 'charismatic' democracy."[66] Unfortunately, Schüssler Fiorenza's opinion in regards to the equality of all gifts and gifted seems rather naïve to me. I am well aware that within my Canadian Pentecostal community with its regular emphasis on the gifts of the Spirit and the supposed equality of the distribution of those gifts for the benefit of the community, there are gifts that are more highly prized. Therefore, those so gifted are granted greater status.[67]

Schüssler Fiorenza insists that feminist biblical interpretation within women church derives its criteria for "discerning of the spirits" as a deliberate rhetorical practice from "the experience and analysis articulated in feminist struggles for transforming kyriarchy."[68] While "discerning the Spirit" is supposedly a regular practice in Canadian and American Pentecostal circles, rarely has anyone dared to ask what "spirit" is being manifested in a community where patriarchy/kyriarchy silences and restricts Spirit gifted and called women and less powerful men? And what "spirit" is being manifested when Scripture is appealed to in order to undermine the Spirit's authority to blow where she will?

While some scholars argue "that feminists should not challenge conservative women's acceptance of patriarchal biblical texts because the Bible gives religious meanings to the lives of countless women," Schüssler

66. Ibid., 117. I wonder if Schüssler Fiorenza would include Pentecostal women as "sisters of the Spirit" and vice versa. While Pentecostal women consider themselves sisters in Christ and Spirit filled, they may not be inclined to extend that designation to feminists. As well, Schüssler Fiorenza's mention of Sophia would be highly suspect. While Wisdom is regularly personified within the worship and teachings of the Pentecostal community, this personification is a literary device with Wisdom viewed as an attribute of God. As feminists, such as Schüssler Fiorenza, remain the primary promoters of insights regarding Sophia, and the Pentecostal community tends to be blatantly anti-feminist, suggestions about Sophia's place in the life of the Christian Church are either ignored or quickly dismissed by Pentecostals.

67. E.g., Gifts of preaching and teaching are considered of great value. Therefore, a professional clergy has developed with institutions established and staffed by educated professors to train them. Both are highly esteemed. On a more controversial note, gifts of healing can lead to a flamboyant ministry with a huge following.

68. Schüssler Fiorenza, *Sharing Her Word*, 88.

Fiorenza claims that such an approach is "unable to fashion critical tools and interpretative religious strategies for liberation and transformation. To enable such transformations, a critical feminist hermeneutics must explicitly problematize the theological claim that the Bible speaks with divine authority and is normative for Jewish or Christian identity." This is "necessary because of the historical function of biblical-theological authority claims in sociopolitical struggles for emancipation." "Through the centuries the Bible has been invoked as a weapon against women and other subordinates."[69] Therefore, a feminist hermeneutic must shift attention away from the text and focus on how women read and internalize authoritative texts thus enabling women to become conscious of what they are internalizing in their reading. "As long as scripture is used not only against wo/men struggling for emancipation and in support of kyriarchy but also for shaping wo/men's self-understandings and lives, feminist biblical interpretation must seek to enable wo/men to engage texts critically, to reclaim their own spiritual authority for adjudicating what they read, and to value the process of biblical readings as a process of conscientization."[70] Schüssler Fiorenza insists that the four crucial moments in a critical feminist hermeneutic (ideological suspicion, historical reconstruction, theoethical assessment, and creative imagination)[71] "can only be sustained when contextualized in a feminist critical process of 'conscientization,' or learning to recognize sociopolitical, economic, cultural, and religious contradictions."[72]

According to Schüssler Fiorenza, a feminist critical process of conscientization "strives to create critical consciousness and has as its goal both a praxis of solidarity and a commitment to feminist struggles that seek to transform patriarchal relations of subordination and expression." Accompanied by cognitive dissonance, conscientization includes "'breakthrough' and 'disclosure' experiences" which bring into question the "'common-sense' character of patriarchal reality."[73] She points out that "since wo/men have internalized and are shaped by kyriarchal 'common-sense' mind-sets and values" (and, in my opinion, that includes many

69. Schüssler Fiorenza, *But She Said*, 137.

70. Schüssler Fiorenza, *Sharing Her Word*, 82.

71. She labels these moments the "hermeneutic of suspicion, hermeneutic of remembrance, hermeneutic of proclamation and hermeneutic of liberative vision and imagination." Schüssler Fiorenza, *But She Said*, 52.

72. Schüssler Fiorenza, *Sharing Her Word*, 53.

73. Ibid.

Canadian and American Pentecostal women), "the hermeneutical starting point of critical feminist interpretation can only be wo/men's experience of injustice as it has been critically explored by a hermeneutics of
suspicion in the process of 'conscientization.'"[74] She also points out, and
rightly, I think, that,

> Insofar as biblical readings of conservative wo/men do not start
> from a critical consciousness and with a critical feminist analysis
> of kyriarchal sociopolitical and ecclesial-religious subordination
> and wo/men's second-class citizenship, they tend to construe
> the respect and dignity of wo/men in terms of their internalized
> cultural ideological frameworks of femininity and "true woman-
> hood." Consequently, such conservative readings cannot but keep
> the ideological structures of wo/men's oppression in place.[75]

Cheryl Bridges Johns, an American Pentecostal scholar, while explaining that conscientization "refers to the process whereby persons become aware of the socio-cultural reality which shapes their lives and their
ability to transform that reality," also insists that the word "implies that
action will be joined with this awareness."[76] In this sense, conscientization
is similar to consciousness-raising yet it includes a type of self-awareness
that leads to action that in turn leads to new awareness.

Within the Pentecostal community, women must be heard. However,
before they speak they must become aware of their own internalization
of patriarchal assumptions or their speech will simply reinforce their
own subordinate positions and undervalued contributions. Pentecostal
women must become self aware, have their "consciousness raised" and
then act. Perhaps a place to begin is with the recovery of their own history
and hermeneutic.

At this point, a Pentecostal feminist can find herself in a difficult
position. Committed to the authority of Scripture she discovers that some

74. Ibid., 82.

75. She tries to explain that "[b]y continuing to insist that such readings are not
feminist or liberationist and by disagreeing with their often antifeminist interpretations, one does not deny agency and respect to individual wo/men but rather names
these frameworks for what they are" (Schüssler Fiorenza, *Sharing Her Word*, 82).
While sympathetic with Schüssler Fiorenza's assessment, I would want to caution her
against formulating some sort of "essentialist conservative woman." Although I would
want to argue that the biblical readings of conservative women start from a critical
consciousness, it is not that of a *feminist* critical consciousness and is, therefore, different from Schüssler Fiorenza's feminist variety.

76. Johns, *Pentecostal Formation*, 13.

Pentecostal interpretations of this authoritative text are reinforcing the oppression of herself and others. While Schüssler Fiorenza insists that authority be transferred from the biblical text to her concept of women church, a Pentecostal feminist, at least one not married to evangelical methodology, must remain committed to the authority of the Spirit who inspires the proper interpretation of Scripture. However, she can critique the ideology that is informing that interpretation within her Pentecostal community.

Schüssler Fiorenza points out that feminist approaches, being explicitly committed to the struggle to change patriarchal structures, "must disentangle the ideological (religious-theological) functions of biblical texts for inculcating and legitimating the patriarchal order."[77] Within the Canadian and American Pentecostal community, this would include the ideology of male headship reinforced by patriarchal interpretations of Scripture, an altar that has been worshipped at far too long. Schüssler Fiorenza also points out that "there is no place outside ideology from which one can critique ideology. One can only critique an ideology by locating oneself in another one, or by using the contradictions within a single ideology to uncover its disjunctures and opposing relations."[78] Although a difficult position to be in, being both explicitly Pentecostal and feminist could prove fruitful.

TOWARDS A LIBERATIVE PENTECOSTAL FEMINIST HERMENEUTIC

I think that Schüssler Fiorenza is on to something when she insists that many hermeneutical discussions revolve around the issue of authority. My own Canadian Pentecostal community gets caught up in this conversation particularly in respect to the debate concerning the role of women within the church. However, Schüssler Fiorenza's concern regarding the issue of authority tends to overlook the fact that in any relationship power and authority are being exercised, including her own as an "expert" in feminist theology. Schüssler Fiorenza also seems to assume that authority is always exercised as domination. It, of course, can be but does not necessarily have to be. In addition, I am not convinced that relocating authority from the biblical text to a woman affirming community inspired by the Spirit corrects the problem of the misuse of authority. Any

77. Schüssler Fiorenza, *But She Said*, 41.

78. Ibid., 113.

community, even a woman affirming or Spirit inspired one, can misuse authority. The biblical text has always been interpreted by a community, Spirit inspired or not. Within Pentecostalism, which was Spirit focused and woman affirming (as well as racially and socially inclusive)[79] in its beginning, patriarchy and kyriarchy still eventually became the unquestioned model of relationships. Conscientization might help. But even that involves interaction with and interpretation of the biblical text. The problem in my mind is not so much to dismiss, ignore, or argue against the authority of Scripture so much as to exercise that authority in a healthier way. Perhaps this is where Phyllis Trible's approach may be of help.

Trible's method honors the authority of Scripture. In fact, authority does not appear to be an issue with Trible—of Scripture or anything else. Instead, she seems to be allowing the text, and particular people within the text, to speak to whatever other "pilgrims" will listen, without concern for the question of authority. For Trible, the "Bible as literature is the Bible as scripture, regardless of one's attitude towards its authority. And conversely, the Bible as scripture is the Bible as literature, regardless of one's evaluation of its quality."[80]

Trible insists that "liberating the Bible from patriarchy is the first theological consideration."[81] Therefore, she attempts to uncover "neglected traditions to reveal countervoices within a patriarchal document."[82] However, she also insists on the Bible's ability to act as a corrective for feminist thought when she cautions that "prophetic movements are not exempt from sin. Even as feminism announces judgment on patriarchy and calls for repentance and change, it needs ever to be aware of its own potential for idolatry. No document teaches this lesson better than scripture."[83]

I prefer a method that honors the Bible, recognizing that it has the potential to speak to us without assuming that such potential is a dominating misuse of authority. However, Trible's work seems to contain a self-contradiction. While the work of literary criticism attempts to locate meaning intratextually, feminism is external to the text. Attempting to remain committed to an intratextual approach while at the same time

79. See Robeck, "Azusa Street Revival," 31–36.

80. Trible, *God and the Rhetoric of Sexuality*, 8.

81. Trible, "Postscript: Jottings on the Journey," 147.

82. Ibid., 149.

83. Ibid.

hoping to rid that same text of patriarchal assumptions using extratextual insights seems to me to be rather a dialectical position.[84]

Trible, Schüssler Fiorenza, and Pentecostals are not primarily concerned with the historical facts of the biblical text (although historical questions do enter into the interpretative process).[85] Instead, all three focus on the symbolic meaning of the text. That is what I call a "what's the point" reading that ascertains meaning through the "inner hermeneutic of Scripture" (Trible), "imaginative reconstruction" (Schüssler Fiorenza), or "Spirit illumination." At the same time, the meaning of the text is understood to apply to us today as "pilgrims" (Trible), "women church" (Schüssler Fiorenza)," or "Spirit-filled believers" (Pentecostals). Again the approach seems dialectical—"inner hermeneutic of Scriptures" and "pilgrims," "imaginative reconstruction and women church" or "Spirit illumination" and "Spirit filled believers."

CONCLUSION

I am a Pentecostal and a feminist.[86] The preceding has been my attempt to introduce feminist thinking into the fledgling discussions of Pentecostal hermeneutics before the discussion solidifies. In my attempt, I briefly examined the hermeneutical approaches of two feminists, Elisabeth Schüssler Fiorenza and Phyllis Trible and then compared their thinking with Pentecostal ideas. I also utilized my own insights and experiences

84. As Trible herself attempts to explain her approach through an example derived from Gen 1:27, "Within scripture, my topical clue is a text: the image of God male and female. To interpret this topic, my methodological clue is rhetorical criticism. Outside scripture, my hermeneutical clue is an issue: feminism as a critique of culture. These clues meet now as the Bible again wanders through history to merge past and present. Using them, let us trace first the journey of a single metaphor in the traditions of Israel, a metaphor that highlights female imagery for God." Trible, *God and the Rhetoric of Sexuality*, 23.

85. For an example of how Trible appeals to historical meaning see *Texts of Terror*, 93; for Schüssler Fiorenza see, *But She Said*, 88–92; for Pentecostals, see any book on evangelical hermeneutics.

86. Elisabeth Schüssler Fiorenza has encouraged feminists from various branches of the Christian church to "speak in their own particular voices to their own communities and traditions in order to change them, just as Jewish, Muslim, or Buddhist ones do." She assumes that "the critical insights and constructive visions that are articulated by feminists in diverse religions and denominations do not seek to revive malestream confessional controversies but must be seen as strengthening each other in global feminist struggles for liberation. Schüssler Fiorenza, *Sharing Her Word*, 27.

as a Pentecostal and as a feminist. My hope in this work is to take the first steps towards the formulation of a Pentecostal Feminist Hermeneutic of Liberation capable of discerning, analyzing and correcting domination within Canadian and American Pentecostalism. Feminist scholars Schüssler Fiorenza and Trible have proven to be helpful dialogue partners in this endeavour particularly in terms of analyzing the role of authority and its effect on Canadian and American Pentecostal women and the necessity of conscientization. As this is a Pentecostal project, particularities— including the emphasis on the ongoing work of the Spirit, the authority of the Bible, the necessity to experience and live out the Spirit-filled life and not simply assent to rational creeds or doctrines and the understanding of the community as a continuation of book of Acts, an Acts 29 community —must be included.

Therefore, I would like to explore the possibilities and the potential of a quadrilectical model that brings together the role of the *community*, the role of the *Bible*, the role of *experience* and the role of *Spirit* in the process of interpretation. While a project of this size is not possible within the confines of this work, recognition of the need for it is an important first step. The Canadian and American Pentecostal *community* must have its consciousness raised. The community's involvement in a hermeneutic circle must be acknowledged. The results, sometimes domineering, of interpretations of the Bible on men and women within the community must also be discerned.

Within this quadrilectic the *Bible* would act as a meta-narrative or a "historical prototype" as Schüssler Fiorenza might call it. As a meta-narrative, the Bible would provide the consistency for the ongoing living out of the biblical narrative in a creative fashion acting as an authoritative text that must be constantly re-examined to determine whether or not it is promoting abundant life for all—that is in accordance with the Spirit—or only for a privileged few.

The Canadian and American Pentecostal community's *experience*, its attempt to continue to live out the implications of its Christian commitment in creative ways consistent with its contexts, would be another side of the quadrilectical relationship. Pentecostals often speak of being an "Acts 29 people" indicating that they consider the story of the Bible to be ongoing.[87] The attempt must be regularly examined to see if it continues the story of the Bible. As the Bible is considered not essentially a

87. Mittelstadt, "Scripture in the Pentecostal Tradition," 129.

doctrinal treatise but a "record of testimonies, a story of the relationship between God and [God's] creation," it witnesses to the "diverse ways in which the biblical authors *experienced* the revelation of God."[88] This lends itself to the attempt to continue to experience the revelation of God.

It would be the *Spirit* that brings the various aspect of the biblical text to life, which the community would then recognize as relevant and authoritative and attempt to apply experientially to particular continuing contexts in the power of the Spirit. The Spirit illuminated Scriptures serve as judge and corrector of experiences while at the same time pushing towards the possibilities of new realities being recognized and realized by the men and women within the community. The Spirit would inspire the innovative and creative application of the Bible by illuminating the biblical text and by empowering the experience of living it out.

While *Spirit-illuminated Scripture* may be the final authority, such authority does not become concretized in doctrinal positions. Rather, it is exercised through *Spirit-filled people* telling and retelling their stories within a *Spirit-birthed community* of how the Spirit is at work in their lives, thereby examining and re-examining their interpretations of Scripture in the light of the insights of all Spirit-filled believers. Intentional effort must be regularly made to make certain that all are allowed to participate and are being heard, particularly women and non-elite men from various races and social classes who are often silenced. Based as it is on real life experiences of a community attempting to discern authentic ways to live out their faith in the power of the Spirit, authority remains fluid, ever blowing where it will. Such an approach should be conducive to the conscientization process because all voices are being heard and considered.

Part of the living out of "Acts 29" for Pentecostals includes paying attention to our context, discerning the Spirit at work in the world drawing the world to God, while at the same time noting the evil that must be confronted and challenged. This would include paying attention to voices, to perspectives, which we may not care to hear, prophetically calling us into account for how we are living out the gospel in the power of the Spirit. This includes voices like those of feminists, including Pentecostal ones like myself.

"Come, Holy Spirit we need You . . ."

---

88. Ellington, "Pentecostalism and the Authority of Scripture," 29.

BIBLIOGRAPHY

Anderson, Gordon L. "Pentecostal Hermeneutics." Paper presented at the Twenty-Second Annual Meeting of the Society for Pentecostal Studies. Springfield, MO. November 12–14, 1992.

Appleby, Blanche A., and Beatrice Simms. "South China." *Canadian Pentecostal Testimony* 2.12 (December 1922) 1–4.

Archer, Kenneth J. *A Pentecostal Hermeneutic for the Twenty-First Century: Spirit, Scripture and Community.* New York: T. & T. Clark, 2004.

———. "Pentecostal Hermeneutics: Retrospect and Prospect." *Journal of Pentecostal Theology* 8 (1996) 63–81.

Arrington, French L. "The Use of the Bible by Pentecostals." *Pneuma: The Journal for the Society of Pentecostal Studies* 16 (1994) 101–7.

Blumhofer, Edith L. *The Assemblies of God: A Popular History.* Springfield, MO: Gospel, 1985.

Brumback, Carl. *A Sound from Heaven: The Dramatic Beginning of the 20th Century Pentecostal Revival.* 1961. Reprint, Springfield, MO: Gospel, 1977.

Cargal, Timothy B. "Beyond the Fundamentalist-Modernist Controversy: Pentecostals and Hermeneutics in a Postmodern Age." Paper presented at the Twenty-First Annual Meeting of the Society for Pentecostal Studies. Lakeland, FL. November 7–9, 1991.

Ellington, Scott A. "Pentecostalism and the Authority of Scripture." *Journal of Pentecostal Theology* 9 (1996) 16–38.

Gibb, Margaret. "A Woman's Place in Ministry." *Pentecostal Testimony* 69.7 (July 1988) 0–11.

Hollingsworth, Andrea. "Spirit and Voice: Towards a Feminist Pentecostal Pneumatology." *Pneuma: The Journal for the Society of Pentecostal Studies* 29.7 (2007) 189–213.

Holm, Randall. "Organizational Blues: The Struggle of One Pentecostal Denomination with the Bugbear of Institutionalism." Paper presented at the Twenty-Fourth Annual Meeting of the Society for Pentecostal Studies. Wheaton, Illinois, November 10–12, 1994.

Holmes, Pamela. "Ministering Women in the Pentecostal Assemblies of Canada: A Feminist Exploration." In *Canadian Pentecostalism: Transition and Transformation,* edited by Michael Wilkinson, 171–96. Montreal-Kingston: McGill-Queen's University Press, 2009.

———. "The 'Place' of Women in Pentecostal/Charismatic Ministry Since the Azusa Street Revival." In *The Azusa Street Revival and Its Legacy,* edited by Harold D. Hunter and Cecil M. Robeck Jr., 297–316. Cleveland, TN: Pathway, 2006.

Israel, Richard D., Daniel E. Albrecht, and Randal G. McNally. "Pentecostals and Hermeneutics: Texts, Rituals and Community." Paper presented at the Twentieth Annual Meeting of the Society of Pentecostal Studies, Dallas, TX, November 8–10, 1990.

Johns, Cheryl Bridges. *Pentecostal Formation: A Pedagogy among the Oppressed.* Journal of Pentecostal Theology Supplement Series 2. Sheffield: Sheffield Academic, 1993.

Johnston, Robert K. "Pentecostalism and Theological Hermeneutics: Evangelical Options." *Pneuma: The Journal for the Society of Pentecostal Studies* 6 (1984) 51–66.

McLean, Mark. "Towards a Pentecostal Hermeneutic." *Pneuma: The Journal for the Society of Pentecostal Studies* 6.2 (1984) 35–56.

Menzies, William. "The Methodology of Pentecostal Theology: An Essay on Hermeneutics. In *Essays on Apostolic Themes*, edited by Paul Elbert, 1–14. Peabody, MA: Hendrickson, 1985.

Mittelstadt, Martin. "Scripture in the Pentecostal Tradition: A Contemporary Reading of Luke-Acts." In *Canadian Pentecostalism: Transition and Transformation*, edited by Michael Wilkinson, 123–41. Montreal-Kingston: McGill-Queen's University Press, 2009.

Robeck, Cecil M., Jr. "Azusa Street Revival." In *Dictionary of Pentecostal and Charismatic Movements*, edited by Stanley M. Burgess and Gary B. McGee, 31–36. Grand Rapids: Zondervan, 1988.

Schüssler Fiorenza, Elisabeth. *Bread Not Stone: The Challenge of Feminist Biblical Interpretation*. Boston: Beacon, 1984.

———. *But She Said: Feminist Practices of Biblical Interpretation*. Boston: Beacon, 1992.

———. "Cartography of Struggle." *Discipleship of Equals: A Critical Feminist Ekklesialogy of Liberation*, 1–12. New York: Crossroads, 1993, 1994.

———. "Introduction: Feminist Liberation Theology as Critical Sophialogy." In *The Power of Naming: A Concilium Reader in Feminist Liberation Theology*, edited by Elisabeth Schüssler Fiorenza, xiii–xxxix. Maryknoll, NY: Orbis, 1996.

———. *Jesus: Miriam's Child, Sophia's Prophet*. New York: Continuum, 1994.

———. *Sharing Her Word: Feminist Biblical Interpretation in Context*. Boston: Beacon, 1998.

———. "The Will to Choose or to Reject: Continuing Our Critical Work." In *Feminist Interpretation of the Bible*, edited by Letty M. Russell, 125–36. Philadelphia: Westminster, 1985.

Spittler, Russell P. "Scripture and the Theological Enterprise: View from a Big Canoe." In *The Use of the Bible in Theology: Evangelical Options*, edited by Robert K. Johnson, 56–77 and 233–36. Atlanta: John Knox, 1985.

Stronstad, Roger. "Pentecostal Experience and Hermeneutics." *Paraclete* (1992) 16–26.

———. "Pentecostalism, Experiential Presuppositions and Hermeneutics." Paper presented at the Twentieth Annual Meeting of the Society of Pentecostal Studies, Dallas, Texas, November 8–10, 1990.

Thomas, John Christopher. "Women, Pentecostals and the Bible: An Experiment in Pentecostal Hermeneutics." *Journal of Pentecostal Theology* 5 (1994) 41–56.

Trible, Phyllis. "Eve and Miriam: From the Margins to the Center." In *Feminist Approaches to the Bible*, edited by Hershel Shanks and Phyllis Trible, 5–24. Washington, DC: Biblical Archaeology Society, 1995.

———. *God and the Rhetoric of Sexuality*. Overtures to Biblical Theology. Philadelphia: Fortress, 1978.

———. "Postscript: Jottings on the Journey." In *Feminist Interpretation of the Bible*, edited by Letty M. Russell, 147–49. Philadelphia: Westminster, 1985.

———. *Rhetorical Criticism: Context, Method, and the Book of Jonah*. Guides to Biblical Scholarship. Minneapolis: Fortress, 1994.

———. *Texts of Terror: Literary-Feminist Readings of Biblical Narratives*. Overtures to Biblical Theology. Philadelphia: Fortress, 1984.

Yong, Amos. *Spirit-Word-Community: Theological Hermeneutics in Trinitarian Perspective*. Burlington, VT: Ashgate, 2002.

Issues of Ecology

9

Globalization and the Environment as Social Problem

Assessing a Pentecostal Response

Michael Wilkinson

INTRODUCTION

The literature on ecological issues continues to grow as do the debates among scholars and Christians about a number of points including whether or not the planet is experiencing an ecological crisis and if so, what to do about it. For example, in *Hot, Flat, and Crowded,* Thomas L. Friedman says we need a green revolution to deal with decreasing energy resources, the extinction of plant and animal species, America's dependence on oil, political instability over resources, and long term climate change.[1] Not everyone agrees with Friedman, although he makes an excellent case. Evangelicals likewise have disagreed over the nature of the problem and how to respond. Many of the debates include the scientific

1. Friedman, *Hot, Flat and Crowded.*

questions as well as theological arguments for creation care and steward-ship as biblical principles.[2] In this chapter, I explore one particular re-sponse to the debate on ecological issues as represented among Canadian Pentecostals. I also offer a globalization framework to make some sense of the issue from a sociological perspective.

Scholars suggest that globalization offers a valuable theory by which researchers can examine the responses of religious groups to social is-sues.[3] While sociologists of religion have explored the theoretical rela-tionship between globalization and religion,[4] there is still much work to examine how these theories explain the ways in which religious groups address social problems.[5] More specifically, there is very little research to explore the discourse of religious groups about the environment in spite of the view that ecological issues would become increasingly important to religious groups as an area of concern.[6]

The literature on religion and the environment has focused on a wide range of issues, theories, and methodologies, including the positive and negative relationships between religion and environmental concern, the lack of influence religion has in shaping environmental concern and the need to recognize multiple factors for explaining the relationship between religion and environmental concern.[7] The literature on religion, global-ization, and the environment has tended to focus on the more damaging aspects of social change for the environment and the need for responses rooted in social justice including ecofeminism, economic reform, and policy based political action.[8] The position adopted here incorporates the viewpoints of Roland Robertson and Peter Beyer to explain the seem-

2. See *Christianity Today* and its online edition on "Global Warming, Creation Care and the Environment." Online: http://www.christianitytoday.com/ct/special/global warming.html#opinion.

3. Robertson, *Globalization*; "Globality" 2:524–26 and Scholte, *Globalization*.

4. For example, see Beyer, *Religion and Globalization* and *Religions in Global Society*; Robertson, *Globalization*; "Globalization Theory 2000+," 458–71; and Simpson, "Glo-balization and Religion," 1–17 and "Great Reversal," 115–25.

5. Beckford, *Social Theory and Religion*, 103–49.

6. Beyer, *Religion and Globalization*, 207.

7. For example, see Greeley, "Religion and Attitudes toward the Environment," 19–28; Guth, et al., "Theological Perspectives and Environmentalism among Religious Activists," 373–82; Sherkat and Ellison, "Structuring the Religion-Environment Connection," 71–85; and Woodrum and Wolkomir, "Religious Effects on Environmentalism," 223–34.

8. Gottlieb, *This Sacred Earth*; Eaton, *Ecofeminism and Globalization*; Lofdahl, *Envi-ronmental Impacts of Globalization and Trade*.

ingly contradictory responses among Canadian Pentecostals about the environment.

GLOBALIZATION AND THE PENTECOSTAL MOVEMENT IN CANADA

Following Roland Robertson, globalization is defined as the increased interconnectedness of the world's societies into a single socio-cultural reality.[9] Robertson's view of globalization is that it represents a long historical process that has developed over the past 500 years. Outlining five major phases, Robertson highlights in skeletal form the main points including: Phase 1: The Germinal Phase from the early 15th to mid 18th century; Phase 2: The Incipient Phase from the mid 18th century to the 1870s; Phase 3: The Take off Phase from the 1870s until the 1920s; Phase 4: The Struggle for Hegemony Phase from the 1920s until the 1960s; and Phase 5: The Uncertainty Phase from the 1960s until the 1990s.[10] Of importance here are the last two phases which parallel the development of twentieth century Pentecostalism, and especially the Uncertainty Phase for understanding Pentecostal responses to social issues like ecological concerns. Robertson characterizes this final phase as displaying crisis tendencies in the 1990s with much uncertainty over such things as ethnic unrest, civil rights, conceptions of identity, access to nuclear weapons, anti-globalization movements, world civil society, and ecological threat. More recently, Robertson has added a new category which he calls the millennial phase to highlight the apocalyptic qualities of contemporary life.[11] His historical overview points to the necessity of researching different phases for the specificities of global change.

A related concept is globality which refers to the reflexive consciousness of humanity about the conditions associated with the process of globalization.[12] Change in the ecology of Earth represents an important example in the late twentieth century of human awareness about social change on a worldwide scale. It also draws our attention to the particular discourse of religious groups, like Pentecostals, on the nature of the problem, a range of solutions, and the specific action one should consider. This chapter explores the religious responses of one denomination, the

9. Robertson, *Globalization* and "Globalization Theory 2000+," 458–71.

10. Robertson, *Globalization*, 58–59.

11. Robertson, "Global Millennialism," 9–34.

12. Robertson, "Globality," 524–26.

Pentecostal Assemblies of Canada (PAOC), to assess the various ways in which it addresses ecological issues as a global social problem.

Sociology provides an important window into understanding the nature of social change through the framework of religious groups. Specifically, it shows how religious groups define the nature of the problem, the ways in which they propose solutions and what specific action they ought to take in response to the problem. Additionally, it provides insight into how religious groups are motivated internally to respond to social issues; whether the group embraces change or rejects it and what resources are mobilized in response. Among Canadian Pentecostals, there are multiple, often conflicting responses to social issues that do not fit neatly the categories of "liberal" or "conservative" and require further analysis and discussion to explain a possible range of responses. This is precisely what Robertson's view of globalization allows one to see—unconventional responses to the problems of the environment that may not fit the standard categories that often frame the kinds of explanations on religion and social issues. Pentecostalism also consists of a cultural pattern of flexibility, innovation, and fluidity which may account for how multiple discourses can exist within a single denomination.

My interest in Pentecostal responses to ecological issues led me to examine the PAOC, a "classical" Pentecostal denomination with roots in the Methodist-holiness movement of the nineteenth century. The PAOC was influenced by the events surrounding the Azusa Street revival held in Los Angeles between 1906 and 1909 as well as important revivals in Toronto and Winnipeg. In 1901 the Canadian Census reported no responses for religious identification as Pentecostal. By the next Census in 1911 just over 500 Canadians self-identified as Pentecostal. These numbers continued to grow, reaching a peak in 1991 when over 436,000 Canadians indicated they were Pentecostal on the Census. The largest denomination of Pentecostals in Canada is the PAOC which reported over 220,000 adherents in the 1990s.[13]

One of the founders of the PAOC, holiness preacher Robert McAlister, travelled by train from Ontario, Canada to Los Angeles where he "spoke in tongues" returning almost immediately to spread the news of revival in Quebec, Ontario, and Manitoba. McAlister was one of the founding members of the PAOC which officially formed in Eastern Canada in 1919. Pentecostals in Western Canada were affiliated with the

13. Wilkinson, "Canadian Pentecostalism: An Introduction," 3–12.

Assemblies of God, headquartered in Springfield, Missouri. The PAOC and the Western Pentecostals worked closely together with the Western group officially joining the PAOC shortly after they received a Canadian charter as an organized religious group. It was not until 1925 that the PAOC became fully independent from the US based Assemblies of God, maintaining strong transnational ties through the exchange of ministers, ideas, and doctrinal statements.[14]

The PAOC grew considerably during its formative years expanding throughout the country with some of its largest congregations located in the cities of Winnipeg and Toronto. Winnipeg became the center for theological education with the Anglican James Eustace Purdie as its first principle. The denomination also expanded into the Maritime Provinces although it faced much difficulty with the large number of Baptist, Wesleyan, and "oneness" Pentecostals, a non-Trinitarian group which also faced much opposition from "Trinitarian" Pentecostals. Pentecostalism in Canada also grew at a higher rate among aboriginal peoples in British Columbia and throughout the northern territories. By the 1950s, the PAOC was experiencing many of the institutionalization issues other denominations faced. Still, growing signs of renewal among mainline churches and the Catholic charismatic renewal challenged "classical" Pentecostals to reconsider the view that God could not "visit" the liberal churches they often denounced as "dead churches."

During the 1970s and 1980s, the PAOC was quite confident in its ministry programs, mission activities, theological training colleges, and overall administration until the late 1980s when a crisis of identity began to appear with the failings of Assemblies of God evangelists Jim Bakker and Jimmy Swaggart. Following the "Congress on Pentecostal Leadership" in Toronto in 1986, questions were raised by PAOC ministers about Swaggart who was one of the keynote speakers. Reports from the General Superintendent indicated the PAOC was also facing financial pressures. A very large International office located in the Toronto region would prove to be too costly leaving the denomination to sell it and move into a smaller office building. Along with a crisis of leadership, the PAOC was experiencing a decline in the rate of growth so that nearly all of the new growth in the 1990s was among new immigrant congregations.[15] Furthermore,

14. Kydd, "Pentecostal Assemblies of Canada," 961–64; Di Giacomo, "Pentecostal and Charismatic Christianity in Canada," 15–38.

15. Wilkinson, *Spirit said Go.*

there was much debate over divorce and remarriage, the role of women in ministry, theological education and social concerns.[16] While women were finally recognized with ordination and ministers were allowed to marry divorced persons, the largest denominational college in Canada, Eastern Pentecostal Bible College in Peterborough, Ontario did not fare so well. With major philosophical changes and relocation to Toronto, the college lost significant numbers of students and the PAOC had to re-evaluate the decisions it made about theological education for its ministers.

The PAOC also developed a "Social Concerns and Public Relations" department with Hudson T. Hilsden appointed as the National Coordinator in 1983. A number of statements written by Hilsden in the article "Evangelism and Social Concerns in Partnership" illustrate the denomination's viewpoints.[17] The main point of the article is that social concern is biblical and a partner with evangelism. In Hilsden's view, social concern is not equal with evangelism but it must be an integral part of evangelism and discipleship. Hilsden says Pentecostals must "speak out against the actions of those who have advanced to places of leadership in politics, law, education and civil service and who are rapidly turning our society to secular humanism and paganism. But we have a responsibility to prepare our young people to enter these influential professions in order to bring a Christian perspective to the public market place."[18] Yet the issues he focuses on are abortion, homosexuality, sexually transmitted diseases, and poverty which are primarily the conservative concerns of some evangelical groups. Hilsden is silent on what most considered the pressing social issues of the time such as the environment, gender inequality, nuclear threat, the cold war, economic issues, etc. The irony is that while the PAOC does not include these issues in its official statements, the *Testimony* did publish numerous articles by its ministers and members on these topics. Often the viewpoints were inconsistent with each other including statements on the environment which I will address later. Finally, Hilsden states:

> It is understood that the positions and actions taken by the Pentecostal Assemblies of Canada in regard to social concerns will be influenced by our strong theological positions of the affirmation of the Bible as our all-sufficient source of faith and practice,

16. These issues are examined in a number of chapters in Wilkinson, *Canadian Pentecostalism*.

17. Hilsden, "Evangelism and Social Concerns in Partnership," 4–6.

18. Ibid., 5.

> our subscription to the historic creeds of the universal Church, our belief in the fall of man and the provision for our salvation through belief in Jesus Christ as Saviour, Healer and Coming King and the Baptism of the Holy Spirit, with speaking in tongues as the initial evidence to empower the believer to live and work for God.[19]

This final thought about Spirit Baptism as the source of empowerment is a unique Pentecostal position but little else is said by the PAOC to articulate how this experience shapes social concern. In fact, I did not read anything in the cases examined that linked a pneumatological position on any social problem. Still, the tension among the "official" voices needs some explanation and understanding. The events of the 1990s left the PAOC in a state of questioning and while it appears to have weathered the stormy decade, it was perhaps the most difficult decade for the PAOC.

As a "classical" Pentecostal denomination we would expect to find a "conservative" response to social problems making them "negatively" oriented towards issues like the environment. This hypothesis assumes that conservative religious groups are also ideologically on the right of the political spectrum while liberal groups are on the left. Beyer distinguishes between "liberal" and "conservative" responses to globalization with the concepts of function and performance.[20] The basic idea is that in global society a specialized functional system for religion has emerged among others. Religions within the religion system are highly specialized offering differing views of the world. Yet when addressing the problems of other spheres of global society like economics or politics, religions rely on "performance" or the offering of responses based in one system to the problems of another (i.e., in economic or political terms). While religions may be motivated by theological values, responses are typically in economic or political terms. A range of solutions falls on a continuum between "liberal" and "conservative" responses. Liberal responses, for example, are prosystemic, characterized by pluralism, ecumenism, inclusion, and a generally positive role of religion, economics, and politics for solving social issues. Conservative responses are antisystemic and illustrate a reassertion of the religious tradition as a normative response to social issues. It is through "right" practice of the religion that one finds order in the world. Both responses, however, represent a public role for religion in global society.

19. Hilsden, "Evangelism and Social Concerns in Partnership," 5.
20. Beyer, *Religion and Globalization*, 86–94.

The existence of inconsistent, if not unconventional, responses within a religion raises questions about "conservative" and "liberal" categories as exclusively within the domains of single religious traditions. What happens when a religious group, like the PAOC, allows for responses among its ministers that are representative of each end of the spectrum? How can we begin to explain the variation of responses to social problems, and more specifically, ecological issues? Is there any evidence of a unique Pentecostal perspective on global social issues in North America? I hypothesize that some Pentecostals will envision a public role for the church on ecological issues that is shaped by such things as ecumenism, while others will offer a public role for the church that reasserts tradition as a response. The range of responses within any religious group, however, is contested especially during a period of change and uncertainty.[21]

METHOD

The data used in this study come from a content analysis of the *Pentecostal Testimony*, the official denominational magazine of the PAOC. *Testimony* was first published in 1920 by the PAOC and founded and edited by Robert McAlister.[22] The *Testimony* played an important role in the development of Canadian Pentecostalism. A free publication, it was the main source of communication for spreading Pentecostal viewpoints across the country, advertising evangelistic campaigns, camp meetings, church openings, conferences, Bible schools, theological viewpoints, and social critique. Early Pentecostal publications served to promote and preserve renewal and revival.[23] For example, in the USA, Seymour's *Apostolic Faith* ran a press run of 40,000 copies in 1906, growing to 80,000 a year later. The paper promoted the Pentecostal movement throughout the world, lending to an emerging Pentecostal culture. The *Apostolic Faith* and *Pentecostal Testimony* occasionally published the same reports, lending to the global quality of the early movement. For the Pentecostals, the stories were signs that God's Holy Spirit was poured out over the entire world.

The PAOC made available the *Pentecostal Testimony* on CD Rom in 2003. The twelve CDs reproduce the entire series of magazines since 1920. A search engine allows researchers to look for key words that may

21. Beyer, *Religions in Global Society*.

22. Miller, *Canadian Pentecostals*, 64 and 119–21.

23. Warner, "Publications," 742–52.

be found in all instances including editorials, advertisements, news pieces, articles, and reader responses. For this study I searched for all cases and instances of "global" and its cognates (e.g., globalization) from 1920–1999. First, I wanted to discover the number of times in which "global" was referenced to see if there was some correlation between Robertson's historical development of globalization and a Pentecostal awareness of global issues. Second, I conducted an analysis of those specific cases that focussed on ecological concerns to illustrate the discourse among Canadian Pentecostals in the PAOC. Documents are an important source of data for researchers with secondary analysis or content analysis being a standard method in social science.[24]

FINDINGS

As anticipated, there was an increase in the usage of "global" in the *Testimony* since it was first published in 1920. Between 1920 and 1939 there were no cases of "global" published in the *Testimony*. From 1940 until 1969 there were twenty-four cases and fifty-four instances. The first occurrence was in 1943 in which an article appeared about World War II as a "global" war. While five of the nineteen instances were in reference to "global" war, eleven referred to the churches mission as a "global" one. The remaining three instances were in reference to world religions as "global" religions. However, it is during the next phase from the 1970s with increasing tension during the 1990s that a substantial increase in usage appears in the magazine. In this period, there were 105 cases with 176 instances in which "global" was referenced between 1970 and 1999. Overall, between 1920 and 1999 there were 129 cases with 230 instances of "global." The vast majority occurred since 1970 with a significant number in the 1990s.

Table 1: Overview of "Global" in *The Pentecostal Testimony*, 1920–1999

Year	Cases	Instances
1920–1939	No cases	No instances
1940–1969	24 cases	54 instances
1970–1999	105 cases	176 instances
TOTAL	129 Cases	230 Instances

24. Prior, "Doing things with Documents," 76–94 and Neuman, *Social Research Methods*, 292.

Taking a closer look at the 1990s, there were sixty-four cases containing 117 instances. Not surprisingly, there is not only an increase in the number of cases but a substantial increase in the usages of "global" with reference to globalization themes. The various themes of globalization were categorized in the following topics: missionary activity, religion and religions, social issues, theology, and worldwide Pentecostalism. While missionary activity accounted for nearly 50% of the cases, social issues was the next highest accounting for 31.3% of the cases. The types of documents included advertisements, articles, news reports, reader responses, and one special issue which focused on worldwide Pentecostalism. The type of document used most often in relation to "global" themes was the article, totaling forty-two.

Table 2: Global Themes: Number of Cases and Percentage, 1990–1999

Theme	Number of Cases	Percentage
Missionary Activity	31	48.4%
Religion and Religions	2	3.1%
Social Issues	20	31.3%
Theology	6	9.4%
Worldwide Pentecostalism	5	7.8%
TOTAL	64	100.0%

Focusing specifically on social issues, it is interesting that the kinds of concerns raised with global themes are not the kinds of issues the Social Concerns and Public Relations department were particularly interested in. None of the issues were concerned with conservative sexual issues like abortion or homosexuality. AIDS/HIV received attention but the focus was on the issue as a global problem with attention given to the worldwide crisis. Not surprisingly, the 1990s witnessed much concern about technology, computers and the possibility of microchips failing all over the planet. Of particular interest for this chapter are those cases that focus on the environment. Overall three of the twenty cases in the 1990s focused on ecological concerns.

A closer examination of the discourse on the environment in the magazine shows divergent viewpoints. The two articles written by Rev. W. H. Moody, a retired PAOC minister living in Burlington, Ontario questions whether or not we need to be alarmed about these issues. In "Global

Warming?" Moody states: "There are more important future events to concern us than the alarmist warnings of the environmentalists."[25] For Moody, the catastrophe that awaits Earth is a sign of God's judgment on the planet and upon a materialistic and unbelieving world. Pollution of the planet is not the real problem, he argues. Rather, the pollution of sin is a far greater issue. He says "By all means let us keep the 'greenhouse' clean, but more importantly let us avoid the pollution of sin which will keep us from entering into our heavenly Father's house of purity and safety."[26]

Table 3: Global Themes: Type of Case, Number and Percentage, 1990–1999

Type of Case	Number of Cases	Percentage
Advertisement	1	1.6%
Article	42	65.6%
Editorial	4	6.2%
News Report	9	14.1%
Reader Response	7	10.9%
Special Issue	1	1.6%
TOTAL	64	100.0%

Table 4: Global Themes: Kinds of Social Issues, Types of Cases, Numbers and Percentage, 1990–1999

Issues	Types of Cases	Number of Cases	Percentage
AIDS/HIV	Article	2	10%
Economics	Article	1	5%
Environment	2 Articles, 1 Reader Response	3	15%
Feminism	Article	1	5%
Nature of Global Problems	Article	1	5%
Politics	Article	1	5%
Popular Culture	Reader Response	1	5%
Refugees	Article	1	5%
Technology (Y2K)	5 Articles, 3 Reader Responses, 1 News Report	9	45%
TOTAL		20	100%

25. Moody, "Global Warming?" 15.

26. Ibid., 23.

Moody wrote on the topic again in an article called "Green! A New Religion?" where he argues that the environmental movement is a godless social movement blessed by Gaia, the goddess of Mother Earth. The environmental movement is a diabolical ploy to deceive people into a new religion masked in the ideology of environmental concern. Further, the environmental movement is the new left green ideology to replace the former red Marxist philosophy of socialism. Earth Day is the new pagan holiday devoted to a socialist world. According to Moody, the philosophy of the "Green New Age One World" movement is anti-God and anti-Christian. He concludes by saying: "Above the red of socialism and the green of environmentalism is the white of God's righteousness, possessed by true born again believers in Christ the Saviour. What colour is your flag?"[27]

Moody's view is illustrative of a conservative position based upon a pre-millennial view that the world will increasingly get worse and then the Kingdom of God will come. Clearly, Moody does not share in the values of the environmental movement he is concerned about. Yet, there is nothing distinctly Pentecostal about the position held here from other conservative Protestants who saw the movement in negative or antisystemic terms. Neither does his view reflect a number of positions among evangelical Protestants of the time on "Earthkeeping."[28] His view does represent something of an official view as he is an ordained PAOC minister writing in its official denominational magazine.

Testimony published in January 1992 a response to Moody's articles by Rev. Roger Rayner who completely disagrees with Moody. Rayner is actually quite critical of Moody who he feels does not adequately define the ideology of the environmental movement. Rayner also believes he has overstated his position when he suggests that ecological concern is inspired by Satan. Moody's view, according to Rayner , is "an affront to ecologically-minded Christians."[29] He goes on to say: "I do not find the sweeping generalizations biblically justified nor scientifically accurate."[30] Rayner quotes a number of people including David Suzuki, a well known left leaning socially minded Canadian environmentalist, to support his

27. Moody, "Green! A New Religion?," 11.

28. See Loren Wilkinson, *Earthkeeping in the 90s* and Kearns, "Saving the Creation," 55–70.

29. Rayner, "Environmental Issues," 32.

30. Ibid., 32.

viewpoints. Rayner also asks the PAOC to review articles of this nature in the future to avoid losing credibility and to not appear so gullible. While Rayner is critical of Moody, there is no development of a Pentecostal theology articulated in his or any other articles on the environment as a global social issue. Yet, his view fits well the prosystemic analysis of Beyer that allows for a more ecumenical and scientific approach referred to as "liberal" in response to social issues.

In sum, the findings show a substantial growth in publication on global social issues in the 1990s. But the PAOC official position as represented through the Social Concerns and Public Relations department is inconsistent with the positions of those writing in the official denominational magazine. There is also an inconsistency with views that religious organizations are typically "conservative" or "liberal" on social issues. Finally, there is tension within the denomination over an appropriate response to ecological issues.

EVALUATING PENTECOSTAL DISCOURSE ON GLOBAL ISSUES

A Pentecostal Distinctive or Pluralization of Viewpoints?

There are several lines of explanation that can be explored to make sense of a Pentecostal response to the environment. First, Allan Anderson argues that Pentecostals have wrongly been accused of withdrawing from global issues like politics and the struggle for liberation and social justice.[31] He writes about "Pentecostal Liberation," a unique perspective that is developing especially outside of North America. Pentecostal Liberation is characterized by a concern for issues surrounding race, class, and gender. Anderson says Pentecostals have wrongly been accused of withdrawing from global issues like politics and the struggle for liberation and justice and that it is incorrect to apply the conservative viewpoints of American politics and religion elsewhere in the world. He then goes on to provide a number of examples to illustrate a more complicated and ambiguous position among Pentecostals on social issues from Chile, Korea, South Africa, Zambia, etc. He argues that from a worldwide perspective the stereotype of Pentecostals as politically conservative or apolitical needs to be seriously challenged. Anderson says "the Spirit of God brings a liberation that is holistic, not only in that which is confined to the 'spiritual' sphere.

31. Anderson, *Introduction to Pentecostalism*, 269.

If freedom is always the result of receiving the Spirit, then true freedom or liberation is an integral part of Pentecostal experience."[32]

Pentecostalism's emphasis on Spirit encounter is also about the transforming power of the Spirit personally and socially. He agrees that much of western Pentecostalism is shaped by conservative viewpoints and prosperity gospel schemes but those views are not representative of all Pentecostals in theory or practice. Further, he argues that Pentecostalism, even in North America, is characterized by left/right political views that are always in tension. The case in the USA is the left leaning African American Pentecostals versus the right leaning "white" Assemblies of God Pentecostals. While the tensions may exist within those two generalizations I do not know if we have any evidence to make a firm conclusion. For example, we have no evidence from the findings in this chapter that the viewpoints of Canadian Pentecostals are shaped by Pentecostals outside of North America. Neither do we have any evidence of a unique pneumatological position on social issues in North America surrounding the ecology, even in proto form in this period. Nor do we see any evidence among Canadians of a developed "Pentecostal Liberation" view.

Another possible explanation is offered by Peter Beyer.[33] Beyer argues that the ambiguity represented in the responses of religions to ecological concerns is an important aspect of the globalization debate. While most religions are "liberal" or "conservative" in their response to other global issues, the environment is one area that is not as clear. For Beyer, most responses tend to be "liberal" even those from more conservative groups. His reasoning is that ecological concern is typically prosystemic and not antisystemic. Following Laurel Kearns, Beyer expands on a threefold typology of religious response which includes eco-spirituality, eco-justice, and stewardship.[34] Eco-spirituality focuses on the holistic relationship between human and natural worlds. The eco-justice type treats environmental problems in the context of inequality and marginalization. Thirdly, the stewardship type represents those religious responses that focus on restoring the creation which is in its current state of disaster because humans have strayed away from the traditional message. This type is also the most conservative and what Beyer calls eco-traditionalism. The articles by Moody, while focusing on the environment, do not appear

---

32. Ibid.

33. Beyer, *Religion and Globalization*, 206–24.

34. Ibid.

to fit into any of these categories. In my view Moody's writings represent a "conservative" response which is antisystemic. However, the response by Rayner fits well the "stewardship" view illustrating well the ambiguity of viewpoints among Pentecostals. God and the Bible contain the answers to the ecological crisis, but not alone. Pentecostals are encouraged by Rayner to understand the problem from other environmental activists, regardless of religious viewpoint, as well as science.

Finally, Roland Robertson's view of globalization and the reflexive responses to social issues deserves some attention.[35] The Pentecostal responses are illustrative of a discourse that attempts to make sense of a particular disruption in the social environment. It is also illustrative of a response to the restructuring of global society and how religions respond to the systematization of the religion system, through negotiation, often with conflict.[36] This accounts for the variations in responses within one religious group to the environment as a social issue. It does not mean that both views will continue or that one will become the central view. There is no predictive power in the theory to say where Pentecostals will come down on the issue. It only represents a specific point in history where Pentecostals were wrestling (in this case openly in an official magazine) about their viewpoint. There is no evidence to suggest that the differing opinions were part of a strategy by the editor of the magazine to explore it in any systematic way either. Still, the viewpoints are part of the public discourse of Canadian Pentecostalism and both represent something of an "official" view as published in the denominational magazine by two of the PAOC's ordained clergy. It also highlights the contested nature of globalization and more specifically, religious responses to social problems in the 1990s.

CONCLUSION

In conclusion, there does not appear to be anything uniquely "Pentecostal" about the response to social concerns among PAOC clergy. The views of Moody and Rayner are not theological statements about the nature of creation. Nor do the responses represent a distinct Pentecostal theology on the environment. Rather, the definition of the problem, the proposed solutions, and the action to be taken, is similar to other evangelical

35. Robertson, "Globalitiy," 524–26.
36. Beyer, *Religions in Global Society*.

Protestants. No doubt there is a tension among Canadian Pentecostals over how to respond to environmental issues. Divergent viewpoints do not suggest a movement toward one end of the liberal/conservative continuum, however. In my view Beyer's thesis is correct. Pentecostals in Canada adopt a largely eco-traditionalist perspective. Yet, while Beyer observes religious responses to ecological concern as primarily "liberal" and prosystemic, the Moody viewpoint illustrates a "conservative" or antisystemic viewpoint. Overall, the responses to the problem necessitate a return to the correct practice of the tradition or toward solutions based in the scientific and political realm. There are limitations to this research as it focuses on only one Pentecostal denomination during a specific historical period. Comparisons with other Pentecostal denominations like the Assemblies of God need to be conducted to show how similar denominations in different countries responded to global change.[37] Research could be conducted to compare PAOC responses with other evangelical Protestants in Canada. The research, however, does show the need for understanding the particularities of globalization contextually, including the range of responses to global change during a period of uncertainty.

BIBLIOGRAPHY

Anderson, Allan. *An Introduction to Pentecostalism: Global Charismatic Christianity.* Cambridge: Cambridge University Press, 2004.

Beckford, James A. *Social Theory and Religion.* Cambridge: Cambridge University Press, 2003.

Beyer, Peter. *Religion and Globalization.* London: Sage, 1994.

———. "Defining Religion in Cross-National Perspective: Identity and Difference in Official Conceptions." In *Defining Religion: Investigating the Boundaries Between the Sacred and Secular,* edited by Arthur Greil and David G. Bromley, 163–88. New York: Elsevier, 2003.

———. *Religions in Global Society.* New York: Routledge, 2006.

Di Giacomo, Michael. "Pentecostal and Charismatic Christianity in Canada: Its Origins, Development, and Distinct Culture." In *Canadian Pentecostalism: Transition and Transformation,* edited by Michael Wilkinson, 15–38. Montreal-Kingston: McGill-Queen's University Press, 2009.

Eaton, Heather, and Lois Ann Lorentzen, editors. *Ecofeminism and Globalization: Exploring Culture, Context, and Religion.* Lanham, MD: Rowman & Littlefield, 2003.

37. Beyer, "Defining Religion in Cross-National Perspective," 163–88.

Friedman, Thomas L. *Hot, Flat and Crowded: Why We Need a Green Revolution, and How It Can Renew America.* New York: Farrar Straus & Giroux, 2008.

Gottlieb, Roger S., editor. *This Sacred Earth: Religion, Nature, Environment.* New York: Routledge, 2004.

Greeley, A. "Religion and Attitudes toward the Environment." *Journal for the Scientific Study of Religion* 32 (1993) 19–28.

Guth, J. L., L. A. Kellstedt, C. E. Smidt, and J. C. Green. "Theological Perspectives and Environmentalism among Religious Activists." *Journal for the Scientific Study of Religion* 32 (1993) 373–82.

Hilsden, Hudson. "Evangelism and Social Concerns in Partnership." *The Pentecostal Testimony* 9 (1990) 4–6.

Kearns, Laurel. "Saving the Creation: Christian Environmentalism in the United States." *Sociology of Religion* 57 (1996) 55–70.

Kydd, R. A. N. "Pentecostal Assemblies of Canada." In *The New International Dictionary of Pentecostal and Charismatic Movements*, edited by Stanley M. Burgess and Eduard M. Van Der Maas, 961–64. Grand Rapids: Zondervan, 2003.

Lofdahl, Corey L. *Environmental Impacts of Globalization and Trade: A Systems Study.* Cambridge, MA: MIT Press, 2002.

Miller, Thomas William. *Canadian Pentecostals: A History of the Pentecostal Assemblies of Canada.* Mississauga, ON: Full Gospel, 1994.

Moody, W. H. "Global Warming?" *The Pentecostal Testimony* 2 (1991) 15, 23.

———. "Green! A New Religion?" *The Pentecostal Testimony* 8 (1991) 10–11.

Neuman, W. Lawrence. *Social Research Methods: Qualitative and Quantitative Approaches.* Boston: Allyn & Bacon, 2000.

Pentecostal Testimony. (CDs, vols. 1–12). Mississauga, ON: The Pentecostal Assemblies of Canada, 2003.

Prior, Lindsay. "Doing things with Documents." In *Qualitative Research: Theory, Method and Practice,* edited by David Silverman, 76–94. Thousand Oaks, CA: Sage, 2004.

Rayner, Roger. "Environmental Issues." *The Pentecostal Testimony* 1 (1992) 21.

Robertson, Roland. "Global Millennialism: A Postmortem on Secularization." In *Religion, Globalizaiton, and Culture,* edited by Peter Beyer and Lori Beaman, 9–34. Leiden: Brill, 2007.

———. "Globality." In *Encyclopedia of Globalization,* edited by Jan Aart Scholte and Roland Robertson, vol. 2, 524–26. New York: Routledge, 2007.

———. *Globalization: Social Theory and Global Culture.* London: Sage, 1992.

———. "Globalization Theory 2000+: Major Problematics." In *Handbook of Social Theory,* edited by George Ritzer and Barry Smart, 458–71. London: Sage, 2001.

Scholte, Jan Aart. *Globalization: A Critical Introduction.* London: Palgrave MacMillan, 2005.

Scholte, Jan Aart, and Roland Robertson, editors. *Encyclopedia of Globalization.* 4 vols. New York: Routledge, 2007

Sherkat, Darren E., and Christopher G. Ellison. "Structuring the Religion-Environment Connection: Identifying Religious Influences on Environmental Concern and Activism." *Journal for the Scientific Study of Religion* 46 (2007) 71–85.

Simpson, John. "Globalization and Religion: Themes and Prospects." In *Religion and Global Order,* edited by William Garrett and Roland Robertson, 1–17. New York: Paragon, 1991.

———. "The Great Reversal: Selves, Communities, and the Global System." *Sociology of Religion* 57 (1996) 115–25.

Warner, W. E. "Publications." In *Dictionary of Pentecostal and Charismatic Christianity,* edited by Stanley M. Burgess and Gary B. McGee, 742–52. Grand Rapids: Zondervan, 1988.

Wilkinson, Loren, editor. *Earthkeeping in the '90s: Stewardship of Creation.* Grand Rapids: Eerdmans, 1991.

Wilkinson, Michael. "Canadian Pentecostalism: An Introduction." In *Canadian Pentecostalism,* edited by Wilkinson, 3–12. Montreal-Kingston: McGill-Queen's University Press, 2009.

———, editor. *Canadian Pentecostalism: Transition and Transformation.* Montreal-Kingston: McGill-Queen's University Press, 2009.

———. *The Spirit Said Go: Pentecostal Immigrants in Canada.* New York: Lang, 2006.

Woodrum, E., and M. J. Wolkomir. "Religious Effects on Environmentalism." *Sociological Spectrum* 17 (1997) 223–34.

10

Looking the Wrong Way

Salvation and the Spirit in Pentecostal Eco-Theology

A. J. Swoboda

INTRODUCTION

Recently, during my annual pilgrimage to the UK to continue my doctoral work, I discovered an unfortunate statistic many American tourists probably do not know.[1] My dissertation advisor confirmed this sad
trend. In the UK, an unfortunately large number of American tourists
and students die each year after being hit by cars while looking the wrong
way as they cross the street due to the flow of traffic being in the opposite
direction in the UK. I even had my own experience when I nearly walked
directly into an oncoming bus unawares. Looking the wrong way metaphorically speaks to the problem for Pentecostals and an underdeveloped
eco-theology, which this chapter attempts to address.

1. My PhD dissertation under Dr. Mark Cartledge is the development of a Pentecostal
eco-Pneumatology asking how Pentecostals and Charismatics view the Holy Spirit and
how their view informs the way they view, care for, and envision the environment.

In its century-old history, Pentecostals have matured in their theological imagination, shown increased academic rigor, exercised denominational repentance, developed an enriched sense of conviction of the Holy Spirit's power and role in social justice, and all marched with continued passion for the salvation of the world. One can see why Pentecostal movements have inspired believers worldwide. It is in this sense that Pentecostals follow the reformation Spirit that yearns for endless reform: *Ecclesia Reformata, Semper Reformanda*.[2] Nevertheless, in regards to ecological care and eco-theology, Pentecostals have been at least looking the wrong way if not altogether unwilling to cross the street. It is my conviction that before Pentecostals can cross the street into new levels of cultural influence and theological breadth, especially in North America, they must train themselves to look both ways, giving fresh attention to the salvation of the world, which includes all creation and not just individuals.

Recently, Pentecostals have been forced to develop an eco-theology. Yet, they remain the last numerically large Christian tradition to be by and large *en absentia* from the eco-theology conversation table.[3] To their credit, eco-theology in the more long-standing traditions of the Christian faith (e.g., Roman Catholic, Orthodox, and Protestant) benefit from being enriched both by a historic systematic, and in some cases mystical, theology.[4] Having only one short century of theological development under its wings, American Pentecostalism lacks the luxury of waiting for such further developments to address the ecological crisis. I contend that eco-theology in the twenty-first century will be perceived in church history as a theology of crisis, and at this point, Pentecostals cannot afford to wait for a systematic theology before addressing the crisis upon them and all human beings.

---

2. That is, "the Church Reformed, Always Reforming."

3. While this is of course not universally the case, as some Pentecostal thinkers have taken up the crucible of developing this eco-theology, such as Harold Hunter, Murray Dempster, Steve Studebaker, Amos Yong, Matt Tallman, Shane Clifton, and Augustinus Dermawan, to name a few. Keep in mind the first Pentecostal publication on the topic came in 1988, the work of then-Pentecostal Jean-Jacque Suurmond.

4. For instance, Roman Catholic Teilhard de Chardin's cosmology relies heavily on Roman Catholic systematics. See for instance Chardin, *Phenomenon of Man*. See also Chardin, *Man's Place in Nature*. This is as well the case for Protestants who often rely heavily on the works of Calvin, Luther, and Kuyper. The Orthodox have a much less developed eco-theology but do have a long standing tradition of systematic thinking that in the long run will benefit them.

In the midst of this crisis, Pentecostals need a sort of ecological *aggiornamento* similar to the Roman Catholic breath of fresh theological air, post-Vatican II. Yet ecology is notoriously a difficult topic with which to get Pentecostals engaged.[5] While they may be reassured this chapter does not argue that the initial sign of the baptism of the Holy Spirit is recycling, it does, nevertheless, argue ecological care is a subsequent sign of the Spirit-filled life, a life deeply concerned with God's created cosmos. It must emerge as a major topic of discussion as Pentecostal theology, praxis, and social justice have a unique opportunity to present the larger ecumenical body a model of Spirit-filled creation care. To that end, I will argue for a distinctively Pentecostal eco-theology based on two primary foci that may have a potentially powerful complement to a larger ecumenical eco-theology. I would like to suggest that a robust and re-invigorated Pentecostal soteriology and pneumatology of creation will play key roles in developing a praxis-centered creation care and relationality-centered ecological stewardship that will bring Pentecostals into a more effective role.[6]

THE PNEUMATOLOGICAL ROOT

Pentecostals worldwide experience the 'groaning of creation' every day by living in relationship to the world around them.[7] We have a worldly existence and a personal relationship to it, a cosmos baptized with the same Spirit that baptizes the believer.[8] Clark Pinnock challenges Pentecostals to develop a theology based on its strength, which he perceives to be relationality.[9] Pinnock, somewhat critical of Pentecostalism's lack of systematic theology, nevertheless contends that its contribution remains in

5. This may be for a number of reasons: fear of the 'liberal' agenda, a turn from the importance of evangelism, eschatological presuppositions. Many Pentecostals may have many reasons to remain absent from the conversation.

6. There are undoubtedly more streams in Pentecostal theology for development of a Pentecostal eco-theology such as the historical and eschatological strain, but for our purposes here, I will focus on these two. My current research focuses primarily on the soteriological, eschatological, historical, and pneumatological streams.

7. Romans 8:18–27 is a key eco-theology text that speaks of the groaning of creation.

8. This is in the sense of Michael Polanyi's classical argument that knowledge comes through personal interaction and relation, not dispassionate observation. His overall argument is a major criticism of so-called "scientific detachment." Knowledge comes through relationship. See Polanyi, *Personal Knowledge*, introduction.

9. Pinnock, "Divine Relationality," 3–26.

emphasizing a relational theology. The notions of the immanent presence of God and God's nearness to earthly life (and non-human life) provide theological categories to emphasize a praxis relationality that Pentecostalism can use to construct new avenues for theological imagination. Could this be its strength creationally? I argue that a pneumatological framework will prove constructive in bridging the God/world gap. The experience of relational nearness with God and the rest of creation through the Spirit will provide a focus for a Pentecostal eco-theology.[10]

Once developed, a Pentecostal eco-theology could further conversation on Pentecostal cosmology and create space for Pentecostals to discover a living cosmology based on the Spirit's life-giving presence in creation. This very well may culminate in a more integrated cosmology that goes beyond mere existence within the world to a more fully interrelated presence in the creation and universe.[11] Cosmological imagination is not an emphatic element of Pentecostal God-talk, academically or ecclesiastically. Pentecostals seem to be experiencing, in the words of John Haught, a cosmic homelessness.[12] But what cosmologist and theologian William Brown, among others, has done to emphasize the importance of cosmological work, imagination, and development within theological systems should not be ignored by Pentecostals. William P. Brown's *The Ethos of the Cosmos* offers Pentecostalism a significant challenge to recapture the story of creation.[13] He suggests that morality and ethical construction flow primarily from a cosmological vision.[14] Without cosmology there

10. Pinnock, "Divine Relationality," 9. In this sense Pentecostalism has an embedded form of empiricism or knowledge that follows experience. Pentecostal experience is dependent on how one defines Pentecostalism. I follow Juan Sepulveda's argument that Pentecostalism does not consist of new doctrine, but rather "Pentecostalism offers a new and direct experience of God, bypassing any foreign cultural or priestly mediation." It is relational over and above doctrinal. See Sepulveda, "Future Perspectives for Latin American Pentecostalism," 191.

11. I was helped in my thinking about the inter-relatedness of creation and all time-centered activity in Page, *Ambiguity and the Presence of God*.

12. A creative phrase borrowed from John Haught in Haught, "Religious and Cosmic Homelessness," 159.

13. See Brown, *Ethos of the Cosmos*. In the same way, Narrative Medicine as a branch of the medical field seeks to bring health to individuals through engagement of their story. In the same way, Pentecostals must re-integrate the story of the creation to its overall theology in order to bring healing to Earth. I was introduced to Narrative Medicine in Pink, *Whole New Mind*, 52.

14. Brown, *The Ethos of the Cosmos*. Brown's main thesis appears to be that the central importance of cosmology within religious and theological discourse is for ethical

is no theology. It follows, therefore, that an ethical treatment of creation would be imbued by what I call a pneumatological cosmology.

The concept of a pneumatological cosmology has already been suggested in the literature. For instance, in Hollenweger's "All Creatures Great and Small," which compares pneumatology in the East with that of the Pentecostals, he argues that a roadblock for Pentecostal pneumatology is its derivative relationship to Western Philosophy, sharing, what he calls, "the deficiencies of the pneumatologies of the western tradition."[15] He argues that the Pentecostal pneumatological apple has landed way too close to the Western tree. Hollenweger suggests that Pentecostals must cautiously, yet intentionally, be mindful of the logs in their theological eye. What he perceptively observes is possibly one of the greatest potential pitfalls for a Pentecostal eco-theology. Pentecostal theology, in particular the American and European forms, has given Western frameworks of theological and philosophical discourse (Baconian utilitarianism) prominence, having, intentionally or not, more or less silenced Eastern influences that traditionally construct a more dignified and respectful view of nature. In essence, the deficiencies to which Hollenweger alludes remain a Western perennial loss of creation's Spirit-centeredness. Yet these deficiencies meet a Pentecostal pneumatology undergoing major rethinking and creative development.[16] Hollenweger proposed a sort of pneumatological evolution, the idea of the Spirit's role in seeing organic life live to its fullest.[17] His prophetic call centered on the Spirit in creatures great and small gives Spirit-centered expression room for a creative and innovative pneumatology. It is within this context that Pentecostalism begins its engagement of creation and eco-theology, especially through a pneumatological lens.

What can Pentecostal pneumatology learn from the East? Edmund Rybarczyk's irreplaceable study *Beyond Salvation* contrasts the theological and spiritual themes within Pentecostal and Eastern Orthodox traditions, proposing very stimulating insights for an eco-theology.[18] From a historical perspective, Rybarczyk makes the case that even Wesley, an

---

and moral constructions. For the intersection of theology to science in the development of a meta-cosmology, see Russell, *Cosmology*, 110–271.

15. Hollenweger, "All Creatures Great and Small," 41 and 44.

16. Hollingsworth, "Spirit and Voice." This is an intriguing example of how Pentecostal Pneumatology is engaging new areas of research previously un-engaged.

17. Martin and Mullen, *Strange Gifts?* 7.

18. Rybarczyk, *Beyond Salvation*.

early forerunner of American Pentecostalism, drew heavily on the Eastern Fathers in his theology, even potentially favoring the East over the West.[19] Although Wesley was a forerunner, Rybarczyk argues that the one key element that gives them similarity is their emphasis on the Holy Spirit and a robust pneumatology. Although Pentecostals struggle with eastern mysticism, he leads us to a vision of mysticism inherent in both traditions. Yet one element remains illusively different. The Eastern traditions will often situate the mystical Spirit holistically in creation throughout its theology while Pentecostals emphasize the mystic Spirit individually through the Spirit-infilling of the individual believer.[20] Striking difference is found in the primary residence of the Holy Spirit's activity. Likewise, Pentecostals view the *imago dei* throughout the Genesis account more anthropocentrically, relating primarily to Adam and Eve as the primary agents, while Eastern theology will often view the *imago dei* resident throughout the cosmos beyond Adam and Eve.

A significant strength of Pentecostal pneumatology is its necessary connection to the biblical account. While a full exegesis is impossible here, we do find focal points throughout the biblical narrative. The Genesis account begins with a prelapsarian Ruach "hovering" over the chaotic creation, which gives life to every creature within the created order. Luke's account strategically alludes to Joel's prophecy of God's Spirit "poured out on all flesh."[21] Paul's theology develops a motif in Romans 8:18–27 of the "groaning creation." There is a clear stream within the biblical tradition of the Spirit's presence, solidarity, and suffering with all creation.

Yet, in speaking of this apparent absence of creation pneumatology within Pentecostal theology, Frank Macchia comments that "Pentecostals are thus not accustomed to detecting the presence of grace in all of life reaching for liberation and redemption through the Spirit of creation (and) . . . neglects the insight that social transformation can be viewed as a legitimate sign of the redemption yet to come in Christ."[22] Macchia highlights two essential elements of a Pentecostal theology that we assume would be integral to a creation theology. First, he mentions the difficulty of seeing the Spirit in all creation. Second, Macchia observes a skeptical

---

19. Ibid., 10.

20. Rybarczyk, *Beyond Salvation*, 9.

21. Acts 2:17–21 is the full text of Joel 2:28–32. Amos Yong's text gives a full-fledged description of Pentecostal theology on this topic. See Yong, *Spirit Poured out on All Flesh*.

22. Macchia, *Baptized in the Spirit*, 279.

view towards social transformative practice. Although liberation theology and social action have been a major thrust outside North America it is unclear as to how Pentecostals view social justice in the West.

Illustrative of indifference among Pentecostals about ecological issues is an article in *Mountain Movers*, an Assemblies of God magazine, written in March of 1989. It says: "The Bible clearly warns that believers will not make this world better . . . Christ did not ask His followers to renovate this place. This place is condemned. Jesus raised up His disciples to pluck men and women out of this world and set them on the path that leads to a heavenly home."[23] This is not to say that Pentecostals always have a negative view of creation as they will sometimes argue the charismatic nature of all creation with the Spirit's ability to speak through the believer.[24]

Jean-Jacque Suurmond speaks of the horizontal yet vertical harmonious lifestyle "not only with the ecological structure of the whole creation, but even the inner life of the triune God."[25] We must note this emphasis on harmony and connectedness, which should develop from a Trinitarian framework. The model, interweaving through Suurmond's work, leads to what we might call an ecclesiological ecology, a view of the charismatic church interconnected with God, creation, and destined to become the *oikos*, or the dwelling place, of the Spirit.[26] A fully charismatic church should live at peace with the fully charismatic creation. But despite this emphasis on pneumatology implicit in Pentecostal theology, Suurmond makes the case that neither "Pentecostalism nor the charismatic renewal has produced a consistent theology involving the whole of life."[27] But it is here that we begin to find an emerging Spirit-centered view of creation that needs to develop.

Additionally, relationality is found often in ecological movements arguing for social justice without a religious basis. The point must be made that a charismatic theology of the Earth and recent scientific findings of its inter-dependence are strikingly similar. While we may agree

23. Dempster, "Christian Social Concern in Pentecostal Perspective," 51–64.

24. Rybarczyk, *Beyond Salvation*, 345.

25. Suurmond, "Christ King," 28. It is important to note historiographically that this is the first substantive academic piece published by a Charismatic or Pentecostal on eco-theology, written in 1988.

26. In this section, Suurmond speaks of the "Holy ecology of the Father, Son, Holy Spirit, and Creation."

27. Suurmond, "Christ King," 28.

with Travis Ables that trinitarian theology is not the necessary element to understanding nature relationally, it very well may be the best place to start. Relationality is central to the organic philosophies of Whitehead and others that emphasize the ontological category of becoming over being and is central to Chardin's omega point theory that sought to conceive a future moment when all creation would find harmony with God and each other. Terry Cross recognizes this strain of relationality in Pinnock's work as well.[28] I would contend that the Pentecostal view of God's relationality is a corrective of Frederick Elder's famous criticism that "Christianity has fostered a dangerous subject-object attitude toward nature, which separates man from nature and promotes a utilitarian mentality, leading to exploitation."[29]

If Pentecostals desire to go further in this discussion, on whose shoulders are they to stand given the dearth of Pentecostal eco-theologians? And in a culture that has an updated Cartesian spirit of "I consume, therefore I am," how will Pentecostals find their footing to engage the golden calves of consumerist society? I propose a reinvigorated pneumatology that imagines the whole of creation as the Spirit's home. While Pentecostal theology is helpful for recapturing the sanctifying nature of the Spirit's role in the life of individuals, it is doubtful whether this vision includes the sanctification and ongoing care of the created order.

THE SOTERIOLOGICAL ROOT

As a foundation, soteriology is core to Pentecostal theology.[30] Early twenty first century-American Pentecostals zealously sought the salvation of all people as they anticipated the imminent return of Jesus. Dispensational Premillenialism coupled with the influence of the Wesleyan/Holiness movement coalesced into a soteriological focus on the salvation and holiness of the individual believer. However, "Now we must seek the salvation

28. Cross notes that "Pinnock has made a good case that Pentecostals readily ward to the concept of a relational God—a God who interacts with his creation." Cross, "Rich Feast of Theology," 32.

29. Elder, *Crisis in Eden*, 19.

30. I borrow "foundation" language from Carl Raschke, who argues for a "minimal Foundationalism," or a foundation that includes only essential and important issues. It is unlikely ecological issues will be a foundation of Pentecostal theology as long as it is not included in soteriology. If it is included therein, ecological issues must be foundational for any biblical theology. See Raschke, *Next Reformation*. This is similar to what Douglas Webster calls "limited dogma" in Webster, *Yes to Mission*, 18.

of all creation."[31] These words of Pentecostal historian and theologian Harold Hunter have in many ways opened the door for a Pentecostal engagement of ecological issues, especially for soteriological purposes. His article, "Pentecostal Healing for God's Sick Creation," written in 2000, was a breakthrough for Pentecostals who were frustrated with a lack of soteriology beyond the individual person.[32] Hunter's work, which examines models in South Korean Pentecostalism, typifies a trend within Pentecostalism to re-frame salvation beyond the individual to a cosmologically and holistically-centered salvation. For Hunter, soteriology must outgrow its early Pentecostal mold and begin to shape the way we understand what full-gospel means beyond individual salvation.[33] From a soteriological perspective, this full-gospel should include the salvation and healing of all creation (human and non-human), which has been baptized in God's Spirit as it yearns for Jesus's return to the Earth.

Miroslav Volf sees a disconnection in Pentecostal language about this full-gospel.[34] Volf comments that "a 'full-gospel'—to use a favorite Pentecostal aphorism—can consist only in the unity of personal-spiritual, individual-physical, socioeconomic, and ecological aspects of salvation."[35] In other words, the need for a more holistic approach to the Pentecostal "full-gospel" knocks at the door. His article on the "Materiality of Salvation" discusses the main differences between Liberation and Pentecostal theology while examining the nature of a bodily salvation.[36] For Volf, this "materiality of salvation" depends on its influence in all spheres of existence, not just the personal and individual. Pentecostalism in North America has often become intertwined with traditional Reformation and evangelical Protestant theology and many within the Pentecostal tradition, like

31. Hunter, "Pentecostal Healing for God's Sick Creation?" 154.

32. It should be noted that this is one of the first published academic articles written by a Pentecostal about ecological issues and the need for engagement.

33. Thanks to Shane Clifton for posing this question in his conference paper at the 2008 SPS/WTS conference at Duke University. Clifton, "Preaching the 'Full Gospel' in the Context of the Global Environment Crises." The "full-gospel" is a term often used of Pentecostalism's view of Jesus Christ as healer, savior, baptizer, and soon coming King.

34. For an explication of this "Four-fold" or "Full-gospel" Pentecostal theology of "Jesus Christ as Healer, Baptizer, Savior, and Soon Coming King," see Dayton, *Theological Roots of Pentecostalism*.

35. Volf, "Materiality of Salvation," 467.

36. Ibid., 448. For a well-argued perspective on the connections between liberation and Pentecostal theology, see Sepulveda, "Pentecostalism and Liberation Theology," 51–64.

Volf and Hunter, have called for a renewed vision of salvation beyond the anthropocentric to a more cosmos-centric soteriology. Australian Pentecostal Shane Clifton envisions this full-gospel to include all aspects of life, especially ecological, in a Pentecostal theology. Aside from an emphasis on the nearness of the Spirit in enabling spiritual gifts such as glossolalia and healing, there does seem to be among Pentecostals a lack of a sense of the materiality of salvation.

The drive of this soteriological refinement has no doubt been fueled by conversations with prominent non-Pentecostals, such as Jürgen Moltmann. Surely this newfound relationship has provided Pentecostals a much needed dialogue partner and theological conversant, especially in discussions on the nature of salvation.[37] Important aspects of Moltmann's thinking have focused on the pathos (suffering) of God, God's solidarity with creation, and the eschatological hope of creation, drawing heavily on Kazo Kitamori's suffering-centered theology and Martin Luther's theology of the cross. Moltmann highlights God's relationship to the world and re-contextualizes a theology based on relationality.[38] For God to feel the pain of the world is for God to be in relationship to the world, a relationship and desire for salvation that goes beyond human beings. Salvation in this regard echoes the Hebraic idea of shalom (wholeness), which consistently goes beyond the individual, and includes the community, the nation, the world, and the land.[39] In this regard, human community and relationality have always played a key role within Pentecostal movements.[40] Volf agrees with Moltmann that soteriological zeal is important, but of the kind that never needs to escape from the world.[41]

37. So influential among Pentecostals and Charismatics was Moltmann that he was the keynote guest at the 2008 joint WTS-SPS conference at Duke University, which allowed many Pentecostals and Wesleyans an opportunity for face-to-face feedback from Moltmann on their developing theology.

38. Moltmann, *Crucified God*, 11. Moltmann has made it clear that a large part of his theology of the *pathos of God* arises from his experience in prison camps as well as the theology of Japanese Kazo Kitamori. See Kitamori, *Theology of the Pain of God*.

39. The Hebrew word for "salvation" is wholeness. There is a constant connection in the Hebrew Bible between the sin and righteousness of Israel to the health of the land. See Studebaker, "The Spirit in Creation." As well, in particular, see Dempsey, "Hope Amidst Crisis," 269–84.

40. Keep in mind William Seymour's vision for blacks and whites to worship together at the Azusa Street revival. Trans-cultural and bi-racial relationships have since Seymour's work in Los Angeles been a key theme of Pentecostal community. See the introduction to Burgess and Maas.

41. Volf, "Rhythm of Adoration and Action," 40.

The escapist bent and focus on the Christian's inner-life are often marks of classic Pentecostalism that inevitably shape its views of the Spirit's role in salvation.[42] Andre Drooger's intriguing article, "The Normalization of Religious Experience," examines, among other items, the constant tension Pentecostals face in relationship to cultures around them.[43] This is often fueled by a Pentecostal view of being called out of the world as a sanctified people preparing for the return of the Lord. As the Spirit sanctifies, people become less like the world around them. The Spirit's work within the individual, and not outside, becomes the primary workplace of the Spirit. Drooger argues that Pentecostals rely on "[the Spirit's] role in the Creation and on Pentecost [which] is continued in the life of the believer."[44] The believer, and not creation, becomes the continued agent of God's Spirit. This indwelling always forces Pentecostals to integrate their theology into daily life. Drooger eloquently concludes, "While nature is not explicitly valued in religious terms, it makes itself felt in the lives of Pentecostals. Where the growth of Pentecostalism is explained on the basis of problems with which people were confronted, nature becomes relevant. If and when illness is the cause of these problems, nature's role is obvious. Especially in Latin America, local growth has been linked to natural disasters like floods, droughts, and earthquakes."[45]

Volf, once again, speaks of our *Cooperatio Dei*, the believer's cooperation in healing the world and its ills.[46] Yet Pentecostals outside of a liberationist view, especially in Latin America, Korea, and South Africa, often fail to see their cooperation with God in both the spiritual and the social. The unfortunate existence of a difference between the two remains. Social justice and spirituality are not always parallel programs in Pentecostal thinking and practice. Volf makes the argument that the second creation account makes the case for cooperation with God as necessary for the world to function.[47] Christian spirituality as an extension of the Jewish faith finds more purpose than the mere salvation of souls, but also of trees, animals, and all physical matter in which God placed human beings.

42. Ruether calls this escapism prevalent in Christian thought "salvation from nature" as opposed to salvation of nature. See Ruether, *Sexism and God-Talk*, 79.

43. Droogers, "Normalization of Religious Experience," 46–49.

44. Ibid., 46.

45. Ibid., 48.

46. Thanks to Miroslav Volf for introducing me to this idea in Volf, *Work in the Spirit*, 98.

47. Volf, "God at Work."

Denton Lotz, one time general secretary for the Baptist World Alliance, says: "There seems to be a conflict between those who emphasize saving souls and those who emphasize saving trees."[48] Pentecostals often fully embrace cooperation with God in personal salvation, healing, and Spirit-baptism, but not in the wider arena of creation.

Salvation in the Hebrew tradition goes beyond the individual to include a broader social and corporate idea. Although rarely engaging the Creation/Spirit tradition immanent in the Old Testament, some Pentecostals have found rich fruit in the Hebrew tradition for their theology.[49] For instance, Wonsuk Ma argues this may be the case because for most Pentecostals the Hebrew Bible as a whole is not a Charismatic category.[50] However, Murray Dempster argues that there is a possibility for a Pentecostal social concern based on the Hebrew Bible. In his construction, five features of Old Testament social ethics remain relevant for the contemporary church. These are: a theocentric foundation, the *Imago dei*, the portrayal of a covenant people, the prophetic tradition of social criticism, and Jubilee teachings.[51] Dempster's theology raises a question: Can we see the *Imago dei* in non-human creation? He further makes the case that Pentecostals must engage social justice because "the church's evangelism efforts need to be authenticated by a ministry of social action that puts into practice what it preaches."[52] Thorleif Boman also argues that Pentecostal spirituality is much more compatible with Hebrew ways of thought as dynamic, vigorous, and passionate than with Greek forms of thought that tend to be static, peaceful, and moderate.[53]

So we return again to a relationally focused spirituality that offers a robust perspective for a soteriology that seeks the salvation of the whole world. Travis Ables proposes that a trinitarian theology is not necessary to understand creation relationally but rather should inform more practically "the kind of people we are."[54] Ables and others have been quick to

48. Campolo, *How to Rescue the Earth without Worshipping Nature*, 10.

49. For instance see the important work of Ma, *Until the Spirit Comes*. See also Yong, "Ruach, the Primordial Chaos, and the Breath of Life," 183–204.

50. Ma, Menzies, and Spittler, *Spirit and Spirituality*, 16.

51. Dempster, "Pentecostal Social Concern and the Biblical Mandate of Social Justice," 129.

52. Ibid.

53. Boman, *Hebrew Thought Compared with Greek*.

54. Ables, "Ladder Leading toward God: Pneumatology and the Environmental Crisis," 15.

utilize the social trinitarianism of Jürgen Moltmann and Miroslav Volf, which has been influential not only in theological abstraction, but also in ecclesiological contexts.[55] We ought to have before us a new perspective in soteriology that very well may shape a renewed commitment to see creation freed from its bondage.

In large part, a roadblock for Pentecostal theology and praxis for developing an eco-theology is its emphasis on the salvation of the individual, particularly in light of the Pentecostal view of the return of the Lord and the end of all things. This soteriological passion must not be lost, simply enlarged. As with pneumatology, our challenge is to re-imagine the salvation of the world not simply in human-centered modes, but rather to capture the larger cosmic vision of Christ in the recapitulation of all creation to its unified state of inter-relation with humanity and God. Christ came so that God could be "all in all" and "the reconciliation of all things" (Rom 15:28 and Col 1:20). Pentecostal passion is one of its hallmarks and it must be continued, but in a way that includes care for all of God's creation: the birds of the air, the fish of the sea, the trees of the land, all of the groaning created order.

Endeavors to construct a Pentecostal eco-theology must lead to a praxis-centered end. To a degree, what is needed is what Jeff Astley calls ordinary theology or the theology of the formally uneducated.[56] There must always be a central element of Pentecostal eco-theology that is praxis-centered, able to be practiced in congregational life, and somewhat concrete for the ordinary everyday believer. To their praise, Pentecostals perennially ask the question, "Great idea, how can we do it?"[57] As well, any Pentecostal eco-theology with primarily an esoteric focus and thus un-doable would do little to see actual change take place unless the goal was wasting more paper, which would in turn be the opposite of its goal. This is a perfect ground in which Pentecostals, who are seen as ordinary individuals, especially through their growth outside North America, can engage with developing forms of theological discourse. This issue is simply waiting to be addressed. Is a Pentecostal engagement of social issues such

55. As an excellent example of social Trinitarianism, in particular as it relates to ecclesiology, see Volf, *After Our Likeness*.

56. See Astley, *Ordinary Theology*.

57. Thank you to Charles Lee's *Cultural Ministry* course at Life Pacific College in San Dimas, California for listening to a one-hour presentation on Pentecostal eco-theology and responding with this simple classic Pentecostal question. This is similar to Aristotle's idea of *Phronesis*, which is the interdependence of theory and practice.

as debt reduction, poverty eradication, or even ecological destruction ever going to make it through the academic ranks to a lay-level lifestyle? As well as being praxis-centered, it must be constructed biblically for "the starting point and very foundation for Pentecostal faith and practice has been the Biblical text."[58] Since Pentecostals often claim to be a "people of the book," a Pentecostal eco-theology must be biblically rooted.[59]

CONCLUSION

To conclude, this chapter has argued that soteriology and pneumatology are two promising areas for Pentecostals to critically engage eco-theology through resituating a more holistic pneumatology and envisioning a more expansive soteriology. Yet, balance is necessary. It must be clear that it should never be our intention to focus entirely on the ecological crisis at the risk of neglecting theological development, biblical exegesis, and other important issues engaging Pentecostal thinkers. At the same time, our vision must go beyond simply recycling the Sunday morning bulletins to a more life-enriching vision that shapes not only our church policy, but also the depths of our personal piety. Clearly, focusing solely on the ecological problems we face will never lead to a sustainable Pentecostal lifestyle that honors the Spirit-baptized creation. Staring at the problems never solved them. Yet, Pentecostals serve a God who cares for the salvation of souls and trees alike. And as we envision a salvation that includes all creation and a Spirit that lives throughout that creation, we can begin to have a more holistic vision of God's salvation as a Spirit-filled church called to care for the Spirit-filled creation. We end where we began, back in the U.K. ready to cross the street. I suppose we should listen to the advice and look both ways.

BIBLIOGRAPHY

Anderson, Allan. *An Introduction to Pentecostalism: Global Charismatic Christianity.* Cambridge: Cambridge University Press, 2004.

58. Arrington, "Use of the Bible by Pentecostals," 101.

59. Pentecostals have developed excellent works finding these charismatic strains throughout the Bible. For instance, an excellent engagement of the Charismatic strain in the Lukan tradition (including Acts), see Stronstad, *Charismatic Theology of St. Luke.*

Arrington, French L. "The Use of the Bible by Pentecostals." *Pneuma: The Journal of the Society for Pentecostal Studies* 16 (1994) 101–7.

Astley, Jeff. *Ordinary Theology: Looking, Listening, and Learning in Theology.* Aldershot, UK: Ashgate, 2002.

Boman, Thorleif. *Hebrew Thought Compared with Greek.* Philadelphia: Westminster, 1960.

Brown, William P. *The Ethos of the Cosmos: The Genesis of Moral Imagination in the Bible.* Grand Rapids: Eerdmans, 1999.

Burgess, Stanley M., and Eduard M. van der Maas. *The New International Dictionary of Pentecostal and Charismatic Movements.* Rev and expanded ed. Grand Rapids: Zondervan, 2002.

Campolo, Anthony. *How to Rescue the Earth without Worshipping Nature: A Christian's Call to Save Creation.* Nashville: Nelson, 1992.

Clifton, Shane. "Preaching the 'Full Gospel' in the Context of the Global Environment Crises." Paper presented at the 2008 Gathering of the Society of Pentecostal Studies. Raleigh, NC.

Cross, Terry L. "The Rich Feast of Theology: Can Pentecostals bring the Main Course or only the Relish?" *Journal of Pentecostal Theology* (2000) 27–47.

Dayton, Donald W. *Theological Roots of Pentecostalism.* Studies in Evangelicalism 5. Peabody, MA: Hendrickson, 1987.

Dempsey, Carol J. "Hope Amidst Crisis: A Prophetic Vision of Cosmic Redemption." In *All Creation is Groaning: An Interdisciplinary Vision for Life in a Sacred Universe,* edited by Carol J. Dempsey and Russell A. Butkus, 269–84. Collegeville, MN: Liturgical, 1999.

Dempster, Murray W. "Christian Social Concern in Pentecostal Perspective: Reformulating Pentecostal Eschatology." *Journal of Pentecostal Theology* 2 (1993) 51–64.

———. "Pentecostal Social Concern and the Biblical Mandate of Social Justice." *Pneuma: The Journal of the Society for Pentecostal Studies* 9 (1987) 129–53.

Dempster, Murray W., Byron D. Klaus, and Douglas Petersen. *Called and Empowered: Global Mission in Pentecostal Perspective.* Peabody, MA: Hendrickson, 1991.

Droogers, Andre. "The Normalization of Religious Experience: Healing, Prophecy, Dreams, and Visions." In *Charismatic Christianity as a Global Culture,* edited by Karla Poewe, 33–50. Columbia: University of South Carolina Press, 2002.

Elder, Frederick Milton. *Crisis in Eden: A Religious Study of Man and Environment.* Nashville: Abingdon, 1970.

Faupel, D. William. *The Everlasting Gospel: The Significance of Eschatology in the Development of Pentecostal Thought.* Sheffield, UK: Sheffield Academic, 1996.

Fitch, David E. *The Great Giveaway: Reclaiming the Mission of the Church.* Grand Rapids: Baker, 2005.

Haught, John F. "Religious and Cosmic Homelessness: Some Environmental Implications." In *Liberating Life: Contemporary Approaches to Ecological Theology,* edited by Charles Birch, William Eakin, and Jay McDaniels, 159–81. Maryknoll, NY: Orbis, 2002.

Hofstadter, Richard. *Anti-Intellectualism in American Life.* New York: Knopf, 1974.

Hollenweger, Walter J. "All Creatures Great and Small: Towards a Pneumatology of Life." In *Strange Gifts?: A Guide to Charismatic Renewal,* edited by David Martin and Peter Mullen, 41–53. Oxford: Basil Blackwell, 1984.

———. *Pentecostalism: Origins and Developments Worldwide.* Peabody, MA: Hendrickson, 1997.

Hollingsworth, Andrea. "Spirit and Voice: Toward a Feminist Pentecostal Pneumatology." *Pneuma: The Journal of the Society for Pentecostal Studies* 29 (2007) 189–213.

Hunter, Harold D. "Pentecostal Healing for God's Sick Creation?" *The Spirit & Church* 2 (2000) 145–67.

Hunter, Harold D., and Peter Hocken, editors. *All Together in One Place: Theological Papers from the Brighton Conference on World Evangelization.* Sheffield, UK: Sheffield Academic, 1993.

Karkkainen, Veli-Matti. *Introduction to Ecclesiology: Ecumenical, Historical and Global Perspectives.* Downers Grove, IL: InterVarsity, 2002.

Kitamori, Kazo. *Theology of the Pain of God.* 1965. Reprinted, Eugene, OR: Wipf & Stock, 2005.

Ma, Wonsuk. *Until the Spirit Comes: The Spirit of God in the Book of Isaiah.* Journal for the Study of the Old Testament Supplement Series 271. Sheffield, UK: Sheffield Academic, 1999.

Macchia, Frank D. *Baptized in the Spirit: A Global Pentecostal Theology.* Grand Rapids: Zondervan, 2006.

Marsden, George M. *Fundamentalism and American Culture.* New York: Oxford University Press, 2006.

Martin, David, and Peter Mullen. *Strange Gifts?: A Guide to Charismatic Renewal.* Oxford: Blackwell, 1984.

Moltmann, Jürgen. *The Crucified God.* New York: Harper & Row, 1974.

———. "The Spirit Gives Life." In *All Together in One Place: Theological Papers from the Brighton Conference on World Evangelization,* edited by Harold D. Hunter and Peter Hocken, 22–37. Sheffield, UK: Sheffield Academic, 1993.

Noll, Mark A. *The Scandal of the Evangelical Mind.* Grand Rapids: Eerdmans, 1995.

Page, Ruth. *Ambiguity and the Presence of God.* London: SCM, 1985.

Pink, Daniel H. *A Whole New Mind: Why Right-Brainers Will Rule the Future.* New York: Riverhead, 2006.

Pinnock, Clark H. "Divine Relationality: A Pentecostal Contribution to the Doctrine of God." *Journal of Pentecostal Theology* 16 (2000) 3–26.

Polanyi, Michael. *Personal Knowledge: Towards a Post-Critical Philosophy.* Chicago: University of Chicago Press, 2000.

Price, Lynne. *Theology Out of Place: A Theological Biography of Walter J. Hollenweger.* London: Sheffield Academic, 2002.

Raschke, Carl A. *The Next Reformation: Why Evangelicals Must Embrace Post-Modernity.* Grand Rapids: Baker, 2004.

Ruether, Rosemary Radford. *Sexism and God-Talk: Toward a Feminist Theology.* Boston: Beacon, 1983.

Russell, Robert J. *Cosmology: from Alpha to Omega.* Minneapolis: Fortress, 2008.

Rybarczyk, Edmund J., and Cecil M. Robeck. *Beyond Salvation: Eastern Orthodoxy and Classical Pentecostalism on becoming like Christ.* Carlisle, UK: Paternoster, 2004.

Sepulveda, Juan. "Pentecostalism and Liberation Theology." In *All Together in One Place: Theological Papers from the Brighton Conference on World Evangelization,* edited by Harold D. Hunter and Peter Hocken, 51–64. Sheffield, UK: Sheffield Academic, 1993.

———. "Future Perspectives for Latin American Pentecostalism." *International Review of Mission* 87.345 (1998) 189–95.

Spittler, Russell P. "Are Pentecostals and Charismatics Fundamentalists?: A review of American uses of these Categories." In *Charismatic Christianity as a Global*

Culture, edited by Karla Poewe, 103–16. Columbia: University of South Carolina Press, 2002.

Stronstad, Roger. *The Charismatic Theology of St. Luke*. Peabody, MA: Hendrickson, 1984.

Studebaker, Steven M. "The Spirit in Creation: A Unified Theology of Grace and Creation Care." *Zygon* 43 (2008) 943–60.

Suurmond, Jean Jacques. "Christ King: A Charismatic Appeal for an Ecological Lifestyle." *Pneuma: The Journal of the Society for Pentecostal Studies* 10 (1988) 26–35.

Teilhard de Chardin, Pierre. *The Phenomenon of Man*. New York: Harper, 1959.

———. *Man's Place in Nature*. New York: Harper & Row, 1966.

Volf, Miroslav. *After Our Likeness: The Church as the Image of the Trinity*. Sacra Doctrina. Grand Rapids: Eerdmans, 1998.

———. "God at Work." *Word & World* 25 (2005) 381–93.

———. "Materiality of Salvation: An Investigation in the Soteriologies of Liberation and Pentecostal Theologies." *Journal of Ecumenical Studies* 26 (1989) 447–67.

———. "A Rhythm of Adoration and Action." In *All Together in One Place: Theological Papers from the Brighton Conference on World Evangelization*, edited by Harold D. Hunter and Peter Hocken, 38–45. Sheffield, UK: Sheffield Academic, 1993.

———. *Work in the Spirit: Toward a Theology of Work*. 1991. Reprint, Eugene, OR: Wipf & Stock, 2001.

Warrington, Keith. *Pentecostal Theology: A Theology of Encounter*. New York: T. & T. Clark, 2008.

Webster, Douglas. *Yes to Mission*. London: SCM, 1966.

Wells, David F. *The Search for Salvation*. 1978. Reprint, Eugene, OR: Wipf & Stock, 2000.

Wilber, Ken. *A Theory of Everything: An Integral Vision for Business, Politics, Science, and Spirituality*. Boston: Shambhala, 2001.

Wirzba, Norman. *The Paradise of God: Renewing Religion in an Ecological Age*. New York: Oxford University Press, 2003.

Yong, Amos. "Ruach, the Primordial Chaos, and the Breath of Life: Emergence Theory and the Creation Narratives in Pneumatological Perspective." In *The Work of the Spirit: Pneumatology and Pentecostalism*, edited by Michael Welker, 183–204. Grand Rapids: Eerdmans, 2006.

———. *The Spirit Poured out on All Flesh: Pentecostalism and the Possibility of Global Theology*. Grand Rapids: Baker, 2005.

11

Creation Care as "Keeping in Step with the Spirit"

Steven M. Studebaker

INTRODUCTION

I remember changing the oil in my car and pouring the old oil on the weeds that grew along the backside of my parents' garage. Of course I knew that doing such was illegal and harmful to the environment, but at the time I did not give it much thought; after all, I would not get caught and Jesus would return soon and ultimately destroy the earth and its evil inhabitants. What is important to note is that I dumped that oil as a Christian and that I did not sense that it was in any way at odds with my confession of Christ. Moreover, my indifference toward the earth had a direct theological foundation in dispensational premillennial eschatology and the traditional Pentecostal concern for spiritual matters over worldly ones. The problem is that Pentecostals often are unaccustomed to think of environmental efforts as a dimension of Christian formation.

248

Pentecostals are trained to consider their decision about which DVD to rent at Blockbuster as an issue of Christian formation. For example, should I watch a film that is rated "R" for violence, language, and nudity? But, how often do we consider a visit to the car dealer and our decision about the type of car we buy and drive an issue of Christian formation? Does this not implicitly say that as Christians we care about what pollutes our minds, but are less concerned about what pollutes the air we breath? I served in a church as a youth pastor in which a board member thought that it was a bad testimony for the youth pastor to be seen attending movies at the local theatre. What the board member meant was that my presence at the theatre gave a tacit affirmation of the values and behaviors promoted in Hollywood movies. Yet, the same fellow did not consider being seen driving around town in a full-size pick-up truck a poor testimony. Now my point is not to suggest that we should not go to movie theaters and that it is un-Christian to own certain vehicles. However, I want to encourage us to consider that our decisions and actions that have an impact on the health of planetary life are just as much a part of our Christian formation as the decisions and actions that impact what we more often think of as our "spiritual" life.

This chapter maintains that creation care is a participation in the redemptive mission of the triune God and, therefore, a dimension of Christian formation. The basis for this is a trinitarian understanding of the Holy Spirit as "the Spirit of Christ." The foundation of this proposal is a version of the Augustinian mutual love trinitarian model influenced by the insights of Roman Catholic David Coffey. In order to develop the proposal, the following first defines Karl Rahner's notion of the *entelechy* of the Spirit as "the Spirit of Christ," second details David Coffey's work that gives Rahner's notion of the *entelechy* of the Spirit a trinitarian articulation, and third extends the theology of the *entelechy* of the Spirit to all of creation and thereby enables it to provide a theological basis for seeing creation care as a way of "[keeping] in step with the Spirit" (i.e., Christian formation).

THE MUTUAL LOVE MODEL OF THE TRINITY AND THE *ENTELECHY* OF THE HOLY SPIRIT

Karl Rahner and especially David Coffey, who follows and develops Rahner's theology, point out that the Holy Spirit bears an *entelechy* toward the Son. An *entelechy* (as the term is used by Rahner and Coffey) is an internal force or principle that drives a being toward its destiny.[1] When applied to the Holy Spirit it refers to the redemptive purpose that motivates and orients the work of the Holy Spirit in redemption. The philosophical term *entelechy* helps to express the theology of the biblical description of the Holy Spirit as "the Spirit of Christ."[2]

Rahner used *entelechy* in two senses.[3] In the first sense, the Holy Spirit is the *entelechy* of the history of revelation and salvation; that is, the Holy Spirit is the intrinsic principle that directs revelation and salvation history. In the second sense, Christ, inclusive of the Incarnation, cross, and resurrection (and the actualization of its grace in human persons), is the *entelechy* of the Holy Spirit. In this second use of *entelechy*, Rahner understands the Christ event as the final cause (the goal or end of an activity that determines the operation of efficient causality) of the Spirit's efficient work in the world. Since Christ is the final cause of the Spirit's work, Christ is the *entelechy* of the Spirit; this is the case because the Christ event informs the Spirit's direction of the history of revelation and salvation. The two senses in which Rahner uses *entelechy* are distinct, but coherent. However, the second use (Christ as the *entelechy* of the Spirit) is foundational (theologically primary) because it informs the first (the Spirit as the *entelechy* of salvation history) or the first follows naturally from the second. Finally, the Holy Spirit is "the Spirit of Christ" because the *entelechy* of the Spirit's work is Christ. Coffey's contribution is to give Rahner's notion of the *entelechy* of the Spirit trinitarian articulation. Coffey relies on the mutual love model of the Trinity to do so, as detailed in the following section.[4]

1. Rahner's use of the terms differs from its traditional Aristotelian sense, according to which *entelechy* denotes something having perfection (see Coffey, "Trinitarian Response to Issues Raised by Phan," 852–74).

2. Coffey notes that the biblical notion of the Holy Spirit as "the Spirit of Christ" has two senses. The one most familiar is the Holy Spirit as "the Spirit of Christ" poured out on the Day of Pentecost by the risen Christ and subsequently in the life of believers and the church. The second sense, and the one that the current essay treats, is "the Spirit of Christ" that 1 Peter 1:11 indicates. In 1 Peter, the Spirit is "the Spirit of Christ" prior to the Incarnation and outpouring of the Spirit at Pentecost; the Spirit is "the Spirit of Christ" who worked in the prophets of the ancient Israelite community to lead salvation history to the Incarnation and the gift of the Spirit at Pentecost. See Coffey, "Spirit of Christ as Entelechy," 365–70.

3. Rahner, *Jesus, Man, and the Church*, 46.

4. The mutual love model of the Trinity has a long history in Western theology. Historians of the Christian traditions identify its origin with Augustine of Hippo (354–430). Although overshadowed by the psychological analogy, it features prominently in

The *Entelechy* of the Holy Spirit in the Mutual Love Model

A social vision of love is central to the mutual love model. The mutual love model posits that the Father from eternity generated the Son and that the Holy Spirit proceeds and subsists as the mutual love of the Father for the Son and of the Son for the Father.[5] The Father and the Son in their love for one another bring forth the Holy Spirit. The assimilation of the Father and the Son occurs in the subsistence of the Holy Spirit as their mutual love. As mutual love, the Holy Spirit's primary characteristic is union. The Spirit is the love that indissolubly unites the Father and the Son. The subsistence of the Holy Spirit as the person who facilitates the communion between the Father and the Son completes the dynamic sharing of love in the Godhead. This describes the relationships that characterize the eternal life of God or the immanent Trinity.

The identity of the Holy Spirit as mutual love does not depersonalize the Spirit. The Spirit is a unique divine person whose activity is that of uniting the other two divine persons.[6] The Spirit is not an impersonal

---

the thought of central Western theological figures such as Thomas Aquinas (d. 1274) and Bonaventure (1217–1274). For background on the mutual love model, see Fortman, *Triune God*, 204–17.

5. Denis Edwards and Mark Wallace both use the notion of the Holy Spirit as the divine love between the Father and the Son, but they do not develop the Spirit's identity as such and its informative power for the Spirit's work in creation within an Augustinian framework. Although appreciating the Western insight of Augustine, Edwards draws on the trinitarian theology of Basil of Caesarea (Edwards, *Breath of Life*, 120 and 148–57). Wallace's interests lie in the performative truth function of pneumatology; that is, the ability of a pneumatological image to inform an environmental ethic that is consistent with love of neighbor (Wallace, *Fragments of the Spirit*, 145 and 168). My project draws explicitly on the Augustinian trinitarian tradition and shows the theological relationship between the Spirit's identity and work that in turn funds a creation care ethic or performative truth concern.

6. Theologians routinely critique the mutual love model as embodying the Western tradition's preoccupation with divine oneness over and against the primacy of divine threeness in the Eastern tradition. For examples of this characterization, see Boff, *Trinity and Society*, 77–85; Brown, *The Divine*, 243–44; Gunton, "Augustine, the Trinity, and the Theological Crisis in the West," 32; LaCugna, *God for Us*, 96–97 and 101; Moltmann, *Trinität und Reich Gottes*, 166 and 193–94; and Zizioulas, *Being as Communion*, 17 and 87–88.

For a criticism of the oneness-threeness/Western-Eastern/Augustinian-Cappadocian paradigm's problematic premise that the mutual love tradition cannot incorporate a relational understanding of the Trinity, see Studebaker, *Jonathan Edwards' Social Augustinian Trinitarianism*; "Jonathan Edwards's Social *Augustinian* Trinitarianism: An Alternative to a Recent Trend," 268–85; and "Integrating Social and Augustinian Theories of Divine Person," 3–19.

unifying power, but the divine person (a subsistence of the fullness of the divine nature) who facilitates the interpersonal and loving communion of the trinitarian God. The Holy Spirit is called "love" because the nature of love is to unite others in fellowship. Stated in more personal terms, the Holy Spirit is the divine person who constitutes the loving fellowship of the trinitarian God.[7]

Coffey maintains that although the Holy Spirit subsists as the mutual love of the Father and the Son, the most basic component of this is that the Spirit is the Father's love that rests on the Son.[8] The reciprocal love of the Son for the Father that completes their mutual love presumes the Father's initial love. Thus, the Spirit is "first" the Father's love directed to the Son. Of course the sequence of the Father loving the Son who then returns love to the Father is one of nature and not of time. In other words, the Spirit does not initially exist as the Father's love and then in the next moment as the Son and Father's mutual love. But rather, the Spirit eternally exists as the divine person who facilitates the fellowship of the Father and the Son. Recognizing the primacy of the Father's love for the Son relative to that of Son's love for the Father does not invoke temporal succession any more than does describing the Son as being eternally *from* the Father. And yet, at the same time, the affirmation of the eternal nature of the immanent relations that constitute the identities of the divine persons does not mitigate a real order to those relations.

For example, the Father cannot be the Father without the Son. This point illustrates the mutually constitutive nature of the relations for the identities of the Father and the Son. However, while recognizing the mutual constitution of personal identities, the Father has priority of order in the relationship because the Son is *from* the Father. In a similar way, to speak of the Spirit as the mutual love of the Father and the Son affirms both the eternity of the Spirit as the divine person who facilitates the communion of the Father and the Son and the priority of the Father's love in the interpersonal or mutual love between the Father and the Son. Thus, the Spirit, as the person who constitutes the Father and Son in an eternal fellowship of love, "first" unites the Father to the Son in love and

7. Although understanding the Holy Spirit as the mutual love of the Father and the Son runs the risk of portraying the Spirit as passive, this is not necessary to the model. For instance, Augustine treats this concern when he clarifies, "he [the Holy Spirit] is given as God's gift in such a way that as God he also gives himself (see Augustine, *The Trinity*, 15.36 [424]).

8. Coffey *"Did You Receive the Holy Spirit When You Believed?"* 97–98.

"second" unites the Son to the Father. Furthermore, the Spirit's role in uniting the Father to the Son is primary in identifying the personal identity of the Spirit. What this means is that the Spirit's orientation to the Son is primary in the Spirit's personal identity. Coffey maintains that this fundamental orientation of the Spirit to the Son is the *entelechy* of the Holy Spirit.[9] The *entelechy* of the Spirit then is to be the one who unites the Father to the Son and, therefore, the divine person who always seeks and rests on the Son.[10]

Christ as the *Entelechy* of the Holy Spirit (or, the Holy Spirit as "the Spirit of Christ")

Coffey's account of the *entelechy* of the Spirit provides the theological, and more specifically the trinitarian, rationale for the biblical description of the Holy Spirit as "the Spirit of Christ." The Bible assumes when it calls the Holy Spirit "the Spirit of Christ" that the Spirit's work in the mission of the triune God always has orientation to Christ. As Pentecostals, our experience coheres with this because we describe the Spirit as the one who testifies to and glorifies Christ in us. The Holy Spirit has an orientation to Christ because the Spirit is the divine person who proceeds as the Father's love for the Son.

The Spirit is "the Spirit of Christ" in the sense that the Spirit is always moving toward the Son as an expression of the Father's love. What the Spirit does from eternity is what the Spirit does in the economy of redemption. This is the case because the Spirit's identity informs the Spirit's actions. Since the Spirit is the one who eternally brings the Father into loving union with the Son, the Spirit seeks to draw all things to their form of participation in the Son. The description of the Holy Spirit as "the Spirit of Christ" (or Christ as the *entelechy* of the Holy Spirit) captures the way the Spirit's role in the immanent Trinity is played out in the economy of redemption. In other words, reciprocity characterizes identity and work of the Spirit in both the eternal Godhead (immanent Trinity) and the work of redemption in creation (economic Trinity). Coffey specifies the concrete form of the Holy Spirit as "the Spirit of Christ" in terms of a Spirit Christology and a pneumatological concept of grace.

9. Coffey, *"Did You Receive the Holy Spirit When You Believed?"* 98.

10. Coffey's integration of the *entelechy* of the Spirit with the Spirit's personal identity in the immanent Trinity gives the notion its trinitarian rationale that is not found in Rahner's usage.

Spirit Christology and the *Entelechy* of the Holy Spirit

In the Incarnation, the fellowship of the trinitarian God comes to realization in the humanity of Jesus Christ. What is important for our discussion of the Holy Spirit as "the Spirit of Christ" is that the Spirit's identity and role in the immanent Trinity as the divine person who constitutes the fellowship of the Father and the Son informs the Spirit's economic work. In Coffey's Spirit Christology, the Holy Spirit is "the Spirit of Christ" because the Spirit achieves the union of the humanity of Jesus with the divine person of the Son. The Incarnation is an event in which the Father bestows love on humanity by sending the Holy Spirit and through that sending of the Spirit achieves the creation, sanctification, and radical union of the humanity of Jesus Christ with the Son.[11]

The Spirit's role in bringing about the Incarnation corresponds with the primal dimension of the Spirit's personal identity; namely, the Spirit as the Father's love for the Son who always seeks and rests on the Son. Since the Father's bestowal of love in the Holy Spirit inevitably terminates on the Son, Jesus Christ, the union of humanity with the Son, is the *entelechy* of the Spirit. In other words, the work of the Spirit in the economy of redemption always has as its goal the realization of the Incarnation and the redemption that it yields. The Father's expression of love to creation in the person of the Holy Spirit reaches the zenith of its historical mediation in the creation, sanctification, and union of Jesus's humanity with the Son. Thus, in the economy of redemption, the Holy Spirit is always "the Spirit of Christ."[12]

Grace and the *Entelechy* of the Holy Spirit

The Holy Spirit has a similar role in grace. Since Christ is always the *entelechy* of the Spirit, the Spirit draws human persons toward union with Christ and does so for the same reason that the Spirit unites the humanity of Jesus with the Son. When the Father economically directs his love as the communication of the Spirit to human persons, his love still has the Son as its ultimate term or goal. The Spirit then seeks to bring human persons into communion with the Spirit's proper/original term, who is the Son. The purpose for this is to make human persons children of the Father. As

11. Coffey, "Spirit Christology and the Trinity," 315–38 and "Theandric Nature of Christ," 425–30.

12. For a fuller development of Spirit Christology, see Studebaker, "Integrating Pneumatology and Christology," 5–20.

Coffey puts it, believers are "sons (and daughters) in the Son."[13] However, the Incarnation and grace are not identical. In the Incarnation, the Spirit unites the humanity of Jesus with the Son. In grace, the Spirit unites believers or human persons with the Son. Believers experience union with Christ by participating in the Spirit as "the Spirit of Christ;" that is, by participating in the *entelechy* of the Spirit as "the Spirit of Christ."[14]

To conclude this section, the work of the Spirit in redemption includes Incarnation, grace, and final consummation. The Spirit brings the humanity of Christ in the Incarnation and human persons in grace into union with the Son and ultimately gathers them together in the everlasting kingdom of God. The *entelechy* of the Spirit is to constitute the fellowship of the redeemed divine and human community. Having outlined the way the *entelechy* of the Spirit informs the Spirit's role in Christology and the redemption of human persons, the discussion can turn to the question: "what does this have to do with a trinitarian theology of creation and, more specifically, how does this theology promote the notion that creation care is a dimension of Christian formation?"

THE *ENTELECHY* OF THE SPIRIT AND THE COSMIC SCOPE OF REDEMPTION

As Pentecostals we are accustomed to think of salvation in terms of Christ saving our souls for heaven. As the pastor I served with routinely proclaimed, "I can't wait to leave this bag of bones and go to heaven to be with Jesus." Such perspectives hardly fund positive attitudes toward the body, let alone ecological ethics. Although affirming the resurrection of the body, Pentecostal premillennial eschatology tends to fuel an otherworldly orientation in which the Christian is to pursue personal holiness and await final deliverance from this evil world. Indeed, in this eschatology, rather than being something to prevent, ecological crises often are interpreted as harbingers of the second coming of Christ and the rapture. However, Scripture casts a vision of redemption that is cosmic in scope. The following material illustrates that the Spirit's redemptive work encompasses all of creation.

13. Coffey, *"Did You Receive the Holy Spirit When You Believed?"* 34 and *Grace*, 148.
14. Ibid.

The Holy Spirit and Cosmic Redemption

Scripture extends redemption to all of creation and does not restrict it to the "spiritual" dimension of the human.[15] Romans 8:21 promises "that the creation itself will be liberated from its bondage to decay." Moreover, the passage correlates the suffering of creation with the human yearning for eschatological renewal: "We know that the whole creation has been groaning as in the pains of childbirth right up to the present time. Not only so, but we ourselves, who have the firstfruits of the Spirit, groan inwardly as we wait eagerly for our adoption as sons, the redemption of our bodies" (Rom 8:22–23).[16] The groaning of creation parallels the groaning of the Christian community for final redemption.[17]

The Romans passage also casts the longing for cosmic redemption in pneumatological terms. Romans 8:23 and 26–27 see the human yearning for final redemption as arising from the sustaining presence of the Spirit. The inference seems appropriate that if the human "groans" for redemption arise from the Spirit, then so also do creation's moans for its liberation from its current travail. The Spirit who cries out from the breast of every forlorn human also groans within creation and yearns for the same eschatological redemption.

What is more, the physical creation and human bodies are the objects of the hoped for redemption. The Spirit groans in and with all living creatures and, just as the Spirit raised Christ from the dead, the Spirit promises to redeem all life.[18] The groans of creation are the anticipation of its liberation from the bondage to decay and participation in the "glorious freedom of the children of God" (Rom 8:21). The Spirit who longs for the coming of the everlasting kingdom in the human heart longs for the same kingdom to come for all of creation. The agency of the Spirit in redemption encompasses the human and all of creation. Thus, redemption has to do with restoring human persons to their proper relationships with their Creator, each other, and creation and this is why the final redemption

15. Barbour, *Nature, Human Nature, and God*, 126.

16. Denis Edwards illustrates the Spirit's work in liberating creation from its travail in terms of a midwife who facilitates the new birth of creation (Edwards, *Breath of Life*, 110–12).

17. Dale Moody also notes that this text links the groaning of creation and of the children of God with the sighs of the Spirit (Moody, *Word of Truth*, 135).

18. Elizabeth Johnson applies the pattern of cross—Spirit abiding in solidarity with the suffering—and resurrection—Spirit ushering in the new creation—on a cosmic level (*Quest for the Living God*, 189–91).

envisioned in Revelation 21 and 22 includes the restoration of relationship with God ("'now the dwelling of God is with men, and he will live with them'"), the human community, human culture ("the Holy City, the new Jerusalem coming down out of heaven from God"), and creation (the "new heaven and a new earth" and the "river of the water of life," "the tree of life," and its bountiful fruit and curative leaves).[19]

The *Entelechy* of the Holy Spirit and Cosmic Redemption

The *entelechy* of the Spirit informs the cosmic scope of the Spirit's work. Traditional theology readily recognizes that the Spirit is the breath of life in creation, but it often overlooks that the Spirit is at the same time the Spirit of redemption *in* creation. Since the Spirit who is present within the Christian is the same Spirit present within all of creation and since both are recipients of the promise of redemption, the Spirit's work in both should converge. That is, human persons and creation at large have the same intrinsic *entelechy*, which is the Holy Spirit drawing all of creation to its eschatological renewal.

All work of the Spirit ultimately has an orientation to draw creation into its particular mode of fellowship with the Father and the Son.[20] To be sure, pine trees will not participate in the eschaton in the same way that human beings will do so, nonetheless, in some way God promises to redeem creation and, therefore, it will share in the eschaton in a way appropriate to its life form. Because the *entelechy* of the Spirit is constitutive of the Spirit's personal identity, all work of the Spirit in redemption bears that character. This means, therefore, that the Spirit ever and everywhere seeks the particular eschatological end of all created life forms.

19. J. Richard Middleton points out that a biblical view of creation comprehends what we often think of as the natural world and all the dimensions of existence in the world, such as cultural production, and that this stands in contrast to the modernist notion that limits creation to the natural world and physical aspect of the human ("New Heaven and a New Earth," 74). Thus, the redemption of creation includes the New Jerusalem and the new heaven and earth.

20. Others who also draw a connection between the Spirit's role in facilitating relationships in the Godhead and creation are Dabney, "Nature of the Spirit: Creation as a Premonition of God," 81; Denis Edwards, *Breath of Life*, 46–47, 120, and 127; Pinnock, *Flame of Love*, 56–57 and 61; and Wallace, *Fragments of the Spirit*, 145–47.

CREATION CARE AS "[KEEPING] IN STEP WITH THE SPIRIT" OR AS CHRISTIAN FORMATION

My sister and I were in college and graduate school at roughly the same time. She earned degrees in environmental science and management and I in ministry and theology. Her work concentrated on tending the earth and mine on the church and "souls." I thought I had pursued a higher calling than her and thought her somewhat crazy for "saving" the spotted owls and old growth forests. Now, I believe she was hearing the groans of the Spirit within creation and "[keeping] in step with the Spirit" (Gal 5:25).

Many Pentecostals will have little trouble considering their religious and moral activities of prayer, Bible study, and fasting as empowered by the Spirit and acts of Christian formation. But, few Pentecostal Christians consider creation care as an arena of the Spirit's work and, much less, as a form of sanctification. However, creation care, no less than the traditional disciplines of Christian formation is a way the Christian can "keep in step with the Spirit" (Gal 5:25). In other words, buying organic fair trade coffee and turning the heat down may be just as much a way "to work out your salvation with fear and trembling" as praying, attending church, and fasting (Phil 2:12). Just as the activities that Christians typically classify as religious and moral are participations and foretastes of the eschatological kingdom through the Spirit, so also are efforts in creation care. The purpose of this section is to show that creation care is a dimension of Christian formation that participates in the *entelechy* of the Spirit or "the Spirit of Christ." In order to do this, the first step is to explain that redemption and Christian formation are proleptic participations in or foretastes of the everlasting kingdom of God through "the Spirit of Christ."

Redemption and Christian Formation as Participation in the *Entelechy* of the Spirit

As Pentecostals, we often think of salvation in very evangelical terms. For instance, we easily adopt the language of salvation as a personal relationship with Jesus Christ and a born again experience. Without dismissing the importance of those categories, a Pentecostal account of redemption should give the Holy Spirit a central role. The trinitarian theology outlined earlier provides a theological framework to do just that. From a trinitarian and Pentecostal perspective, redemption is to be caught up in the eschatological work of the Spirit as *entelechy* of Christ. That is to say, to be redeemed is to be drawn into union with the Son through "the Spirit of Christ" and to experience the renewal of life through the Spirit. However, redemption is also an eschatological experience of the consummation of the triune God's redemptive mission. Redemption is a foretaste of the everlasting kingdom; it is an hors d'oeuvre of the great banquet feast of the coming kingdom of God. In grace, believers participate in part in the full consummation of God's redemption that will be realized in the everlasting kingdom of God.

The eschatological character of the Christian life means that Christian formation is a proleptic experience of that future redemption. Proleptic means something that *anticipates* and *participates* in a future reality. The Apostle Paul recognizes the proleptic nature of the Christian life when he states that "we ourselves, who have the firstfruits of the Spirit, groan inwardly as we wait eagerly for our adoption as sons, the redemption of our bodies" (Rom 8:23). He suggests the proleptic nature of the Christian life when he refers to it as an experience of the "firstfruits" of a full harvest that remains outstanding and that although the Spirit now "testifies with our spirit that we are God's children" (Rom 8:16), our full adoption as God's children awaits the final resurrection of our bodies. For example, when believers experience the renewal of their lives in this life in Christ they both receive in part their future full redemption and anticipate that future redemption. Or, when believers experience physical healing they experience a foretaste of their resurrection in the everlasting kingdom of God.

Christian formation is also a participation in the *entelechy* of the Spirit. Christian formation is embracing what the Spirit seeks to do in our lives as the Spirit draws us into more intimate relationship with Christ and ultimately into the everlasting kingdom and fellowship of the trinitarian God. Another way of saying this is that Christian formation is the convergence of the work of the Spirit as *entelechy* of Christ or as "the Spirit of Christ" in the life of the believer with the Spirit's work in the world as *entelechy* of Christ. Christian sanctification is the process in which believers allow "the Spirit of Christ" to form them in the image of Christ; hence, the call to be Christ-like. The Holy Spirit seeks to foster ever more intimate union between believers and Christ and to empower patterns of life that reflect their union with Christ. Christian formation is to embrace the Spirit's work and thereby "keep in step in with the Spirit" (Gal 5:25).

Creation Care as Participation in the *Entelechy* of the Spirit

This final section brings together the theology already set forth to suggest that creation care is a dimension of Christian formation because it is a way that the Christian participates in the *entelechy* of the Spirit or "the Spirit of Christ." As previously mentioned, many Christians/Pentecostals readily recognize prayer, Bible study, and church attendance as Christian formation, but are less inclined to do so with creation care. However, the recognition that 1) redemption has cosmic scope; 2) the Spirit as "the Spirit of Christ" (the *entelechy* of the Spirit) is the agent of redemption; and 3) redemption and Christian formation are proleptic participations in the everlasting kingdom suggests that creation care can be a participation in the *entelechy* of the Spirit that is at the same time a proleptic participation in the eschaton. As that is a bit dense, let me express this theology in more concrete terms.

The Spirit who works in Christians and fosters their participation in the eschatological new creation is the same Spirit at work throughout the cosmos.[21] When Christians engage in traditional ministries of preaching the Gospel, ministering to the abused and impoverished, and opposing injustice, they are responding to and being caught up in the work of the Spirit. They do so because the work of the Spirit in their lives corresponds to what the Spirit seeks for the lives of others. For example, when a local church ministers to people disenfranchised from the consumer culture and seeks ways to empower and liberate their lives, the church's ministry correlates with what the Spirit seeks for the lives of those specific people. The correlation is not an abstract one, in the sense that ministry corresponds to the will of God in some generalized sense, but rather the correlation is concrete. The work of the Spirit *in* the lives of Christians meets the work of the Spirit *in* the lives of those to whom they minister.

Similarly, since the Spirit's work extends to the redemption of all of creation and is not limited to the "spiritual" dimension of the human being, then when Christians engage in creation care the work of the Spirit in them meets the work of the Spirit in creation.[22] And again, this meeting is not at the level of thematic abstraction, as in that it is God's will to be stewards of the earth, but in a concrete and specific sense. The Spirit who is present and

21. Denis Edwards aptly remarks that "the story of the Spirit . . . is coextensive with the *total* life of the universe" (Edwards, *Breath of Life*, 33).

22. Carol J. Dempsey articulates the Old Testament prophetic tradition's promise of the eschatological renewal of life that takes in all of creation; see "Hope Amidst Crisis," 269–84.

working in the Christian is present in and seeking the well-being of every part of creation. Christian formation is the process in which the work of the Spirit in the lives of people meets the presence and work of the Spirit throughout creation, both in its human and non-human dimensions.

The realization of the cosmic scope of redemption entails that the Spirit who works to redeem Christians is also at work to redeem all of creation. The Spirit, who breathes life into all living creatures and who breathes new life into Christians, empowers patterns of behavior that foster the flourishing of all of life.[23] The Spirit who gives life to the creature inhabiting the wetland is the same Spirit who redeems human life. It seems plausible that the Spirit working redemptively in humans will lead them to behave in ways that are commensurate with the Spirit's life-giving work in other creatures. Creation care, then, is a dimension of Christian formation because it is our embracing what the Spirit seeks to do in and through our lives in respect to creation. Thus, creation care is the convergence of the *entelechy* of the Spirit as "the Spirit of Christ" in us and in creation.

In closing this section, a cosmic vision of the mission of the triune God, that is one that comprehends all of creation, enables Christians to see creation care as a dimension of their Christian formation and sanctification. Just as the traditional acts of sanctification and Christian formation can be understood as a participation in the *entelechy* of the Spirit and as proleptic experiences of the everlasting kingdom so also creation care can be so understood. This is because the Spirit who is at work in the human person and who ever orients them to Christ and the final consummation of redemption is also the intrinsic principle of life *and* redemption in creation. Creation care, therefore, is the convergence of the work of the Spirit in the human person and in the broader arena of creation. In application this means, for example, that the restoration of an anadromous fish passage is just as much a work of Christian formation and worship as prayer because both activities are concrete manifestations of "the Spirit of Christ" that presage the eschatological renewal of all life.[24]

23. Note: the above is not an endorsement of a radical biocentric model in which the life of virulent viruses and bacteria receive the same regard as humans and other living creatures. For instance, to protect human life from Ebola virus and indigenous trees from invasive and destructive insects would be considered acts of creation care.

24. E.g., Portland General and Electric's removal of the Marmot Dam on the Sandy River in Oregon that once again opened the entire river to wild Salmon and Steelhead migration and facilitated the restoration of its riparian zone to a natural state.

CONCLUSION

Although Pentecostals have not always been at the forefront of ecological sensitivity, they can draw on trinitarian theology to fund a vision of creation care as a dimension of Christian formation. This chapter resources the traditional Augustinian mutual love model of the Trinity, influenced by the formulations of Roman Catholic David Coffey, to suggest that creation care is a participation in the redemptive mission of the triune God and, therefore, a dimension of Christian formation. Based on the Spirit's identity as the divine person who constitutes the loving communion of the trinitarian God, the Spirit has a primordial orientation to the Son. Transposed to the economy of redemption, this means that the Spirit is "the Spirit of Christ." As "the Spirit of Christ," the Holy Spirit bears an *entelechy* toward the Son. An *entelechy* is an internal force that drives a being to its intrinsic destiny. The *entelechy* of the Spirit then is to be the divine person who always seeks and rests on the Son. Christian formation is a process in which believers participate in the Spirit who ever and everywhere seeks to draw creation to its unique way of participating in the cosmic scope of Christ's redemptive work. Thus, whether the Christian participates in "the Spirit of Christ" in terms of the traditional disciplines of Christian formation or in efforts that embrace the broader cosmic breadth of redemption, they are "[keeping] in step with the Spirit" (Gal 5:25) and "[working] out [their] salvation with fear and trembling" (Phil 2:12).

BIBLIOGRAPHY

Barbour, Ian. *Nature, Human Nature, and God.* Edited by Kevin J. Sharpe. Minneapolis: Fortress, 2002.

Boff, Leonardo. *Trinity and Society.* Translated by Paul Burns. 1988. Reprinted, Eugene, OR: Wipf & Stock, 2005.

Brown, David. *The Divine Trinity.* La Salle, IL: Open Court, 1985.

Coffey, David M. *"Did You Receive the Holy Spirit When You Believed?" Some Basic Questions for Pneumatology.* The Père Marquette Lecture in Theology. Milwaukee: Marquette University Press, 2005.

———. *Grace: The Gift of the Holy Spirit.* Faith and Culture 2. Sydney, Australia: Catholic Institute of Sydney, 1979.

———. "Spirit Christology and the Trinity." In *Advents of the Spirit: An Introduction to Pneumatology,* edited by Bradford E. Hinze and D. Lyle Dabney, 315–38. Marquette Studies in Theology 30. Milwaukee: Marquette University Press, 2001.

———. "The Spirit of Christ as Entelechy." *Philosophy and Theology* 13 (2001) 365–70.

———. "The Theandric Nature of Christ." *Theological Studies* 60 (1999) 405–31.

———. "A Trinitarian Response to Issues Raised by Phan." *Theological Studies* 69 (2008) 852–74.

Dabney, D. Lyle. "The Nature of the Spirit: Creation as a Premonition of God." In *The Work of the Spirit: Pneumatology and Pentecostalism*, edited by Michael Welker, 71–86. Grand Rapids: Eerdmans, 2006.

Dempsey, Carol J. "Hope amidst Crisis: A Prophetic Vision of Cosmic Redemption." In *All Creation is Groaning: An Interdisciplinary Vision for Life in a Sacred Universe*, edited by Carol J. Dempsey and Russell A. Butkus, 269–84. Collegeville, MN: Liturgical, 1999.

Edwards, Denis. *Breath of Life: A Theology of the Creator Spirit*. Maryknoll, NY: Orbis, 2004.

Fortman, Edmund J. *The Triune God: A Historical Study of the Doctrine of the Trinity*. Philadelphia: Westminster, 1972.

Gunton, Colin. *The Promise of Trinitarian Theology*. 2nd ed. Edinburgh: T. & T. Clark, 1997.

Johnson, Elizabeth. *Quest for the Living God: Mapping Frontiers in the Theology of God*. New York: Continuum, 2007.

LaCugna, Catherine Mowry. *God for Us: The Trinity and Christian Life*. New York: HarperCollins, 1991.

Middleton, J. Richard. "A New Heaven and a New Earth: The Case for a Holistic Reading of the Biblical Story of Redemption." *Journal for Christian Theological Research* 11 (2006) 73–97.

Moltmann, Jürgen. *Trinität und Reich Gottes: zur Gotteslehre*. München: Kaiser, 1980.

Moody, Dale. *The Word of Truth: A Summary of Christian Doctrine Based on Biblical Revelation*. Grand Rapids: Eerdmans, 1981.

Pinnock, Clark H. *Flame of Love: A Theology of the Holy Spirit*. Downers Grove, IL: InterVarsity, 1996.

Rahner, Karl. *Theological Investigations*. Vol. 17, *Jesus, Man, and the Church*. Translated by Margaret Kohl. New York: Crossroad, 1981.

Studebaker, Steven M. "Integrating Social and Augustinian Theories of Divine Person: A Proposal from the Theology of Jonathan Edwards and David Coffey." *Canadian Evangelical Review* 34–35 (Fall 2007–Spring 2008) 3–19.

———. "Jonathan Edwards's Social *Augustinian* Trinitarianism: An Alternative to a Recent Trend." *Scottish Journal of Theology* 56 (2003) 268–85.

———. *Jonathan Edwards' Social Augustinian Trinitarianism in Historical and Contemporary Perspectives*. Piscataway, NJ: Gorgias, 2008.

Wallace, Mark I. *Fragments of the Spirit: Nature, Violence, and the Renewal of Creation*. New York: Continuum, 1996.

The Works of Saint Augustine: A Translation for the 21st Century. Edited by John E. Rotelle. Vol. 5: *The Trinity*. Edited by Edmund Hill. Brooklyn: New City, 1991.

Zizioulas, John D. *Being as Communion: Studies in Personhood and the Church*. Contemporary Greek Theologians 4. Crestwood, NY: St. Vladimir's Seminary Press, 1985.

Name Index

Subject Index